A
FOOTBALL
BAND OF
BROTHERS

Forging The University of
Washington's First
National Championship

W. Thomas Porter

Note for Librarians: A cataloguing record for this book is available from Library and Archives
Canada at www.collectionscanada.ca/amicus/index-e.html
ISBN 1-4251-0662-5

Offices in Canada, USA, Ireland and UK

Book sales for North America and international:
Trafford Publishing, 6E–2333 Government St.,
Victoria, BC V8T 4P4 CANADA
phone 250 383 6864 (toll-free 1 888 232 4444)
fax 250 383 6804; email to orders@trafford.com
Book sales in Europe:
Trafford Publishing (UK) Limited, 9 Park End Street, 2nd Floor
Oxford, UK OX1 1HH UNITED KINGDOM
phone 44 (0)1865 722 113 (local rate 0845 230 9601)
facsimile 44 (0)1865 722 868; info.uk@trafford.com
Order online at:
trafford.com/06-2420

10 9 8 7 6 5 4

To the coaches and players whose performance permanently affixed the 1959 and 1960 teams at the top level of Washington's football history and whose commitment, team unity, and resolve forged the Huskies' first football national championship.

Contents

Introduction

Almost fifty years ago, a group of student-athletes entered the University of Washington. As freshmen, they were not eligible to play varsity football so they began their collegiate football on a team that went unbeaten against Northwest opponents.

College football was very different then. There was no Sports Center, no Bowl Coalition Series, no 24-hour sports talk shows. An athlete did not leave a university before he graduated thereby using the university as a farm system for his athletic objectives. There was little or no trash talking. There was no chest thumping, high five's, or end zone celebrations when an athlete made a sack, a touchdown, or some other significant play. Most coaches cared about the academic success of their players, recognizing that very few of them would be successful professional athletes.

There were about 50 players on a team, most playing offense and defense. Some had to work part-time to finance their education. The single ones lived with other students in dormitories and fraternity houses. Some were married and had children.

In 1955, Washington had been rocked by a player revolt which led to the firing of the head football coach who went public about a slush fund used by zealous boosters to directly pay players more than the Pacific Coast Conference allowed. The Husky athletic program was put on probation for two years along with Cal, UCLA, and USC.

It was a difficult period for a once proud and successful program. Thirty-one year old George Briggs was hired as Athletic Director to clean up the mess and hire a new coach. Darrell Royal, an All-American quarterback for the Oklahoma Sooners and the head coach at Mississippi State, accepted a four-year contract in 1956 and put the Husky football program on the road to recovery.

However, after the season ended, Royal resigned to take his dream job at the University of Texas where he forged a very successful career which included three national championships.

Briggs then hired 29-year old Jim Owens, a teammate of Royal and an All-American end. He had been a top assistant under Bear Bryant at Kentucky and Texas A&M. He was one of the architects of the "Junction Boys" ten days in hell that helped build the Aggies into a conference champion three years later.

Owens and his staff brought a philosophy that included an emphasis on team unity, defense, tough physical and mental conditioning. The use of the helmet to tackle and block and punish opponents and the willingness to pay the price for success were also primary elements of their approach.

I first saw a Husky team coached by Owens in 1958 when I was an MBA student at Washington. They lost to California 12-7 on November 15 nearing the end of a 3-7 season. The Bears, led by quarterback Joe Kapp, won the Pacific Coast Conference title. It was the last season of the conference which was founded in 1916. Cal lost to Iowa in the 1959 Rose Bowl, 38-12. It was the twelfth loss by a PCC team in the 13-year old pact between the Big Ten Conference and the PCC. Clearly, the fortunes of West Coast football were at a low point.

Many of the fans in Husky Stadium that day watched a mostly sophomore team -- the youngest in the United States -- play the Bears to almost a standoff. Kapp was prophetic in his post-game remarks. "I can't understand how Washington ever loses. They hit as hard as any team we've played. And they're all young guys. In another year, that bunch is going to be hard to beat."

He was right. Over the next two years, the Huskies forged the second best record of a collegiate football team in America -- 20 wins and two losses. With 20 victories, one tie, and one loss, only Mississippi had a better resume. In 1959, the Huskies won the conference title, the first for Washington since 1936, and upset Wisconsin in the 1960 Rose Bowl 44-8. It was Washington's first Rose Bowl victory -- the Huskies had played in Pasadena four times before -- and brought respectability back to West Coast football.

In the 1960 season, despite injuries to many key players including 1959 All-America quarterback and Heisman hopeful, Bob Schloredt, the then senior-laden team again went 9-1. They had several fourth quarter come-from-behind wins. They won four games by the combined margin of five points and became known as the "Cardiac Kids." With another Conference championship, they faced Minnesota, the Associated Press' selection as the number one team in the country, in the 1961 Rose Bowl.

In those days, most of the polls completed their final rankings before the bowl games were played. The Huskies beat the Gophers 17-7. The Husky coaches and players believed that the Rose Bowl was a championship bout and when you win a championship match, you get the title. Two polls -- the Helms Foundation Poll founded in 1900 and the Football Writers Association of America Poll started in 1954 -- announced their final rankings after the bowl games were completed. The FWAA selected Mississippi (10-0-1) as its national champion and the Helms Foundation selected Washington (10-1).

Jim Owens and his Husky band of brothers had gone from ashes to roses and a national championship and had, in the opinion of veteran football announcer, Keith Jackson, picked up the entire state and region and revitalized it.

I wrote this book because it is a compelling story. The coaches and players really believed in the importance of team work. They believed that it took a whole team to get the job done. They believed that everybody was in the battle together. Since all of them played both ways, there was no offensive team, no defensive team, no special team. They could come together much more easily with only 50 players on the team. The coaches recruited players with integrity and character who didn't expect extra or different treatment. Nobody expected anything but hard work. They made it through grueling practices, challenge drills, and punishing conditioning exercises because of an intense determination and commitment to the goals of the coaches and to each other. The result of their shared experience, both on the practice field and in games with tough opponents, was a closeness unknown to outsiders.

They knew each other's background, where they came from, and what their capabilities were. They became a band of brothers ready to give up part of their individualism and quest for personal glory for the good of the team. They were committed to do whatever it took to win battles on the football field. Their success didn't lay so much in having the best talent. The difference was their resolve.

My other reason for writing this book is that I believe that many Husky fans today remember only the great success of the Don James era. But even James understands that the 1959 and 1960 teams laid the foundation for Husky football. They were the ones who turned Husky football around. When you talk about the Husky tradition -- endurance, passion, pride, tenacity, and toughness -- it all started in the late 1950's. Their 20-2 record over a two-year span ranks at the very top level of Husky football.

CHAPTER 1

Boosters Mess It Up

Soaring with cathedral grandeur from the shore of Lake Washington upward through rows of stands to the sweep of a cantilevered roof sixteen stories above a grass field, Husky Stadium -- originally named Washington Stadium -- was built in 1920 and presented one of the most imposing football venues in the nation. For almost forty years, it had granted players and fans, some exhilarating and unforgettable moments.

With Lake Washington's Union Bay and the snow-capped Cascade Mountains as a backdrop, the stadium is where Washington's 20th football coach would implement his coaching philosophy and values. Arriving in January 1957, just shy of his 30th birthday, Jim Owens had the task of reviving a once proud football program reeling from a team mutiny, placed on a two year probation by the Pacific Coast Conference, and without a conference football title since 1936.

Four years before, the fortunes of the Husky football program seemed bright. John Cherberg had been selected to replace Howie Odell as Washington's head football coach. Cherberg was an outstanding Washington running back from 1930-32 and winner, in his senior year, of the Flaherty medal as the "most inspirational player." He was clearly a very popular choice. He had been a successful coach at several Seattle high schools and had joined the Husky coaching staff as backfield coach in 1946 under head coach, Ralph "Pest" Welch. After Odell replaced Welch in 1948, he appointed Cherberg as the freshmen coach. During his five seasons, Cherberg's yearlings won 22 straight games, after losing their first one 25-24 to Oregon.

Cherberg, paid $12,000 in 1953, picked an excellent coaching staff including Lou Saban who eventually went on to be the head coach for the Buffalo Bills and Denver Broncos in the American Football League. In Cherberg's first season, the Huskies compiled a 3-6-1 record finishing next to the bottom of the Pacific Coast Conference, a conference with nine schools -- California, Idaho, Oregon, Oregon State, Stanford, UCLA, USC, Washington, and Washington State. In 1954, the Huskies finished last in the conference with a 2-8 record.

Nineteen fifty-five was a pivotal year for not only Cherberg's coaching future but for the entire Husky athletic program. In the season opener, Washington set a school record by fumbling 11 times in its 14-7 win over Idaho. On the road they shut out Minnesota 30-0 and beat Oregon 19-7. Facing tenth-ranked USC at home, they fashioned one of the most memorable plays in Husky football history to beat the Trojans 7-0. With 6:20 remaining, the Huskies had the ball on their 20-yard line. Quarterback Steve Roake threw a 20-yard pass to right end Jim Houston on a crossing pattern, right to left. After running five yards, Houston was hit as left end, Corky Lewis, was coming up to block. As Houston was falling on the 45-yard line, he tossed the ball laterally to Lewis who was in full stride. Lewis raced past a would-be tackler and headed straight downfield 55 yards for the game's only touchdown. It was the Huskies' first win over USC in Seattle since 1945.

Then, things began to unravel. At home, the Huskies lost to Baylor and Oregon State and tied Stanford. Away, they lost to Cal and fourth-ranked UCLA. Before the Bruins' game, Cherberg asked Torchy Torrance, a Washington alumnus and one of the Huskies' most ardent football boosters, to talk to the players. It was a "pep" talk and it worked. The Huskies went out and nearly upset UCLA, who would win the 1955 Pacific Coast Conference title.

Washington led at half-time 14-7 and increased their lead to ten when Dean Derby kicked a field goal early in the third quarter. UCLA stormed back on its next possession to pull within three. Late in the fourth quarter, The Huskies stopped the Bruins one yard short of a first down and took over on their ten. On fourth and 13 on their seven-yard line, the Huskies took a safety to reduce their margin to one. After Derby's free kick from the 20-yard line, UCLA drove to the Washington 18 in six plays. On fourth down and with 19 seconds left, Bruin halfback Jim Decker split the uprights for a 19-17 UCLA victory.

A few days later, Lewis and a few other players visited Torrance to discuss a coaching change. Torrance told them to talk to Athletic Director Harvey Cassill and to go out and play a great game against Washington State in the season finale.

The Huskies did. Credell Green ran for 258 yards to lead Washington to a 27-7 victory. Washington finished 5-4-1 and fifth in the conference.

Soon after the players turned in their equipment, about 30 of them went to see Cassill. Lewis said, "We told Harvey we could not play for Cherberg any more." After the meeting, Cassill immediately went to Cherberg and said, "I think you should meet with the players." So Cassill and Cherberg met with the players. "The players would not repeat what they told me. They were afraid of John. And I had to agree with John at the end of the session that there was no occasion for him to do anything. As far as the player revolt was concerned, there wasn't any," said Cassill.

Several players who were on Cherberg's squad when he was the freshmen coach said he became a different man when he stepped up to the varsity. Some felt "he couldn't take the pressure," particularly as the losses mounted in the later part of the 1955 season. Cherberg started to lash out at the coaches, players, and others in a manner that startled those who were his targets.

Lewis recounts an incident when Cherberg charged into the locker room where the players were dressing for a game. Lewis was standing nude just inside the door to the room, when Cherberg screamed at him, "Are you ready? Are you mad?" Lewis replied, "Coach, I am ready, I'm always ready." Cherberg bellowed, "Are you really ready, I want you mad, really mad." He then stomped his cleated foot right on the top of Lewis' bare one. Was Cherberg's action intentional? Probably not. Was it called for? Definitely not. Did it hurt Lewis? During the game, Lewis had to loosen his shoe because his foot was swollen and bruised.

Players remember Cherberg blowing up on a charter plane ride home in 1955. On team trips during the Cherberg era, the stewardesses, after takeoff, would serve trays of fruit to the coaches and players. On this trip, when Cherberg saw the stewardesses start down the aisle, he charged out of his seat and hit the trays from below with his fist, sending fruit flying everywhere. Then he shouted, "Don't you ever feed fruit to my players without asking me first!"

Some say the deterioration of the players' regard for Cherberg started with Assistant Coach Jim (Suds) Sutherland. Cherberg hired Suthereland, an assistant coach at the University of California, to tutor his backs.

In practices leading up to the season opener against Idaho, Sutherland altered the starting count. He told Husky center Bert Watson to snap on the half count, rather than the normal full count, to get the line off the ball more quickly. Lewis said, "We were, technically, a very poor football team and we did get off the ball poorly." The week after the Idaho game, Cherberg was furious thinking the altered snap count caused the 11 fumbles in the game. However, he did not confront Sutherland at that point. As the Huskies rolled through the early part of their season, the issue became unimportant. When the losses mounted in the remainder of the season, Cherberg started to unleash his frustrations on the coaches and players. He directed most of his concerns and antagonism toward Sutherland. Cherberg rode him constantly. He made fun of him on the field during practice. On November 23, four days after the end of the season, he fired Sutherland who soon became the head coach at Washington State.

Reports of the players' unrest became public. Many of the negative reactions to the attacks on Cherberg were published in the Seattle Times, a sampling of which indicated just how many felt about the players.

"Those kids are squawking like a bunch of babies."

"We've been too considerate of the younger generation. We've been babying them, and when they get into something highly competitive like college football they can't take it."

"The ball players should not run the team. Johnny is running his own show, and he is capable of doing it. He's a fine gentleman and a good coach."

"In my estimation, there are not enough boys with the extreme desire to play football today. Too many are just going along for the ride."

The Quarterback Club, associated with the University of Washington, reported that they were 100 percent behind Cherberg.

Next, quarterback Steve Roake, weighed in on the matter. "All along, I have been in complete accord with the fellows, but I wasn't ready to take any covert action. But when the fellows were labeled 'cry-babies' and 'back stabbers' by persons not close to the situation, I have to speak out." Roake felt that the players who complained were trying to do a service to the University and their actions were a culmination of three years of dissatisfaction with the Husky football situation. "I feel, as they do, that Cherberg lacks the qualities necessary in a head coach. His football plays are good ones, much of his strategy sound, but he lacks those intangibles which make a top coach." Lewis would add, "We were a very poorly coached team. We ran the same standard, unimaginative running plays week after week and never altered our passing patterns. We didn't utilize the varying talents of the good players we had."

The university administration and student governing body weighed in. H.P. (Dick) Everest, the university's Vice President, announced the administration would start a complete investigation of the situation. The Board of Control of the Associated Students of the University of Washington (ASUW) voted 12-2 to fire Cherberg. The students' action was consistent with the ASUW's initial constitution established in 1901. Under the constitution, all enterprises for student activities and all intercollegiate student relations came under the control of the ASUW. At the turn of the 20th century, when student activities were not so large, diverse and complex, student management may have made some sense. Students paid fees to support athletic programs. When Husky Stadium was built in 1920, student fees provided over $123,000 of the total $565,000 needed for construction. Clearly, the ASUW through its Board of Control felt it had the authority and responsibility to manage all student activities, including involvement in the hiring and firing of coaches.

In 1955, the university had grown much more complex and permanent full-time administrators were required to provide effective management and stability to the University. The ASUW constitution had been amended and the Board of Regents became responsible for establishing policies under which the university's intercollegiate program was to be conducted. Similar changes were taking place at other public universities in the Pacific Coast Conference. It was becoming increasingly clear to university presidents that institutional control of athletics would improve if the university had full charge of the program. Leaders of Associated Students organizations in many universities, with their short term of office, lack of time, and leadership inexperience, simply were not equipped to handle the complexities of managing a rapidly expanding athletic program and budget. Nor could they withstand the pressures from alumni groups, boosters, and coaches. In 1962, the Board of Regents, acting on the report of a special committee of alumni, faculty, and students, would reorganize the ASUW and place the Department of Intercollegiate Athletics and the Husky Union Building and other business areas under the University's direction.

Near the end of 1955, the students thought they were in control. Not so, said the Regents. On December 10, a semblance of quiet was restored when the university's Board of Regents voted unanimously on Everest's recommendation to rehire Cherberg on the condition that he mend the situation and develop harmonious relations with the team. In an executive session prior to the public portion of the December 10 meeting, the Regents gave Cassill the responsibility to decide whether or not Cherberg had accomplished the objective of gaining the players' confidence. Cherberg did little to improve the situation. In mid-January, he met with the players after which many came to the conclusion that the situation would not improve with Cherberg at the helm.

It was a touchy situation. Players received bribes and threats. Lewis, a pre-medical student with outstanding grades and campus activities, remembers getting a phone call from an unidentified booster who said he would never get into Washington's Medical School if Lewis did not stop the players' revolt. Lewis then called Vice President Everest about the threat. Everest responded. "Corky, with your grades and activities you should have no worries about getting into medical school. There are not enough strings for anybody to have to prevent your being accepted."

The players had a meeting later in January. Lewis indicated that some players had received a fifty dollar bill before the meeting. One of the team members stood up during the meeting and said, "God came to me and told me to vote for Cherberg." Another player asked, "Did God leave fifty dollars under your pillow?" The whole meeting room rocked with laughter and then the players agreed to meet with Cassill to discuss their decision to ask for Cherberg's firing.

An editorial in the January 26, 1956, University Daily, called for Cherberg's resignation. On January 27, Cassill fired him. Cherberg immediately went public, firing several bullets at the University administration, Cassill, the ASUW, and prominent boosters who paid players. As reported in an article in the February 20, 1956, issue of Sports Illustrated, *Boosters Mess it up in Washington*, Cherberg said, "The filthiest thing in the world is to corrupt young Americans with dough. I may never coach again, but, God willing, I'm not going to let them corrupt any more kids." Later in the article, he added, "I went along all right -- with the full knowledge of my superiors. No coach has any other choice under the unrealistic rules which prevail in the Coast Conference and others like it." In another publication, he said, "For the good of the university and for the benefit of my successor and other coaches out there, right-minded citizens should take affirmative action to fire Cassill, establish an athletic administration that will operate for the benefit of the students, and create a program without any connection with any downtown interests."

Lewis and other teammates felt Cherberg took a 'holier than thou' stance because they knew he had directed players to boosters for financial assistance. Lewis, for example, got into financial trouble at the end of his sophomore year. "I had no money to pay my Sigma Nu house bill. I could not work the required hours for grant-in-aid payments because of my considerable lab studies in the spring quarter. So I went to Cherberg and told him I needed a loan. He sent me downtown to meet with a booster and the booster starts paying me fifty dollars a month to be his 'campus representative.' "

University of Washington administrators denied the allegations. The Pacific Coast Conference (PCC) Commissioner, Victor O. Schmidt, suggested an investigation of Washington's athletic program.

In the PCC in those days, up to sixty student-athletes participating in the men's intercollegiate athletic program -- which consisted of nine major sports and a few minor ones -- could be provided tuition from university funds in any one year and all student-athletes could be given a campus job and/or summer jobs. Other athletes could receive tuition funds from money contributed by boosters. The rate of pay for campus jobs was $1.50 per hour up to a maximum of 50 hours or a total of $75 per month. Any payments in excess of $75 per month were in violation of PCC rules. Some players who had a high grade point in high school could receive academic scholarships.

In the book, Roses from Ashes: Breakup and Rebirth in Pacific Coast Intercollegiate Athletics, co-author Glen Seaborg, the University of California's conference faculty representative from 1952 until 1958, provides clear evidence that several PCC schools were violating the rules well before 1955. Former USC head football coach, Jeff Cravath, wrote a major article appearing in Colliers Magazine in late 1953 about the hypocrisy of college football and how the present system reduced the star players to perjurers, scalpers, and football gigolos. Many conference presidents felt that collegiate football was well on the path to professionalism and big time business and did not want to go farther down that road. Others felt the amounts provided to college football players were insufficient given the demands of education and the time spent in practicing and playing football. They argued the only sensible solution was the athletic scholarship -- tuition, room and board, books, and reasonable fees and living expenses.

There were stories of payments to student athletes at PCC schools well in excess of the $75 limit per month, mainly from sources outside the university. The Bear Backers, Bruin Bench, Ducks Club, Washington Advertising Fund, Southern Seas Society, and Westwood Young Business Men's Club, were just some of the booster clubs dotting the PCC's landscape.

One of the most widely circulated stories related to the payments made to Husky All-American running back Hugh McElhenny, when he was at Washington in the early 1950's. After McElhenny left Washington to join the San Francisco 49ers, his former teammates jokingly said that the star running back was the only college football player to take a cut in salary when he turned professional. During the PCC investigation of Washington in 1956, McElhenny said he and his wife had a combined income of $800 per month while in Seattle. He said he received $75 a month from an on-campus job. His wife earned $300 per month working for King County Medical. The balance of $425 was earned, he reported, for doing "public relations" work for Seattle's Rainier Brewing Company. He signed with the 49ers for $7000 a year and a $500 bonus. "The remark about me taking a cut in pay wasn't entirely off base," McElhenny concluded.

Before and during the Cherberg years, funds were provided to Husky football players by businessmen boosters. The largest source was the Washington Advertising Fund created to receive money earned from a professional football exhibition game in Husky Stadium in August 1955. Torrance was instrumental in establishing the fund through his association with Greater Seattle, Inc., the game's sponsor. Torrance talked the teams into coming to Seattle. He convinced the directors of Greater Seattle to sponsor the game. He persuaded the University's Board of Regents to allow professional teams to play in Husky Stadium for the first time for a percentage of the gate receipts.

Forty-nine thousand fans watched former Husky quarterback Don Heinrich lead the New York Giants to a 28-17 victory over the San Francisco 49ers. His former Husky teammate, 49ers Hugh McElhenny, did not play because of an injury.

It was a whopping success. Each team made $36,586; the ASUW received $28,361 for stadium rental and management fees; Greater Seattle turned a profit of $7,021. After taxes, there was $28,000 left. With a previous agreement with Greater Seattle, Torrance tucked it into the Washington Advertising Fund to pay Husky athletes.

Many groups weighed in after the Cherberg firing and the issues became polarized. The Organization Assembly representing over 200 of the university's student organizations voted 44-9 in favor of Cassill's action. A group of Washington alumni and athletic boosters announced it would circulate a state-wide petition urging Cassill be fired. Cassill didn't need to be fired; he resigned on February 9. As a result of the most tumultuous period in Husky athletics, the University of Washington was without leadership in two important positions. Athletic probation was a very real threat, the community was divided over the Cherberg-Torrance-Cassill hassle, and spring football practice was due to begin in a few months.

To fill one of the two positions, Washington hired George Briggs, the 31-year-old assistant athletic director at the University of California as its athletic director. Everest recommended him because Briggs was young and a capable athletic administrator and because "he had no connection with any factions or any group associated with this University. I feel the best interests of the University will be served by a man from outside the University circles...Mr. Briggs has accepted his post with the definite understanding that the development of all University athletics must be conducted entirely within Pacific Coast Conference rules and policies." Briggs was given complete control of the Department of Athletics.

A former Seattle resident, Briggs graduated from Seattle's Roosevelt High School in 1943. He entered the Marine V-12 program at Washington and graduated in engineering from the University of California. He was a member of Washington's and Cal's swim team and also played on the junior varsity basketball team. He was a veteran of World War II and the Korean War and completed his military duty as a Marine captain and battery commander of an artillery unit.

The appointment of Briggs on February 15 was met with some opposition. A group of Washington alumni conferred with University President Henry Schmitz and declared Briggs would be "unacceptable to a large representative group of alumni." Some prominent alumni proposed their own candidate. It was the same group that wanted Cassill fired. They also wanted Everest fired so that a fresh approach might be taken. The Washington Quarterbacks Club led by former Husky All-American Vic Markov backed the Briggs' appointment. "We are getting tired of the fighting and think it is time it was settled so we can get back to football."

About this time, a Washington State Legislature review of the athletic situation began together with investigations by the Pacific Coast Conference and the National Collegiate Athletic Association. As a result, on May 6, 1956, all Washington teams, except crew, were placed on a two-year probation starting July 1, 1956. The investigations disclosed that 27 football players had received an average of $60 per month over the allowed $75. The PCC ruling prevented any Washington team from winning any conference championships, the football team from appearing in the Rose Bowl, and the basketball team from competing in post-season games. The school could not participate in the distribution of receipts from the Rose Bowl Game, including receipts for radio and television rights, and could not nationally televise any home games or events. It was estimated the loss of receipts from the Rose Bowl would amount to $53,000 over the two probationary years. All other sports, except crew, could not compete for any championships.

The NCAA subsequently declared all Washington teams ineligible to participate in postseason and national championship events. Because sports other than football had not violated the PCC rules, there was a significant outcry. When the NCAA put the crew on probation, the Washington State Senate sent a letter to the NCAA and the Intercollegiate Rowing Association urging them to stop "the unreasonable, uncalled for and unwarranted indictment" of the Washington crew program.

Later in 1956, three other schools in the conference were placed on probation. California for one year, USC for two and UCLA for three years. In January 1959, the NCAA again placed USC on probation until January 1961 for recruiting violations. All schools placed on probation received restrictions similar to those placed on Washington. Cal was fined $25,000, UCLA $15,000 and USC $10,000. In the UCLA case, called by one sportswriter as "perhaps the severest punishment in the history of intercollegiate athletics," the conference faculty representatives voted six to one (USC) with two abstentions -- UCLA and Idaho -- to inform the President of the University of California system, Robert Sproul, and UCLA's Chancellor Raymond Allen:

"that the Conference has reluctantly come to the conclusion that it cannot confidently expect the athletic program at UCLA will

be conducted at the level of honesty and decency expected of a
Conference institution so long as that athletic department is
conducted under those members of the athletic staff at UCLA
who are responsible for the current breakdown in integrity."

San Francisco Chronicle columnist Art Rosenbaum wrote about the future of the conference wondering if all the other conference schools were innocent as not charged. It was inconceivable that the recruitment programs at the other schools were completely unsullied. "To get hot college athletes, a recruiter must outbid the other school... The whole thing has become an 'arms race.' "

Briggs' initial tasks were to stop the funding of players' expenses and find a new football coach. He did not care about what had gone on at Washington before his arrival and certainly was not on any one side in the turmoil. "I have not been involved in any way in (Washington's) athletic picture." He got all the contributors to the Washington Advertising Fund, the Quarterbacks Club, and other booster groups together and declared he was going to form the Tyee Club. He explained the "Tyee" was a Pacific Coast Native American word meaning "the chief." It was also used to describe Chinook salmon 30 pounds or more. So Briggs wanted the "big fish" boosters to contribute to the Tyee organization. All contributions to the athletic program would be funneled through this new group under the control of the university and the administration of the athletic department. The funds would be used for grant-in-aid to athletes, under the PCC rules. In exchange for their contributions, Tyee members could purchase football and basketball season tickets in favorable viewing locations.

Next Briggs focused on hiring a new football coach. He wanted a coach that was tough on conditioning and discipline and could win games in the fourth quarter. "We were getting a reputation in the Pacific Coast Conference as a party, play-time, country club in football. The conference champion would go to the Rose Bowl and get their butts kicked by the Big Ten victor. They would eat our lunch in the third and fourth quarters." He was right.

Since the Rose Bowl Committee formed the pact between the Big Ten Conference and the Pacific Coast Conference champions in 1946, the Big Ten representative won nine of the ten Rose Bowl games through 1956 -- USC had defeated Wisconsin 7-0 in the 1953 contest. Three were lopsided victories -- Illinois over UCLA 45-14 in 1947; Michigan's 49-0 thrashing of Stanford in 1948; and the fighting Illini's win over Stanford 40-7 in 1952.

Briggs continued, "I called the three best coaches in the country -- Michigan State's Duffy Daugherty, Texas A&M's Bear Bryant and Bud Wilkinson of Oklahoma. I didn't expect any of them to accept my offer to be Washington's head coach. Each of them felt he was running a better program and did not want to start all over again." Briggs would ask each of them, "If you were in my spot, who would you hire?" On everybody's list was Darrell Royal, the head coach at Mississippi State. Briggs called Royal and found out that he was interested in the Washington situation. So, Briggs flew to Mississippi to meet Royal and his wife Edith. "I spent the day with them, offered him the job, and Royal accepted it."

Briggs then had to get the University of Washington's Board of Regents approval and also the approval of the ASUW Board of Control because they had been in the thick of the coaching and athletic department situation. "I went in to the Regents meeting and made my proposal for a four-year contract at the magnificent sum of seventeen thousand dollars."

"It was one of the highest salaries paid to college football coaches in 1956. One regent wanted to know why the Board would be so stupid as to approve a four-year contract when it had just fired Cherberg?" Briggs replied, "Who would be dumb enough to come here if you would not give him a multi-year contract when you've got regents who are firing coaches all the time?" The Regents voted unanimously to hire Royal for four years.

Royal's salary created a lot of controversy on campus. The University Daily polled the school's faculty on the matter and reported that 79 percent of the faculty felt football should be de-emphasized and 81 percent thought that the new coach's salary was too high. Time Magazine declared that the faculty had reason for outrage since the average annual pay was $8,469 for a full professor not teaching in the professional schools such as law, business, and medicine. Finally, local sports columnist, Emmett Watson, noted a few days later in the Seattle Post-Intelligencer that football coaches usually were paid more than professors because they got fired more frequently than professors. Any job with a high turnover, Watson explained, usually commands good money. He then went on to quote an unidentified coach. "A biology professor can flunk 25 percent of his class and nobody pays any attention. But let Royal send a football team out next fall that flunks one test in front of 50,000 people and he's in thick soup." Watson added, "The conclusion is clear: big time football is a thing apart from education, and a professor might as well fret over the salary paid Groucho Marx as worry how much the football coach makes. Both are in the entertainment business, and both had better produce -- or else."

Royal was attracted to Washington for several reasons. "I had a good and really understanding athletic director in George Briggs. There were a lot of things related to the Cherberg situation that worked to my benefit. You could see what you could improve. If you come into a situation where everything is greased and polished and running smooth, how do you change anything?" Royal felt that a young coach should be looking for a place that has problems and then set about to solve them. "It gives you a base upon which to build."

When Royal arrived in Seattle, he said he would like to put

his suitcases in the attic and stay awhile. After graduating from Oklahoma in 1950 where he played under Coach Bud Wilkinson and was an All-American quarterback in 1949, he began his itinerate coaching career. His first stop was as the backfield coach at North Carolina State in 1950. He went to Tulsa in 1951, and Mississippi State in 1952. He received his first head coaching assignment in the Canadian Football League in 1953 as the leader of the Edmonton Roughriders. Edmonton won the Western Division Championship with 16 wins and five losses. He returned to Mississippi State as head coach in 1954.

Shortly after Royal accepted Washington's head coaching position, he called Corky Lewis who was deciding whether to play in 1956. Lewis told Royal that he was going to be in medical school in the fall of 1956 and was not going to play. "Anybody can be a doctor. But not everybody can play major college football," Royal replied. Lewis said football had not been fun. "I will make it fun. You stay and I will make it fun," Royal exclaimed. Lewis decided to stay.

The future doctor felt that Royal was very positive and upbeat and a refreshing change from Cherberg. However, in his first meeting with the team, Royal said it was an absolutely horrible thing that the team did in kicking out Cherberg. "Based on my interaction with him before that meeting," Lewis said, " I thought I knew him enough to say 'Coach, that stuff about kicking Cherberg out was the wrong thing to say to the team.' " "What?" Royal asked. "These guys were looking for a little praise -- we have some good players coming back," replied Lewis. Royal agreed to reverse the message. On the next day, the team heard a completely different talk.

Royal began to build a good football program. In the spring, he introduced the Split-T offense he learned under Wilkinson at Oklahoma. By the time practice started in late August, Husky fans were more interested in the team's upcoming season than rehashing the painful past.

The 1956 team had some good players returning. There was strength in the backfield with Credell Green and Jim Jones at fullback, and co-captain Dean Derby, Mike McCluskey and sophomore Luther Carr at halfback. The line featured Whitey Core, Dick Day, Don McCumby, George Strugar, and co-captain Lewis and Jim Houston at ends.

In the season opener, the Huskies rolled up a school single-game record 430 yards (now the second best in school history) and a record 33 first downs (also the second best in history) in defeating Idaho 53-21. It was an impressive debut for Royal. The next week, Minnesota gave Royal his first Husky loss 34-14. Then, 13th-ranked Illinois came to town. Washington beat the Illini 28-13, a contest that featured Derby's 92-yard touchdown run on the Huskies' second play from scrimmage. Washington took over after stopping Illinois' opening drive on the Husky six.

In their fourth straight home game, the Huskies beat Oregon 20-7 in its conference opener. The fans were flying high and thinking about a conference title. They were brought to earth as the Huskies lost their next four games, all to conference foes. They closed out the season with wins over Stanford and Washington State.

With a 5-5 record, Royal had laid a solid foundation. He stressed that team members be great representatives for the university. He believed that "if a player behaved in such a manner as to embarrass the university and the rest of the team, we are better off without him." He emphasized the academic side. "Players must give the same kind of attention to their studies as we expect them to give to football." He wanted his relationships with faculty to be positive. So, he started to invite three professors each week to join the team from the Thursday before the game to the end of the game. Royal wanted them to see what the coaches did and what the team did. Many faculty members believed Royal was a better teacher than most faculty members.

Everybody looked forward to a royal future. However, Royal's future would be elsewhere. After the 1956 season, Texas came calling. At a Husky home basketball game in early December, Briggs was in the athletic director's aisle seat near the court. Royal came down and sat next to Briggs and said that he just got a call from Texas asking if he was interested in the head coaching job. Royal didn't want to respond to Texas before talking with Briggs because he knew what Washington was trying to do, the kind of commitment he had made, the four to five years it would take to turn the program around, and that he didn't want to blow it apart at this time. Briggs asked Royal, "What do you think of the Texas job?" Royal replied, "I think it's the best football coaching job in college today." Briggs said, "Let's go right now and call Dana Bible (the Texas athletic director). "I called Dana and told him he would be crazy if he didn't hire Royal. My theory was, even though I might have been able to convince Darrell to stay, he would be looking over his shoulder all the time wondering why he stayed. He would be thinking, 'Should I have gone, what would I have accomplished?' That's not the kind of situation you want in football coaching or in any other business."

Royal and his wife wanted to be closer to their parents. "I had a young family when I was in Seattle. I'm from Oklahoma. When I got time off -- say a week -- I couldn't afford to fly the whole family back to Oklahoma and rent a car and do all that stuff. We didn't know when the grandparents would ever see our kids. It was too far to drive and turn around and come back within the vacation period. I wasn't running away from anything. I was running to something."

So Royal left for a long and very successful career with the Longhorns. His teams would win three national championships and eleven Southwest Conference titles. He was the first Washington football coach to leave the program voluntarily since Victor Place left in 1908 to coach at Notre Dame.

Briggs went back to the list of head coaching candidates he had compiled just ten months ago. He attended the NCAA coaches convention in early January and talked to some possible candidates. He brought a couple of them to Seattle for interviews. The press would scout the hotels and the airport to try to find who the candidates were. Briggs said it was easy to foil the press by "putting up the visitors in his home, take them around campus, introduce them to university staff, have our own meetings, and take them back to the airport."

One of the names on his list when he hired Royal was Jim Owens. "The reason why he wasn't a candidate for me the first time was that he was not a head coach," Briggs explained. "I didn't believe I could come to Washington with all the turmoil we had and bring in an assistant coach, however good he was, and get away with it. I had to have a head coach then."

Briggs thought the situation in 1957 was much different from the 1956 search. He had been the athletic director for almost a year and had cleaned up the boosters' mess. He had achieved some stabilization and confidence in the program by interacting with fans, faculty, students, alumni, and other supporters. He also felt he had a broader array of candidates. Still, the program had its outside influences. In the midst of his search, he was visited by a prominent group of alumni who said they had already selected a new coach -- Joe Kuharich, the coach of the Washington Redskins.

Briggs unhesitantly and firmly told them he would not pick anyone they had chosen. "If the new coach is not selected by the Athletic Director and the University Administration, then the coach isn't working for us." Otherwise Briggs reasoned, the University would be in the same position as in the recent past when outsiders were actively involved in activities impacting the athletic program.

Owens' skills had been highly developed by several great

coaches. He played at Oklahoma University for two outstanding coaches -- Jim Tatum and Bud Wilkinson. He was an assistant for six years under the legendary Paul "Bear" Bryant during Bryant's tenure at the University of Kentucky and Texas A&M.

Owens first met Briggs at the NCAA coaches convention in early January 1957. He flew to Seattle to meet with Briggs and other university officials in mid-January to discuss the coaching situation. Owens also was interested in the University of Houston's position. He arrived to freezing weather. Having flown all night, he was not concerned as much about the weather as he was about his appearance. The airlines had lost his luggage and the suit he had on looked as if he had slept in it. And he had.

Briggs met Owens at the airport. "When Jim arrived, as near as I could tell, he was fully prepared to stay. He gave the impression that he was going to get the job at Washington."

Owens interested Briggs because of his record as an assistant under Bryant. The Aggie coach would declare that "Jimmy is the best young coach in America." Bryant was not at all vague about Owens' qualities. "Last year, he was in charge of our offense. The year before he was in charge of our defense when we had the best defensive record in the country... He's had great training. He was well-grounded in fundamentals under Jim Tatum and Bud Wilkinson, and he's gone through a couple of building jobs with me, so he knows what it takes to build a team." One Texas newspaper reporter added, "He just looks like one of our cowboys coming in off the range."

Briggs also wanted Owens because of his split-T experience. Owens could continue the same offense that Royal had implemented in 1956.

Owens' return trip included a stopover in Houston. A few days later, on January 18, Houston announced the hiring of ex-Sooner Hal Lahar, giving credence to Owens' interest in Washington.

On January 21, Owens became the Huskies' head coach. He signed a three-year contract for $15,000 a year. An editorial in the University Daily, while bemoaning the size of Owens' salary, cited that football was now big business and a good football coach was a priceless commodity.

In his introduction to the media, Owens was announced to be 30 years old. In fact, he was about a month-and-half shy of his 30th birthday. He silenced any critics who still had thoughts of Royal's leaving after one year. In his first public appearance in Bremerton a few weeks later, he said, "When I first saw Mt. Rainier, I felt like a displaced person seeing the Statue of Liberty for the first time. I'm here to stay."

CHAPTER 2

The Coaches Were Working Sons of Bitches

Growing up in Oklahoma City, Jim Owens knew he wanted to be a football player when he was about five years old. In the late 1930's and 1940's, many boys got involved in the sport of the season on neighborhood and school playfields, open fields and vacant lots. It was not an organized activity -- no coaches and parents were involved -- just boys picking up sides and going at it. Such activity took place until high school when the school you attended had a school team with one or two coaches for a sport.

In the 1930's, sports were much more than running football plays, swinging baseball bats, or shooting set shots; sports were a way to forget the misery people endured in those days, particularly in Oklahoma and the neighboring states.

The Dust Bowl took place in the southwestern Great Plains of the United States in the thirties and early forties. It was caused by misuse of the land and years of sustained drought. Many people, chasing dreams of thriving on their own farms, were attracted to the cheap land opening up in southeastern Colorado, western Kansas, the panhandle of Texas, and the northwestern section of Oklahoma. Over time, they plowed under the world's greatest grasslands which, for centuries, had provided grazing for herds of buffalo and hunting and tribal areas for the Comanche.

The buffalo grass that had held the soil in place had evolved as the perfect fit for the sandy loam of the arid climate. It could hold moisture a foot or more below ground level even during the summer droughts when the scorching hot winds drained the surface land of water-bearing life.

As the price of wheat soared during World War I, millions of acres were put into production. When the farmers tore out the sod, they tore out the roots of the grass and the creatures thriving in this natural habitat disappeared. The intruders left the land naked. The thin veneer of soil, baked from the sun's stifling heat, gave little resistance to the winds of winter in 1932. The soil was picked up and sent skyward. It eventually piled up in homes, schools, stores, farm equipment and people's hair, throats and lungs. Over several years, it resulted in one of the most difficult times in American history.

Millions of hectares of farmland became useless and people were forced to leave their homes. Many, with no alternatives, stayed. They suffered a double disaster as both the Great Depression and the Dust Bowl arrived about the same time. More than a quarter of a million fled west.

Many more -- about two thirds of the population living in the center of the Dust Bowl never left. They stayed for lack of money or lack of sense or a belief that tomorrow would be better.

Owens remembers the Dust Bowl conditions when he was a boy. His grandparents lived on a farm near Hollis, a small town in southwestern Oklahoma close to the border of the northwestern section of Texas. "Their fields had pretty much blown away and the dirt and sand had drifted and piled up against the barbed wire fences on the property," recalls Owens. "There was no rain for two or three years. They had no moisture at all. The water had dried up in the cattle ponds. There wasn't any way anybody could get any water to the cattle. Eventually they all died. My grandparents survived by sheer determination and scratching for what little they could salvage from the land and some government support."

Young boys, in the most severely devastated areas, who had dreams of playing at Oklahoma University couldn't escape the creeping depression and the dust that seemed to collect everywhere -- on fence posts and door-sills and inside homes. Many of them were concerned they would have to leave Oklahoma and never return again. One of the boys once asked his grandmother "Do you think we'll have to leave Oklahoma?" " I certainly hope not. Not yet anyway." The boy prayed each night that they would not have to leave so he could play for the Oklahoma Sooners. His name was Darrell Royal, Owens' teammate at Oklahoma.

Owens' father, James Evan Owens, had worked his way up from a stock room clerk to become the general manager of General Electric's Oklahoma City Division in the early 1940's. One of the division's larger contracts involved supplying lights for high school stadiums in Oklahoma and Texas. It was a source of pride for the depressed communities of the region to have lighted football fields. Owens would recall, "The towns were broke but the football teams had lights. A lighted football field was a rallying point for those towns that had little else." It was the start of "Friday Night Lights" and the passion of high school football in the Southwest.

Owens' path to Oklahoma began in his sophomore year at Classen High School in Oklahoma City. His first real football coach was Leo Higbie. As a sophomore, Owens was lanky and skinny and was initially placed on the junior varsity team that played in small towns outside of Oklahoma City. He performed well in the early season games and soon the assistant coach, Gene Ferguson, talked to Higbie and said, "I think Owens is good enough to move up to the varsity and get some tougher football experience." So

Higbie moved Owens up and he started scrimmaging with the varsity and played in some varsity games during the latter part of the season. "In my junior year, I played a lot," said Owens. "We had a good team that year. In my senior year, we had the best team that had been around in a long time. We won the 1943 state championship and I made the all-state team."

During World War II, the Navy established a program that enabled high school students to take credits toward a high school diploma in the summer before their senior year and graduate early. Owens took advantage of the program and graduated at the end of the fall semester. He had a keen interest in the Navy. Earlier in the year, he had taken a test to get an appointment to the Naval Academy. He decided instead to join the Navy.

Owens was sent to boot camp in San Diego in the winter of 1944. After a short stint in Norman, Oklahoma, he was assigned to the Corpus Christi Texas Naval Station which had been established in 1941. At Corpus Christi, he was part of a squadron that trained pilots for the PBY (Patrol Bomber) flying boats. They could be equipped with depth charges, bombs, torpedoes, and machine guns and were one of the most widely used aircraft of World War II.

Near the end of the war, many pilots who had been in very difficult missions came to Corpus Christi waiting for their next assignments and to help train new pilots. For the first time in his life, Owens was exposed to harassment and streams of profanity as the veterans incessantly ridiculed and tormented the rookies.

Near the end of his Navy career, Owens received a scholarship offer from Oklahoma University. He was discharged in time to begin his freshman year in the fall of 1946.

Oklahoma had a big-time football program. Beginning in 1946, the Sooners were ranked in the top twenty for 14 straight years. During that period, they were crowned national champions in 1950, 1955, and 1956. From the third game of the 1953 season until the eighth game of the 1957 season, the Sooners never lost a game, compiling an NCAA record 47-game winning streak. They broke the 39-game winning record the University of Washington teams established from 1908-1914. After Bud Wilkinson became head coach in 1947, the Sooners won 94 games, lost four, and tied two from 1948 to 1957. During that period they compiled 31 and 47-game winning streaks. It is a record unmatched in collegiate football history.

Owens was ready for such a program. He had grown to 6'4" and weighed about 220 pounds. Since freshmen could play varsity football in the years following World War II, Owens played end on the varsity teams of 1946-1949. Owens was the Sooners' co-captain in 1949 along with All-American guard, Stan West. Darrell Royal was the quarterback. During those years, two platoons were allowed. One platoon football in which players performed on both offensive and defensive, came into existence in 1953 and lasted until 1965. Unlike today, platooning then did not involve separate offensive and defensive units. The most successful football programs had two squads of somewhat equal ability. One squad or platoon would play both offense and defense. The second or alternate unit would be sent into the fray as the game dictated.

The Sooners played the split-T offense that had been introduced by Don Faurot at the Iowa Navy Pre-Flight program during World War II. He experimented with linemen splitting out different distances to get more advantageous blocking angles. All backs ran the ball. With the correct execution of the many options of the split-T, it was very difficult for the defense to see the ball.

During Owens' college career, Oklahoma went to three major bowl games. In January 1947, Oklahoma upended North Carolina State 34-13 in the Gator Bowl; in January 1949, it beat Charlie "Choo Choo" Justice's North Carolina team 14-6 in the Sugar Bowl; in January 1950, the Sooners again won the Sugar Bowl defeating LSU 35-0. LSU had beaten four conference champions during the regular season.

Owens ended his collegiate career as an All-America selection and would be named to the All-Wilkinson team in 1960. He was cited as the best end in Oklahoma football history.

In June 1947, Owens married Martha Jane Wood right after they had completed their freshmen year. A lot of players were married in those days. Many had been in the service and some in combat and so they were older and more mature than many other college students in that period. The GI Bill provided financial assistance to the returning servicemen. Colleges were jammed with such students and some schools had accelerated academic programs to get students graduated more quickly. Owens graduated in three years and entered Oklahoma Law School in the fall of 1949.

One of his fondest memories as a college player was in the College All-Star game played in the summer of 1950 in fabled Soldier's Field in Chicago. The format had the graduated collegians playing the National Football League champions -- then the Philadelphia Eagles. Led by Eddie LeBaron, the passing wizard from the College of the Pacific, the All-Stars beat the Eagles 17-7. Owens recalls, "We were just a bunch of guys who got together for a week and then beat the Eagles' butts. It was wonderful."

Owens signed a contract with the Baltimore Colts in 1950 for $4500 plus a $500 cash bonus. Y.A. Tittle was the quarterback of that team. The lowly Colts won only one game that season. Financially, it was a disaster. Owens recounts that the owner counted the sticks of gum distributed to each player.

Near the end of the 1950 season, the Colts were playing the Steelers in Pittsburgh. Owens played both ways and on a defensive play, he was hit in the kidney. He continued in the game until the finish. In the locker room, he felt pretty sick and the team physician found a blood clot in his kidney. Owens stayed in a hospital in the

Steel City for the next week until the clot dissolved. He didn't play the last two games of the season.

Earlier in the season, Chuck Guy, in his first year as Johns Hopkins' head football coach, had asked Owens to attend afternoon practices and assist him in introducing the split-T offense. The Colts practiced in the morning so Owens was free in the afternoon to assist Guy and his team. Owens' commitment to assist for a couple of weeks turned into a coaching role for the entire Johns Hopkins season. This assignment built on his student assistant role on the Oklahoma coaching staff in the Spring of 1950.

Owens returned to Oklahoma Law School after the Colts' season ended and was a student assistant again during the 1951 spring practice. Owens had several interests at that point -- law, politics, and coaching. However, he had loved football since he was a little boy. "Really good things had happened to me playing football. The feeling of the game, the competition, just being out playing. When I was small we played in the rain and got covered completely in mud. We didn't have to, we just loved it." As Owens continued playing in college and with the Colts, his love for the game grew and, consequently, a coaching career became very appealing. "Part of my interest in coaching was the impact coaches had on young men -- to get to know the players, to work with them, and to see them improve."

His opportunity soon came. In the spring of 1951, Coach Wilkinson conducted a football clinic for high school coaches. Wilkinson invited Paul (Bear) Bryant, Kentucky's football coach, to speak at the clinic. Bryant needed several men to demonstrate a point he was making. He picked several of the Oklahoma student assistants including Owens and Royal. A few weeks later, Owens received a call from Bryant asking him to meet in Dallas. Over lunch, Bryant asked Owens to be his end coach at Kentucky. "By the time that Bryant finished talking to me, I was ready to go. He was very persuasive."

Mrs. Owens had a different perspective. "I thought Jim would finish law school. We would settle down in Norman. We knew so many people there. It was a good fit. I cried for about three days and then packed our bags to go to Lexington, Kentucky."

Owens would spend the next three years at Kentucky helping the Wildcats compile a 19-10-3 record and a victory over Texas Christian in the 1952 Cotton Bowl.

In 1954, Bryant had had enough of Adolph Rupp, the Baron of Basketball at Kentucky. Rupp's teams had won the NCAA championship in 1948, 1949, and 1951 and clearly basketball was "the" sport at Kentucky. Both Rupp and Bryant had very large egos and competed for everything including the side of the room on which each would sit.

Texas A&M courted Bryant with suitcases full of money and a very challenging situation. He asked Owens to join him as the head assistant coach for the Aggies. At that point, Owens had received several offers from other schools to become a top assistant. One was from Coach Wilkinson at Oklahoma. It was Owens' dream job but the timing wasn't right. Owens had just accepted Bryant's offer.

Bryant and his staff faced a monumental rebuilding challenge. The Aggies had not won a conference championship since 1941 and had lost five games in 1953 by a combined score of 133-41. There were some features about A&M that were attractive. The institution had an elite cadet corps with a long tradition and great espirit de corps. However, there were significant drawbacks. In his book, Junction Boys, Jim Dent described the school. "The campus possessed all of the glamour of a stock show -- an all-military, all-male institution that looked like a penitentiary and boasted the color schemes of a grocery bag."

Many schools in the Southwest conference were country clubs compared to the "cow college" in College Station Texas. Football recruiters at rival schools told top prospects that at A&M, "they blow a horn to get you up, ring a bell to put you asleep, no girls, no nothin."

Owens would respond that the student-athletes that came to A&M really wanted to be Aggies. "Such young men were great to work with."

Bryant approached the rebuilding of the Aggie football program with three major tenets -- sacrifice, hard work, and self-discipline. "My approach to the game has been the same at all places I've been. Vanilla. The same way. That means, first of all, to win physically. If you get eleven on a field and they beat the other eleven physically, they'll win. They will start forcing mistakes. They'll win in the fourth quarter."

He also believed that if a group of players is willing to out-condition an opponent, be more aggressive than the opponent, and have a genuine desire for team victory versus individual acclaim, the team will become a champion.

To bake this philosophy into the mind, heart, and soul of each Aggie player returning to College Station for the 1954 pre-season practices, Bryant met them at 10 AM on August 31, and told them they would be going on a little trip. He didn't want them to call anybody about their leaving campus. Bryant wanted to get away from the administration and the "beer-bellied boosters" who would show up at practice every day. Two buses carrying over 100 players left College Station that morning and headed to Junction in West Texas, 200 miles from College Station. Two Quonset huts, a bathhouse, a mess hall, and a dirt field littered with rocks, cacti, and sand spurs, would be home for the A&M football team for the next ten days.

They rose at 4 AM each day and practiced in temperatures sometimes over 110 degrees. About a third of the players survived. The rest left camp at all hours of the day and night, many not wanting to confront Bryant as they left. A big part of the master plan at Junction was to shock the players' systems with conditioning drills and physical and mental intimidation and separate the quitters from the keepers. At the end of day ten, the 35 "survivors" boarded one bus for the return ride. Junction had molded their character and forged a winning spirit. It would take a couple of years to produce results. A&M went 1-9 in 1954, 7-2-1 in 1955 and 9-0-1 in 1956. Eight "Junction Boys" were seniors in 1956, proud members of the fifth-ranked team in the nation and Southwest Conference champions.

With his experience as an All-American end at Oklahoma and the mentorship of Bud Wilkinson and Bear Bryant, Owens would come to Seattle confident he could do a great job as the new head coach at the University of Washington. "I had great role models. It was like being a law clerk under a Supreme Court Justice. Only the judges were Wilkinson and Bryant. Wilkinson was so well organized and was such a believer in perfection and polish, quickness, speed and agility. He looked for players with those characteristics. It was a great experience to play under him and for a short time, to work as a student coach under him." Owens continued about his other mentor. "Bryant was a fundamentalist and was so concerned about the small things that would always be the difference between winning and losing. He made sure that all the small things were done in the correct manner. Then everything else would fall into place pretty well. He was such a great psychologist and he seemed to know what to say and not to say. His actions on the field seemed to inspire the players and bring out a burning desire to win that was unique among coaches." Ending his reflection on the impact of Wilkinson and Bryant, Owens smiled and said, "It couldn't have been any better."

Owens' first meeting with the Washington football team was on January 30, 1957.

He impressed many members of the team. He was an imposing

figure and possessed those characteristics everybody pictured in a football coach -- handsome features, size, energy, straightforward style, a bounce in his step. He was a leader. Dick Day, the 245-pound All-Coast lineman remembers his hand shake. "What a grip!" exclaimed Day. "If he can coach with that power, Washington football will be in good hands."

Many were pleased Owens planned to continue with the split-T offense. They felt they were just getting used to the formation when Royal pulled out. It was great to have a coach who would continue with virtually the same offensive system.

Not all felt positive about Owens. Luther Carr recalls that "I'm walking down the hallway, a little late to the first team meeting, and a few feet from the meeting room door. Owens looks at me and slams the door in my face. The reason I and a few other players were late was that as we were coming down toward campus, the Montlake Bridge was up for boat traffic. We were caught in the delay. Of course, we were all black." Carr said that later in the meeting Owens gave a speech about the need to be on-time. Owens told them, "When I call a meeting, say at 10 AM, I expect you to be in the room, sitting down, and waiting for me." Carr thought Owens' action showed disrespect, maybe racism; other players called it discipline, establishing team rules, and the start of the process to develop team unity.

All the players would soon find out many other aspects of their football lives would be different and, for some, dramatically different. In three months, spring practice would begin.

Twenty-four hours after Owens was hired, he announced the selection of three new coaches -- Bert Clark, Tom Tipps, and Chesty Walker.

Clark was a teammate of Owens at Oklahoma. He played for the Sooners from 1949-1951 and was an all-conference center and linebacker. He played one year in the Canadian Football League with the Calgary Roughriders. After two years in the Army, he joined the coaching staff at Arkansas for the 1956 season.

Tipps was on the coaching staff with Owens at Texas A&M. He grew up in Texas and graduated from Sul Ross State College in 1938 with a degree in economics. He later returned to that school to complete his masters' degree. After graduation, he became the head football coach at Seagraves (Texas) High School located near the border of New Mexico. Seagraves had not won a game in their 20-year history. Tipps immediately turned the program around and had three winning seasons before joining the US Army. He served from 1942-1945, rising to the rank of an infantry first sergeant. He returned to high school coaching at Pampa High School near Amarillo where he made a name for himself in the high school coaching fraternity. In his tenure at Pampa, Tipps compiled a record of 54 victories, 16 losses and 4 ties. Just 30 miles from Pampa was Phillips High School where Chesty Walker was rampaging through his opponents, losing as often as it snowed in the Texas Panhandle.

Tipps and Walker demonstrated their commitment and dedication to football and personal improvement by attending the first day of spring practice at Texas A&M in 1954. They jumped in a car near Amarillo and drove almost 400 miles to College Station to arrive at 5 AM when Bryant normally arrived in his office. Bryant was surprised when he saw the two high school coaches and said, "What are you up to?" "Just came to watch practice." After practice they drove back to Amarillo. They did that for as many days as they could get away to observe the rest of spring practice. Bryant and Owens invited them to sit in on coaches' meetings. Their commitment made a real impression on the Aggie coaches and Tipps was invited to join the Texas A&M staff in the summer of 1954.

Walker, 52 when he joined the Washington staff, was the "old man" of the group. He had earned the title as the "winningest high school coach in Texas." In 18 years as head coach at Phillips, his teams won 173 games, lost 24, and tied 6. They won or tied for the district championship 15 times and garnered the state championship in 1954. In the summers, Walker worked on oil rigs in Texas. "I was a greenhorn. The crew called me 'Educator.' They played merciless tricks on me. The money was fine but I ruptured a disk in my back. The only thing I could do then was to teach and coach football."

Because of his age, the twinkle in his eyes, his Texas drawl and Panhandle character, Walker was the "Father Confessor" type. He would provide a lot of counsel to many Husky players.

All four coaches, including Owens, came from the Southwest and had no experience playing with or coaching black players. Oklahoma did not have a varsity black player until 1957. Bear Bryant, under whom Owens and Tipps coached, had no blacks at Texas A&M. At Alabama where Bryant won six national championships after leaving A&M at the end of the 1957 season, there were no blacks until 1970. The game that persuaded the many racist fans, university administrators, and citizens of the State of Alabama to integrate football at Alabama was the Tide's season opener against USC in 1970. The visiting Trojans, featuring black running back Sam Cunningham, crushed the Tide 42-21. The story told is that Bryant invited USC coach McKay to bring the Trojans to Birmingham knowing that it was going to be a mismatch. The season before, USC finished 10-0-1 and third in the nation; Alabama had a 6-5 record.

Bryant wanted to speed up the process of racial integration on the Alabama team. He wanted to show the Tide's supporters what blacks could do on the playing field. Cunningham was the perfect example of someone who could not only knock down opposing defenses but also knock sense into the heads of the some university officials who were dug in on integration.

The next year, Bryant took a newly integrated Alabama team to Los Angeles and beat McKay's squad 17-10. The Crimson Tide would finish the season 11-1-0 and ranked fourth in the nation. It was a new era for 'Bama' football.

Washington had black players starting early in its football history. Johnny Prim was on the 1920 team but did not letter. Halfback Hamilton Green played in 1921 and was the first black to earn a football letter. He blocked a punt which set up a Husky field goal in the school's worst defeat ever -- a 72-3 thumping by California. Charlie Russell was another black that played before World War II. As a halfback, he lettered in 1937 on coach Jim Phelan's squad. The team beat Hawaii 52-13 in the Pineapple Bowl on January 1, 1938 and five days later trounced the Honolulu Townies 35-6.

In the four seasons before Owens took over, seven black players had been on Washington football teams. In 1957, five blacks would play. Sensing that maybe because of the new coaches' backgrounds there might be a racial bias, a reporter asked Owens shortly after he arrived, what his attitude on black players would be. "I certainly don't have any attitude, one way or the other. I have no feelings on the subject at all. To me, the Negro is the same as any other player and should be treated that way."

In March 1957, Owens selected Pete Susick as an assistant to get some connections and experience with the high school programs in the Northwest. Susick had played fullback on Husky teams in 1940-1943 and received the Flaherty Award as the most inspirational player in 1943. He had been a very successful head coach at Marshland High School in Coos Bay, Oregon, winning several state championships. In July, Susick would resign to return to Coos Bay. He missed high school coaching where he had control of everything and could implement his own coaching philosophy.

Susick was replaced by Norm Pollom, 32, who had graduated from Chehalis High School. After a four-year stint in the Navy, he attended the College of Puget Sound in Tacoma where he played end for three seasons and graduated in 1950. He then began his high school coaching career at Montesano High School, then on to Auburn, and, finally, to Aberdeen where his team finished second in the 1954 state polls. Because of that high ranking, he was a coach in the prep all-star game in the summer of 1955. He moved to Shoreline High School for the 1955 season and went to Morningside High School in southern California in 1956. He joined Owens' staff in July 1957 to provide recruiting connections in the Northwest and California.

Owens again went to the Oklahoma football pipeline to round out his 1957 coaching staff. He enticed Dick Heatly to join the staff. Heatly played for the Sooners for three seasons beginning in 1950. He was a halfback and punter. During the Korean War, he flew jets. In February 1957, Heatly joined the staff at Iowa State and coached through spring practice when he left to join the Washington staff.

All the coaches were winners. Clark, Heatly and Owens had played on some outstanding Oklahoma teams and received the coaching of the great Sooner staff. Tipps, Walker, and Pollom had been very successful high school coaches. The entire staff was clearly focused on turning the Washington program into an outstanding one.

Owens installed much of the same system of coaching responsibilities used by Coach Bryant. None of the coaches had any specific designation such as end coach, backfield coach or line coach. They would each work with all the players and still focus on some specific areas of expertise. Most importantly, they would all work with the freshmen team during the 1957 season. They recognized the future of the program rested with the incoming class, many of whom they recruited and all of whom had the characteristics the coaches wanted. Owens emphasized, "The freshmen came in with clean hands."

The coaches worked very hard during the months before spring practice and looked at lots of film to determine the skills of the returning Husky players. "Film in those days was terrible," Owens said. "The projectors were terrible. When you got film that had been reviewed before by the last group to use it, usually it was burned in several places. It was a nightmare. People wondered why we spent so much time in the film room -- hell, you spent half the time getting something to look at. But that was the only way in the off season you could determine the skills of the players."

The viewing sessions were very long and frequently the coaches would doze off in the late evening or early morning sessions. Sometimes, they would awake with film all over the floor. There was only one projector in the entire athletic department. The department secretary exercised strict control over its use. She was the gate keeper and relished her power.

The coaches also were shaping their approach to spring practice. On the one hand, they had to deal with the fact that the players didn't know much about the coaches. It was the third coaching staff in three years for some of the them. In addition, the players had to become acquainted with many new techniques, drills, and actual on-field work that was at a level much different than they had experienced before. These new expectations would be shaped by the underlying fundamental principles to which Coach Owens and his coaching staff were firmly committed.

The first was team unity. Owens was not interested in players that focused on personal statistics and making all-star teams. His teams had no names on their jerseys. He recruited players that were smart and would sacrifice their own recognition for that of the team. He wanted people who could fit into his system. He certainly was not interested in having the Husky Sports Information Department develop press releases and the hype that now surrounds the college football scene related to individual players. He did not care about the Heisman award, All-America selections, and All-Coast recognition. If it came to some players, that was fine but team success and recognition were more important.

The Washington Media Guide in 1957 was less than 20 pages. It contained no pictures and minimum information about players. When Owens held a copy of the 2005 Football Media Guide -- over 200 pages long -- he quipped that "it weighed more than some of my linemen did in my initial years at Washington."

Defense was another principle of Owens' football. He would get the Huskies to commit to football "from the defense out." Playing defense was the real test of a player's liking for the game. The best defenders ultimately would be the best football players. If a player couldn't or wouldn't play defense , he would not get much playing time under Owens' system.

A third fundamental was conditioning. Owens and his staff believed that being physically and mentally tough was the key to winning football games. They wanted the Huskies to be in better shape than any opponent, to wear the opposition down, and by the fourth quarter, to run over the tired collapsing foe. The coaches believed players could do more than they thought they could do. "You run drills to get a player to a physical and mental point where he believes he can't give anymore and then you continue to push him so he has to fight through the 'breaking point' and so he understands that he can handle more pain and sacrifice." Owens continued. "Football is a game of power and you beat opponents by beating them physically."

Finally, Owens expected his players to "pay the price." He firmly believed that the best football teams were those that did whatever it took on the practice field to prepare for each Saturday afternoon.

"To do that demands sacrifice and the desire to succeed. I want the kind of player who is willing to pay the price," Owens stated.

One drill they would implement integrated many of these basic principles. At the end of a grueling practice, when all the players were tired and hurting, Owens would have the offense attempt to run ten plays perfectly. When the players accomplished that, everybody could go to the locker room.

"To get eleven guys doing everything right for ten plays when they are tired is really difficult. If one guy jumps offside, you have to go back to zero." Owens continued. "The drill did three things. It made you concentrate more. When you are really tired, it is much harder to concentrate on perfect execution. Second, you are doing this drill with ten other guys -- your teammates -- and you are building camaraderie. The players start to say, 'By God, we went through that tough drill together and we are working better as a team.' " Owens summed up the drill by saying, "You find out whether you love football or not. And if you don't love it, you shouldn't play."

During the spring, the coaches also recruited players. Recruiting was pretty much an annual affair. There were no NCAA recruiting rules, no blackout periods, no letters of intent. In fact, a recruited player could participate in pre-season practices with one team and then leave to go to another team as long as he had not enrolled in classes at a particular school. Since Washington had a comparatively late start (near the end of September) of the academic fall quarter, the entire pre-season at Washington was conducted before classes began. So every recruit who participated in the pre-season could leave and go to another school before classes began. Recruiting and re-recruiting went on every day.

On May 1, 1957, Coach Owens welcomed 58 players to the start of spring practice. Twenty were letterwinners. Seventeen were freshmen and two were junior college transfers. Only one returning letterwinner, fullback Jim Jones, was an All-Coast player. Al Ferguson, the starting quarterback in 1956, had an off-season shoulder operation and could not participate in the spring.

Owens wanted to keep things simple. He stressed conditioning, fundamentals, and defensive techniques initially. He introduced a lot of discipline into the practices. Everything was done quickly, with military precision. All players wore their helmets at all times. Emmett Watson reported on a day in spring practice in early May. "Owens moved from group to group, working with quarterbacks and centers, then the backs, then the tackles and finally the guards. Wearing only practice pants and a light T-shirt, he crouched down in front of a bucking sled to demonstrate. Abruptly, he raised up, slammed his elbows and head into the sled, driving it back a few feet. At one point as the players hit the sled, Owens' voice suddenly rose and he said, 'I don't see anybody trying to break the sled. Go ahead, break it -- we'll buy a new one. Deliver the blow! Deliver the blow!' " In another drill Watson observed, Owens invited a 210-pound tackle to charge him at full tilt. The tackle charged, throwing a high block across the coach's body. Owens calmly caught the player in both arms and held him in the air momentarily and went on talking to the squad.

There were many drills -- pass interceptions, tackling, ball handling, stances, starts, drive blocks, and reaction tests. Players were instructed to drop on the ground on any ball that fell on the turf, anytime, anywhere. Kermit Jorgensen, a 195-pound quarterback during the 1959-1961 seasons, tells about his fumbling a few times in a practice session. "Owens didn't like how I got on the ball after I fumbled. So he picked me up by my ass and my helmet and I was dangling in the air. Then he ran me over to the ball and threw me angrily on it. After being picked up several times, I cured the problem. It was very humiliating. The coaches were very physical."

It was a tough spring for the players. Owens had to find out in a hurry which of the players were going to be able to handle the physical and mental part of the program and pay the price. By the end of the four-week spring sessions, the team had dwindled to 35 players. Owens was satisfied with the first unit but bemoaned the lack of depth.

Practices would cease until early September but the coaches worked hard during the summer months. They viewed film after film sometimes without a projector. They wanted to see what each player needed to improve and how they could better mold the varsity team into one which met their coaching philosophy. They discussed the incoming prospects. They discussed passing routes and blocking angles. Each day involved recruiting -- letters and phone calls to high school and junior college coaches and players.

Keith Jackson, the renowned college football broadcaster, was then Director of Sports for KOMO, the ABC affiliate in Seattle. "The coaches worked like no coaching staff I can ever remember. They were working sons of bitches. The coaching staff was just like a bunch of Marines trapped in a lonely place. They backed each other up and committed themselves to each other and to their philosophy."

CHAPTER 3

The Body is the Tool of The Mind

As the 1957 preseason got under way in September, Owens and his coaches continued to see two problems -- lack of depth and inexperience at quarterback. Only 20 of the 53 players who turned out were letterwinners. Al Ferguson, the number one quarterback, was still recovering from shoulder surgery in the spring. Bob Dunn was designated to take over as field general. He had been a halfback in 1953 and 1954 and sat out the next two seasons with injuries.

Washington had a solid core of running backs led by Jim Jones, Luther Carr, Mike McCluskey, and Dick Payseno. The line was mobile but a good deal lighter than in recent years. It averaged 197 pounds. The Huskies only had considerable line experience at the tackle position -- anchored by Don McCumby and Dick Day.

To compensate for the lack of depth and experience, Owens continued to stress fundamentals and conditioning. "When you have less personnel than others, you have to look for any edge you can find. We decided to excel in the conditioning area because we hadn't had much time with the players and hadn't had the time to get our philosophy installed in the program."

After the first week of practice, many players had shed several pounds as a result of the tough practices. Owens, however, was still concerned about their physical and mental fitness. On September 10, he was determined to find out.

In the second of two practices that day and with the temperature over 90 degrees, Owens held a four-quarters scrimmage. He was very disturbed over the play of the first two units and ordered two more quarters. Then, he called everyone over and reamed the players out. He ordered them down to the practice fields east of Hec Edmundson Pavilion. He lined them up in teams and had each squad cover punts. "Nobody fielded the punts. We just went full bore down the field and stayed in our lanes. After covering eight or ten punts, we figured that was going to be it," Dan Wheatley recalls.

The drills continued. Owens ordered all the players to line up on one goal line. Each player started in a three-point stance and on Owens' whistle, they ran up the field about 15 yards. Another whistle, another three-point stance, another whistle. They continued the wind sprints over the entire length of two football fields and then turned around and came back. Back and forth -- maybe 15 times. After several round trips, the group was in a kind of V-shape with the more conditioned and committed players in the middle. Some staggered and fell. Then they crawled. "They babbled and cried like babies as the assistant coaches lined down the field and urged them on," reported sports writer Mike Donohoe.

One of the senior linemen thought it was Owens' way of punishing us, of trying to figure out who wanted to play. "We were the scum, the leftovers from the Cherberg revolt, and Owens was going to get rid of the ones who couldn't stand the physical treatment."

After the drills were over, some players lay on the nearby bank and took their helmets off. When Owens saw that, he charged over to the group and said, "I told you (at the first team meeting) you never take your helmet off when you are on the field and never take it off until you are clear off the field going to the locker room. Put your helmets back on and line up again on the field." The team did wind sprints for another length of the field.

During all of the practice sessions, nobody could drink water. That was the conventional treatment of athletes, military personnel and others in tough conditioning situations in those days. Supposedly, you would get cramps if you drank water.

When the team was finally dismissed, many had severe cramps, seven had to go to the University Hospital for treatment, all were exhausted.

The team stayed in the Conibear crew house before they started classes in early October. They ate there, slept there, and came together there. After dinner that evening, the players watched film of the scrimmage. McCumby said that after the film was over, Owens commented that in the scrimmage, the play wasn't all that bad. "I just went into orbit. I thought 'you(Owens) tell everybody they are lousy football players and then turn around and after seeing the film say...Oh you weren't too bad after all.' I was at the point of quitting right there. I went away for a day and then came back."

Some players had similar thoughts. Some had their spirits broken. Others lost respect for the coaches and didn't want to pay the price required and left the program. Some resolved to stay the course and embrace the principles of the program. All had a little different perspective on the day.

John Owen, a noted sports columnist for the Seattle Post-Intelligencer, remembers Donohoe, who was covering the Huskies for the P-I in 1957, came into the sports department after the practice was over and began talking about what he termed the "Death March." After describing what went on, he exclaimed, "They ran the kids up and down the field. If they fell down, they called them gutless bastards."

Mike Crawford, a lineman in 1957 and 1959, remembers

the impact on him and said that he has done nothing physically tougher than the Death March including Marine Corps boot camp. "Duane Lowell was in the best physical shape of anybody -- he would always do everything ten times more than everybody else. Finally, near the end of the day, they took him out. His whole body was in spasms. He spent one or two nights in the hospital getting saline solution in his body to get his electrolytes back in balance. There were several seniors -- big guys -- that said 'Screw this, this isn't football, this is bull-shit.' "

All of the coaches had gone through strenuous forms of conditioning either in military service or in football practice. Tipps went through some challenging drills at Sul Ross College whose coach at that time had graduated from the United States Military Academy.

"One day he heard some of the squad had broken training rules," Tipps recalled. "He ran us 440 yards, then had us do starts and stops -- 20 yards and fall on your stomach. When we went the length of the field, he ran us another 440 yards. There were 42 of us on the squad. In the first ten minutes three passed out. Three hours later, we were still running laps and falling on our stomachs. And not another man passed out. You can't tell me that among those 39 young men, there wasn't a great variation in strength and endurance. But not one of them dropped out."

"I hated that coach, but he taught me a great thing. I found out that the human body is a lot tougher than the mind gives it credit for. The body is the tool of the mind. I found out what a marvelous mechanism we have under our eyebrows."

John Thompson, the Director of Public Relations for the athletic department, can still remember the Death March. "When it was all over, I had to take the reporters to visit with Jim. He was almost crying. He said, 'I hope I never have to do that again.' The Death March -- physical and mental toughness -- made Husky football and ultimately revived the Pacific Coast Conference." Coach Tipps expressed the same conclusion. "The Death March was a big deal. West Coast football had a reputation of being a soft touch. We went in the opposite direction. People made a big deal of what we were putting the players through at Washington. I think we brought back a hard-nosed approach to football in the Pacific Coast Conference."

Owens would years later say, "There are few times when you really feel it is necessary to test your team as to how much physical and mental conditioning your players have. It (September 10) was certainly one of our toughest days of physical conditioning, but a certain amount of legend built up around that particular day. It's a lot like combat training. There are times when you have to give your men a reasonable facsimile of what they are going to face. It was tough on them, but I had gone through the same experience at Oklahoma, the Navy, (and with the 'Junction Boys' at Texas A&M)."

The Death March would be the defining moment for the 1957 football team. It is etched in the minds of all who went through it. The stories about that day would be told to the incoming freshmen players and transfers from junior colleges for years to come. It would become part of the Husky football lore. Washington's reputation for toughness, tenacity, and endurance that started in 1957 would become the foundation for a very successful football program in the years to come.

Owens also introduced another drill that had been successful at Texas A&M -- the challenge drill. The varsity team was divided into several units -- first through fifth -- and they wore different colored jerseys -- purple, gold, red, green, and black respectively. The challenge drill gave linemen an opportunity to challenge a player in the unit above him for his spot on that team. All the challenger had to do was to inform a coach that he wanted to challenge.

Challenges would take place twice a week as the first activity of the practice session in front of the whole team. A coach would set up two tackling/blocking dummies two yards apart. The drill would involve a quarterback, a running back, and the challenging lineman and the challenged lineman. The challenger would first try to create a lane for the running back by blocking the "opposing" lineman. The challenger would have three opportunities on offense to try to get the running back gain up to ten yards each time. Then the roles would be reversed. If the challenger won, the challenged player and the victor would have to swap jerseys immediately in front of the whole team.

"I don't think the players liked the challenge drills," recalls Tim Bullard. "I think the coaches put them in to keep the gold and red units thinking they had a chance to move up. The drills were vicious."

Some felt the coaches arranged the challenges. In 1961, when Bullard was a senior and Ray Mansfield was a junior, they shared time at the center position. "Every goddam Tuesday and Wednesday, I walk into the locker room and look at the challenge board and go to Mansfield and say 'You son-of-a-bitch, did you challenge me?' " Mansfield told him that he had not. Next week, Mansfield would confront Bullard. "Timmie, did you challenge me?" "No," said Bullard. They figured Tipps was the one putting the names on the board. The coaches believed that some of the players were not getting enough challenges and so they arranged some.

The drill had several advantages. It stopped the players grumbling to coaches about playing time. It was an excellent motivator and morale booster. It helped the coaches field the strongest possible team. The bad news was that the two combatants started the practice with a headache.

Tim's older brother, Barry Bullard, remembers challenges with Dave Enslow and Ben Davidson for the strong side tackle position.

"They made me better and they made all of us better. I was never mad at Dave or Ben but it certainly made us all more focused on our position."

Players could also lose their jerseys right on the spot during other phases of practice. "If you didn't execute well on any given day, Tipps would grab your face mask, shake your head, slap the side of your helmet with his other hand, and order you to change your jersey with the guy one team lower. It happened to lot of players," recounted Dick Dunn, a center on the 1958-1960 varsity teams. The challenge drills were another part of the punishing practices along with conditioning drills, scrimmages, punting drills, and hitting with the helmet.

Coach Tipps in recalling some of their coaching methods said, "We didn't tippy toe around. You can't coach football that way. I think one of the biggest mistakes made in coaching football is to try and be loved by the players. Players don't give a damn. The good ones don't care whether you love them or not. If you respect them, they will play. You cannot fool a football player or any other human being."

Many players felt Tipps was the dominant personality among the coaches. Dunn recalled, "I've never been around anybody with more intensity. Tipps would grab you by the face mask and shake you and hit you on the side of the helmet." Ben Davidson tells this story. "I spent most of my time with Coach Tipps. One day, Tipps thought the whole line was dogging it or I was dogging it. He took off his belt and started whipping me with it." Davidson laughingly concluded, "That probably wouldn't play too good today."

Another innovation of Owens and his staff was the use of the helmet to block and tackle. The conventional football coaching technique was to have a player use his shoulders to hit his opponent. If you missed with your shoulder just a little bit, you would have a difficult time executing the block or tackle. If you used your helmet and face mask, you had less of a chance to miss the opponent.

Tipps explained. "In football, you can't put your one shoulder against your opponent's one shoulder without giving up some advantage. So we taught the players when making a block or a tackle to focus their target on the very center of things. The center of things is the opponent's helmet."

The helmet was not only used for blocking and tackling but for punishing an opponent. Dunn said, "If you get a clear shot at a running back or a quarterback hung up in a pile, you were instructed to spear him helmet on helmet. You put a stop to whatever he was trying to do and he might not get up. We were also encouraged to block anybody still standing. You could be ten yards from the end of the play that was nearly over. If the whistle had not blown and an opposing player was nearby, you just flattened him."

If you didn't block and tackle with your helmet, you got special instruction. "I will never forget one guy who always turned his head when tackling. He was a back," Bill Kinnune recalled. "Finally, Tipps took the player to a brick wall of a building outside the stadium and Tipps held his hand up in front of the wall. He would then instruct the player to hit his hand with his helmet. The kid fired out and Tipps moved his hand before contact and the kid hit his helmet against the brick wall. After hitting the wall three times, he just walked off. There were a bunch of guys who quit saying such drills were just not worth it."

Joe Jones, an outstanding fullback and linebacker, remembers when the team looked at film after the game, "players would get dinged hard by the coaches for not knocking somebody down before the whistle blew. They wanted no opponent standing up. They created an expectation in all of us to take a shot at somebody, to hurt an opposing player, and never let opponents get the upper hand in the battle of punishment."

Davidson remembers a game with UCLA in Los Angeles where three Bruins were lying on the field after one play. "When that happened, we had the game won. They didn't want any part of us after that."

Fire out and hit them with the helmet was a rallying cry of the Husky linemen. "We all still have noses and foreheads with big scars on them," Tim Bullard proudly proclaimed. "When an opponent got hit with the helmet enough times, he was pretty well beat up by the fourth quarter. We went right for the ear hole of the helmet on some plays and tried to knock him out."

Ray Jackson, one of the most outstanding fullbacks on the West Coast and a punishing linebacker said, "We were not very big so we had to use our leverage. We had to position our bodies to execute maximum leverage and to deliver the blow at the point of contact with our head and our helmet. The coaches had many drills to teach us that technique."

Tipps explained. "What we taught the players is to focus their force at the very center of an opponent. The very center is the opponent's upper chest and helmet. Opposing coaches made a big deal about our use of the helmet and that our players were punishing their players. I suspect we were."

Husky linemen were proud of what they called the "purple badge of courage." When you hit with your helmet, the helmet would frequently come down and the front edge would hit the bridge of the lineman's nose pretty hard. "The trainer would paint you with this purple ointment that was supposed to make a scab. It was a scab all right but it was uglier than hell," said Tim Bullard.

To give the players neck strength to hit with the helmet, the coaches introduced a series of isometric neck exercises. Most linemen's neck sizes increased significantly each fall. "One of the exercises was to get down on your hands and knees and have your teammate stand over you and push down on the back of your head which was tilted down initially. The player on the ground would push back up with his neck. Then, the player on all fours would have constant tension. Some guys could roll their heads up against the pressure exerted by the standing player. A few could lift the standing player off the ground. That's hard to do without a very strong neck. That was a big deal," Dunn exclaimed.

Another tough part of the Husky practices was punting drills. Punting -- both kicking and returning punts -- was a major part of the defense and offense of Washington football. When Owens was at Texas A&M, the Aggies allowed an opposing team an average of only two yards on punt returns. During one period during those two years, the Aggies punted 26 straight times without giving any yardage on the return.

On the kicking drills, Washington would have eight players run downfield at full speed to smother the punt returner. These drills would be repeated over and over and over. The coaches stressed high hang time on the punts, good spacing by players running downfield, and keeping leverage inside out on the punt returner and not overrunning the return man. "They kept yelling 'There is a guy called the sideline that has never missed a tackle so use him.' "

Dunn again. "They would scream at you if your spacing got out of whack. You were supposed to be spaced precisely. In practices, the punt returner would receive the punt and run back and forth, sideline to sideline. And we would run crab-like near the receiver back and forth as well. After having sprinted 50 yards down field," he continued, "we would sprint back, huddle up, and do it all over again. You were so gassed. The more gassed you got, the sloppier you got on the spacing and the more they would scream at you."

The Huskies were also very successful on punt returns because of their execution of come-back blocks. Everybody on the punt return team was looking for an opponent's head. They could not wait for an opponent to get around the first block and then drill him with a come-back block -- usually to the helmet. In some games, three or four guys would go down with such blocks on one play. When the coaches showed the game films, guys were screaming as they watched the opponents get slammed and the punt returner go all the way or gain significant yardage to give the Huskies great field position.

Bob Schloredt, one of the nation's best punters in 1959, summed up the objective of the punting game. "We gave up about two yards a punt. We averaged about 10 yards on punt returns. So figure the math. If we played great defense, punted the ball, played great defense, punted the ball -- after about four series without giving up a first down, we would be in the opponent's end of the field, many times in four-down territory. That was as simple as you could make it."

His math was pretty good. By Schloredt's senior season in 1960, the Huskies had an average punt return of 14.2 yards compared to the opponents' average of 3.8. The margin still stands as the best in Washington history.

With his underlying coaching philosophy firmly in place, Owens and his staff turned their attention to the season opener against Colorado on September 21. It would be the first of 187 games for the "Big Fella" over the next 18 years.

CHAPTER 4

The Demise of the Pacific Coast Conference

The 1957 college football season would be exciting for many teams around the nation, The Oklahoma Sooners would increase their unbeaten winning streak to 47 games. Bear Bryant would leave Texas A&M at the end of the season to begin a 25-year career at Alabama, his alma mater. The great Aggie running back, John David Crow, would receive the Heisman Trophy. Auburn and Ohio State would be voted number one in the country -- Auburn in the Associated Press Poll; Ohio State in the United Press International Poll.

Oregon and Oregon State would be the Pacific Coast Conference co-champions with identical 6-2 records. Oregon State beat Oregon in the final game of the season but could not go to the Rose Bowl because conference rules did not allow repeat Rose Bowl appearances. Oregon would lose to Big Ten conference champion, Ohio State, 10-7 in the 1958 Rose Bowl.

Very little of what was happening elsewhere mattered to Coach Owens. He was focusing on the work to be done to carry his team through one of the toughest schedules in Husky history. Before beginning conference play, Washington would face Colorado, Minnesota, and Ohio State.

While Washington had a good group of starters, Owens recognized that he had slim pickings for a second eleven to spell the first unit. Also, he had a questionable picture at quarterback.

Bob Dunn would be the starting quarterback in Washington's home opener against Colorado. He would have to master the split-T formation quickly to lead the Huskies to any success.

Owens was also concerned about the impact on the seniors of the change in coaching staffs. It would be the third change -- to have one change is enough during a college career. "It took some time for the squad not only to become acquainted with us and us with them, and with a lot of techniques, a lot of drills and on-field work we did that was much different than any they had experienced," Owens stated. "We had to be tough on the players. We had to find out in a real hurry which of the fellows were going to be with us and in our program. The 1957 season was an extremely difficult time for the players and coaches."

In the season opener, a crowd of almost 35,000 -- the largest opening day assemblage since 1951 -- greeted the Colorado Buffalos. The game satisfied no one except those who delighted in Indian Summer sunshine. Led by sophomore quarterback and punter Boyd Dowler -- the future Green Bay Packer wide receiver and member of the Packer team that won Super Bowl I in 1967 -- the Buffalos scored in the first period to go up 6-0.

Early in the second stanza, Washington started a series on its own 40. Jones plowed into the line for a two-yard gain. Next, Dunn faked inside and scampered to the right side. Colorado's defensive back gambled on Dunn's keeping the ball and let Payseno run free behind him. Dunn threw the strike, Payseno tucked it in and raced down the sideline all alone for the score. On the extra point try, the football went straight up like a missile and fell woefully short of the crossbar.

The game established the difficulty the Huskies would have with the split-T offense. They fumbled four times and lost three -- they would fumble 46 times in 1957, losing 25. Two defensive stands within the five-yard line enabled the Huskies to escape defeat.

In his post-game interview, Owens sat all alone in the Washington equipment property room, legs stretched straight out, leaning against the wall, and chin in hand. He looked for all the world like a western marshall after some Colorado bad guys had shot up his town and ruined his first day in office. "I feel sick because we didn't win," Owens began. A few minutes later after summarizing his misery in technical football terms, he mustered a grin and said, "A tie game is like kissing your sister." He had a point -- no exhilaration in the act.

Colorado's coach, Dallas Ward, identified what Owens was most concerned about -- lack of depth. "Washington has a good sound team. But they are not as deep as they should be. I thought their second team was definitely weaker than the first. They'll have to have better passing if they are going to have a really good football team."

The next day, Owens and his staff would start their Sunday ritual -- watching game films and starting to put together a plan for the next opponent. It was sixth-ranked Minnesota in Minneapolis. The Gopher quarterback was Bobby Cox, the Husky starting signal-caller in 1954. Cox decided to transfer to Minnesota in the spring of 1955.

Owens' worst fears came true. The Gophers thoroughly trounced the Huskies 46-7, before a sellout crowd of 63,500. They scored in every period. Washington got its single touchdown when Jim Jones returned the second-half kickoff 91 yards. At that time, only Hugh McElhenny's 97-yard runback of the opening kickoff in 1949 -- again against the Gophers in Minneapolis -- was longer than Jones' feat.

Owens was embarrassed. The Gophers rushed for 388 yards to

Washington's 80. Minnesota had 550 total yards, the Huskies 105. The Huskies fumbled seven times losing four. Washington took its worst licking in the series with Minnesota dating back to 1936. After the game, Owens tersely told the press, "We played half as good as we did last week."

When the team arrived back in Seattle, Owens told the spouses and other family members and friends to go home. The team went to the crew house and they turned out on Sunday. As Artie Buerk, the team manager, recalls, "When Owens got embarrassed, it was Katie bar the door. He got tougher and meaner and he stepped up the process at that point. There was not an ounce of fun and laughter."

Owens started the preparation for next week's opponent, Ohio State, with a critique of the Minnesota game. "I know there are times when your team has to lose. You accept those defeats as best you can if your team has played well. But when they let themselves get mauled, fumble the ball, fail to drop on loose balls and miss assignments, there just isn't any way to apologize for a defeat." He then discussed the preparation for the Buckeyes, "It's going to take a lot of hard work. We'll work hard to get ready. We'll have to. And then we'll keep right on working. We've got a long way to go."

Washington did play a little better on October 5 before another large home crowd. They held the Buckeyes even in the first half -- 7-7. A Husky fumble allowed Ohio State to score about five minutes before half-time. Three more fumbles in the second half enabled the Big Ten power-house to breeze to a 35-7 victory.

The next week, the Huskies opened their conference schedule with UCLA in Los Angeles. They suffered their only shutout of the season losing to the Bruins 19-0. The following week, the Huskies put together the best showing in their first five games losing to Stanford 21-14. In the first quarter, Washington drove 80 yards in 18 plays for the score. The Indians answered early in the second period to tie the game. A Husky fumble led to Stanford's second touchdown to put the Indians ahead 14-7 at half-time. The lads from Palo Alto controlled the ball for the last part of the third quarter and more than eight minutes of the fourth and went 75 yards in 20 plays to go up 21-7. The Huskies put life back into the down-hearted partisan fans by going 68 yards in 12 plays to end the scoring. Stanford was glad to leave Seattle with a 21-14 victory.

Owens told the press, " The game was the best team effort of the year. I was real proud of them on the last drive. That's one thing we accomplished this week. We came fighting back in the fourth quarter and outplayed the other team." Near the end of the interview, a California writer asked Owens, "Who've you got next week?" "Oregon State." The writer continued. "Ohhh, they got beat today. They'll be madder than hell next week." "So will we," Owens shot back.

Owens was right. It was his first meeting with Tommy Prothro, the head coach at Oregon State. Not only were the Huskies mad as they ran out of the tunnel onto Husky Stadium but they were ready to show something new to the visiting Beavers.

The rainy season had begun. When it got cold, wet, and windy, the outdoor practice field was called Pneumonia Flats. On the really bad days, the Huskies would practice in the wide-open spaces of Hec Edmundson Pavilion. For the first time in the season, the team practiced a few days indoors in preparing for the Beavers' single-wing offense. The coaches also introduced an unbalanced line on offense. The left end lined up on the right side, split wide of the right end, and making the left tackle eligible for look-in passes. It worked. The Huskies outgained the defending conference champions 335 yards to 236. Jim Jones gained 102 yards including a 53-yard scamper late in the third quarter. The Husky fullback juked and muscled his way into the clear and then turned on the jets. His touchdown run put the Huskies up 19-6, the game ending score.

The game "featured" a few uninvited people. During the Oregon State series at the start of the fourth quarter, a Beaver spectator lined up in the backfield. Seattle police quickly and forcibly ushered the Bremerton sailor off the field. His brother, an Oregon State student, then dashed from the stands and grappled with the policemen. They were booked at the city jail. Immediately following the game, Washington students stormed the field and infiltrated the ranks of the Beavers' band which was playing a post-game air. Two bandsmen were injured and two Washington students were arrested.

While the raucous post-game activities were taking place on the field, the Huskies celebrated by carrying Owens off the field and into the locker room. For the first time in the season, the players danced, yelled and hugged. During Owens' interview with the media, he saw Husky tackle, Jim Heck, come through the door. Heck interrupted the proceedings and seriously and respectfully said, "Coach, there is someone out here to see you -- somebody important." Owens excused himself and started down the hall. In an instant, a boisterous, laughing bunch of Huskies pounced on their coach and packed him into the shower and drenched him under cold water. "The kids will remember this for a long time. Just like I will," Owens said, as water dripped off his broad shoulders.

For his excellent offensive and defensive play, the Associated Press selected Jones as the national "Back of the Week." At season's end, Jones would be named to every all-coast team, to the Hearst All-America second team, and honorable mention on the AP All-America team. When Owens told the players about Jones' selection as back of the week, he respectfully said, "This award isn't so much for what Jones did last Saturday but rather as recognition of the fine football he has played for us every week. He praised Jones for his leadership qualities and physical condition. "He has the marks of a good back. Besides carrying the ball, he fakes well and that's awfully important to us on our belly series. He's a fine boy. We're proud of him and happy for him."

Game number eight was in Portland's Multnomah Stadium against Oregon, the conference leader. Playing with fervor, intelligent defense, and a solid running attack, the Huskies defeated the Ducks 13-6. They presented the game ball to Owens -- an honor which portrayed the admiration the players had for the coaches who had driven them so relentlessly in pursuit of victory. Sitting on the game ball in a crouched position surrounded by the press corps, Owens had one word in reply to a question on how the Huskies won the game. "Desire."

Implicit in that response were the many components that the coaches had drilled into the team during the season. The players were seeing the impact of conditioning, mental and physical toughness, and the commitment to pay the price to succeed.

Click Clark, the Husky head trainer from 1929 to 1961, commented during the 1957 season that Owens worked his team harder than any coach in my years at Washington. "Jim Owens puts great emphasis on physical condition. Yet I seldom hear a squawk. It sure pays off. How many Husky players have you seen carried or helped off the field this season?" The answer was "None."

Clark was another person who was like a father to many of the athletes. Clark, as a trainer, had a unique role in the athletic program. He spent time individually with many players who needed special attention -- medically and psychologically -- due to injuries, bad games and practices, and personal problems on and off the field. Clark helped keep the team together with his modest and unobtrusive manner, his wide grin, and clever wit. His heart and soul were in every game.

Even though the season record was not very good, positive things were beginning to happen on the Washington football scene. Owens was also being recognized as a fine young coach. United Press International named Owens the national "Coach of the Week" for the upset of Rose Bowl bound Oregon.

On November 16, the Huskies journeyed to Berkeley to face quarterback Joe Kapp and his bunch of Bears. Washington completely dominated the first half and took a 21-7 half-time lead. California stormed back but the Huskies hung on to record a 35-27 victory.

Washington ended the season by losing to Washington State 27-7 before 47,000 fans in Seattle. The Huskies finished sixth in the nine-team conference besting Cal, USC, and Idaho. Husky guard Whitey Core and fullback Jones were elected co-captains at the end of the season. Jones was the first black to be named a captain in school history.

In December 1957, actions were taken that would lead to the break up of the Pacific Coast Conference. In May 1956, Washington had been placed on athletic probation for two years beginning July 1, 1956. California, UCLA, and USC were also put on probation. In December 1957, they announced that they would quit the Pacific Coast Conference -- USC after July 1, 1958 and Cal and UCLA on June 30, 1959.

They did so for a variety of reasons including the probationary actions and the voting of Idaho, the two Oregon schools, and Washington State against new athletic policy standards proposed by the three above mentioned California universities. The three California schools also decided that they had all they could take from Orlando Hollis, Oregon's faculty representative to the conference and Dean of the Law School. They felt he had Victor O. Schmidt, the conference Commissioner, in his hip pocket along with the faculty representatives from Idaho, Oregon State, and Washington State.

Then, Washington announced it would pull out if Stanford and the four other Northwest schools remained in the conference. Washington was more aligned with the withdrawing members in size, academic standards, and athletic facilities. Some critics observed that the schools leaving had the biggest stadiums and could derive more revenue by scheduling non-conference opponents that provided the potential for larger crowds.

In May 1958, Washington's Board of Regents voted to have the Huskies join a new athletic conference with the three other withdrawing schools. In a meeting on August 8, 1958, faculty representatives and athletic directors of each of the nine conference member schools voted to dissolve the PCC in June 1959 and distribute its assets. It also voted to participate in the 1960 Rose Bowl with all nine schools, for the last time, participating for the right to be the conference representative.

The decision to dissolve the conference was difficult for all involved because of its history. It had been formed on December 15, 1915. The original members were California, Oregon, Oregon State, and Washington. Conference play began in 1916. Washington State was admitted in 1917 and Stanford in 1918. The PCC expanded to eight with the admission of the University of Southern California and Idaho in 1922. Montana joined in 1924. The conference rounded out at ten when UCLA became a member in 1928. Montana resigned in 1950 to join another conference and the PCC continued with nine members through its final season.

It was unclear at the time what conference would emerge to provide the West Coast team in the Rose Bowl after 1960. On August 23, 1958, the answer became clear. California, UCLA, USC, and Washington representatives agreed to establish the Athletic Association of Western Universities on July 1, 1959. Now the focus was on Stanford. Finally on July 16, 1959, Stanford agreed to join the newly formed conference as the fifth and final member. Don Selby reported on the action in the San Francisco Examiner the next day:

> ....*Stanford made the big leap at long last. They joined the Big Four.... With the University of California, UCLA, USC, Stanford and Washington all pulling together, the West Coast once again has a powerful athletic league, something it has lacked since the 1956 financial aid scandal rocked the Pacific Coast Conference and led to its demise.... Dr. Wallace Sterling, president of Stanford, said the decision was reached after discussions with the presidents of the other universities involved "made clear that at each university the control of and responsibility for the policy and conduct of intercollegiate athletics now rest with the president, and that each president is prepared to discharge that responsibility."*

Another team -- the Husky Pups -- was being forged in 1957. On October 2, the players in the Class of 1961 joined other students in attending their first day of classes at Washington. Five days later, 83 reported for the first turnout of the freshmen football team. Sixty-seven were from high schools in the state of Washington. None were from California. Forty were on some form of financial assistance. Twenty-four of the 40 were good enough to play in annual high school all-star games staged in Montana, Oregon, and Washington.

The most talented players had been initially contacted by Darrell Royal and members of his staff in the fall of 1956. Owens and his coaches actively continued the recruiting process to persuade the prospects to enroll at Washington. They stressed the academic quality of Washington and the potential of putting together an outstanding Husky football program.

Lee Folkins, a rangy, raw-boned end at Roosevelt High School in northend Seattle, was the first player to make a decision to attend

Washington. He remembers that Chesty Walker was his primary contact. One of Walker's daughters attended Roosevelt. Walker would drive around in a 1955 Lincoln with a turquoise finish. Folkins asked the coach "What are you doing driving around with that awful looking Lincoln?" "Because that is the color my daughter chose." Folkins was considering Stanford and Washington State -- Stanford because of its outstanding engineering program and WSU for the excellent veterinary medicine curriculum. Hearing about Folkins' interest in the other conference schools, Walker said to Folkins in his slow Texas drawl and with his eyes looking right at the tall senior, "Let me tell you -- go any place else other than Washington and we are going to beat you."

Owens visited Barry Bullard, an outstanding tackle on three Oregon state championship teams at Marshland High School in Coos Bay. Not only was Bullard impressed with Owens and his coaching philosophy, but his mother, in jest, said after Owens had left, that she was going to leave Bullard's dad for Owens because he was such a stud.

Bob Schloredt, an all-state quarterback from Gresham High School near Portland Oregon, remembers his recruiting trip to Washington. He stayed at the brand new Edmund Meany Hotel a few blocks from campus. "Corky Lewis and a couple of his fraternity brothers took me around. They had enough money to take me out to a nice restaurant and a steak dinner. Hell, we snuck into a movie and went to Hasty Tasty for hamburgers. They pocketed most of the money." Schloredt visited other schools in the conference. "I liked coach Len Casanova. It was a real bitch to tell him I wasn't coming to Oregon. Some Oregon supporter told my dad that if I went to Washington there would be many quarterbacks in front of me. And my dad said, 'Well, that's fine. If four or five quarterbacks are going to beat my son out, they are going to be damn good ones.' I picked Washington because of the assistant coaches -- Chesty Walker and Tom Tipps. Chesty was like your grandfather. Tom had fire in his eyes."

Brent Wooten, from Walla Walla Washington, decided to come to Washington after a talk around the dinner table with his family. He had narrowed his decision down to Washington and Washington State. Finally his Dad said, "Brent, you know where you want to go so why don't you make the phone call? And if you call Washington State, I will sail your plate right out the window." Wooten called Washington but said it was tough to do so with all the Cougar supporters around Walla Walla.

The recruiting of Chuck Allen, an all-state guard and linebacker from Cle Elum, Washington, included riding in an unlimited hydroplane on Lake Washington during the summer Seafair festival. Owens was the key factor in Allen's coming to Washington. "He said some things I wanted to hear. He told me that if we could set some goals and reach them, we would have a pretty good football team." Allen continued. "What he didn't tell me was that he was going to recruit 30 other linebackers. When I turned out for the first practice, there were some really good athletes. I thought 'Oh shoot, they are so much bigger, stronger, faster than I am. I'll never make it.' "

Bill Kinnune, an all-state tackle, was influenced by his father and the Everett Washington connection to the Husky program. "My dad was president of the Washington Boosters Club in Everett. Darrell Royal and his coaches recruited me first. When he left, it was a real shock. The next person who came to see me was Tom Tipps and that was more of a shock," he said laughingly. "I also knew a lot of guys who choose Washington who played in the high school all-star game. And my girlfriend was going to Washington."

When practice started on October 7, the freshmen squad knew about the Death March and the physical punishment the varsity was going through in practices. During fraternity rush week, some of the freshmen would run into varsity players. "It was scary for us to hear about. The doctor who gave us a physical and shots at the beginning of our season would ask us, 'Do you really want to be here? Do you know what this place is like? Guys are getting hurt here,' " recalls Dick Dunn.

Chesty Walker was in charge of the freshmen team, but the entire coaching staff worked with the team. The freshmen team would begin practice about 30 minutes before the varsity started. The coaches knew that the future success of the program depended on this group of players. They were coming in the program unencumbered by the philosophy and methods used by the previous Washington coaches. They were ready to commit to the rugged physical and mental conditioning drills exacted by Owens and his staff.

They practiced on a field east of the stadium, now the Lloyd Nordstrom Tennis center, the Husky Softball stadium, and the Dempsey Indoor facility. The field was full of goose and seagull droppings. They received tetanus shots to deal with this problem. But they could not get any relief from punishing practices. First, there were the new tackling and blocking techniques to master. The basic block was the drive block which involved driving the forehead into the opponent's chest and face mask. The basic tackle was the same maneuver except the tackler would wrap up the ball carrier with his arms at the moment of contact.

In the first years of the Owens' era, collegiate football rules stated that blockers' hands could not extend more than six inches from the blocker's body. The rule made the initial collision very important. In order to execute an effective block, a lineman needed to first drive his forehead directly into the opponent like a sprinter out of his blocks and maintain contact with his legs driving and without the use of his hands. The movement was not a natural act and required lots of practice. When perfected, the use of the helmet in blocking and tackling contributed significantly to the success of the Husky teams in 1959 and 1960.

Most football teams in the fifties -- high school through professional teams -- used Riddell suspension helmets. The Chicago-based John T. Riddell Company patented a plastic football helmet in 1939. The company also devised the first chinstrap worn on the chin and not the Adam's apple in 1940. Army's 1944 team was the first to wear plastic helmets. Soon all teams replaced their leather helmets with plastic ones. The suspension system was a slight modification of the World War II liner system used inside the steel pots worn by GI's during the war. Riddell helmets came in several sizes and the equipment managers would try to get good fits for the players. For some, the suspension system's leather strap/sweatband that went around the head inside the helmet didn't exactly fit. As a result, rough movement of the helmet would irritate the forehead. Also, full-speed, forehead-first collisions tore foreheads open -- day after day. These collisions eventually led to rule changes that prohibited spearing.

The helmet did not have a padded bumper on the front edge in those days. The players would get blood in their eyes. Dick Dunn remembers that "one day, my helmet chin strap broke and the plastic part of the helmet came down on the bridge of my nose and cut it pretty badly. It required several stitches to close. That wasn't too unusual."

Helmet fit probably was not so important when players blocked and tackled with the shoulders rather than the helmet. Prior to the mid-fifties, face masks on helmets were seldom seen. When they were, they were worn by players who were protecting broken jaws and noses. In the mid-fifties, high schools mandated the use of at least a single bar in front of the teeth. Collegiate football teams soon started using more face protection as well. Eventually, players started to use full face masks.

The toughest part of the freshmen practices was when the third and fourth string guys came over from brutal varsity scrimmages to do battle with the freshmen team. Dunn stated, "Imagine how happy they were to do that, how much they liked us. There were so many chicken-shit shots taken. They had been through the Death March and had already been through a tough practice that day." With a chuckle, Dunn continued. "It was a great learning experience for us. We got forearms to the throat when we were doing pass blocking. We got butted in the ear when we were in the open field or standing near a pile. It seemed to get worse later in the season when it rained like hell and it was dark in the late afternoon. Every one was miserable. And then we got these absolutely hostile third and fourth string guys."

Owens' goal was clearly stated. "We may not win a freshmen game. Our job is to get them ready for next year's varsity. We want to get them indoctrinated in our system. We want to get the boys ready to move right into the varsity next spring and fall. All of the coaches are going to spend a lot of time with the youngsters."

Well, they did win games -- all three of them. Thirty-three players traveled to Pullman on Halloween to face the Washington State Coubabes the next day. The Pups split-T attack was directed by Schloredt and Phil Borders, who had led Seattle's Ballard High School to the Seattle prep championship a year earlier. After spotting Washington State seven points on a 68-yard scoring pass in the first period, Washington dominated the play in the final three quarters. Washington went on a 51-yard scoring drive in the second quarter to tie the score. Washington went ahead in the fourth quarter when end Pat Claridge, from Vancouver BC, blocked a Coubabes' field goal attempt on the Pups' 20-yard line, grabbed the ball and took it to the Washington 45. Twelve plays later, Washington was up 14-7. Finally, a recovered Washington State fumble allowed the Pups to score and seal the 20-7 victory.

After getting the team together to watch the film of the Washington State game, Coach Walker gave them hell, Folkins recalls. "Listen, everyone of you were stars in high school and you paced yourself. Now just look at the film and how you are running down the field on the kickoff. Look at you. Are you running as fast as you can? NO, none of you are!" Folkins summarized that coaching moment. "I can guarantee you that from that moment on, we ran as fast as we could. In that one moment, we jumped a level in covering punts and kickoffs. There were a whole series of those kind of exhortations. They put the challenge system in during our freshmen year. Everything worked. And the people who couldn't take it, quit." He added, "On the varsity level, the coaches were trying to do the same thing. It was much more difficult to accomplish success with guys who had been under different coaches and a much different philosophy in the years before."

Next week, the Pups played at home for the only time during the season. Seattle P-I reporter, John Owen, described the setting. "A fair-sized crowd estimated at 2,500, clustered on the sunny side of the stadium like gnats around a light bulb." They saw Washington again suffer a first quarter seizure giving up two fumbles and an intercepted pass to provide Idaho's frosh three chances to score. The defense chased the intruders away from the front gate, stopping the Vandals on the eight-yard line and later inside the three. Washington ended all their gift-giving after the first period and used the split-T sledgehammer to methodically chop Idaho to pieces.

The linemen were consistently tough on defense and opened up jumbo-sized holes on offense. Seven Pups averaged five yards or better per carry. They scored once in the second quarter on a 62-yard scoring drive with Brent Wooten slamming through left guard for the final eight yards. After an intercepted Idaho pass on the Vandals' 21 in the third stanza, the Huskies scored when Schloredt hit the wide-open Brian Stapp. With Sam Hurworth's two conversion kicks, the Huskies were up 14-0. Washington's third score was set up by Gene Bates' 36-yard punt return. After a 15-yard penalty, Schloredt hit Bates on the Idaho 28 and he took it to the nine. Three plays later, Schloredt sneaked into the end zone. The final score in the 26-0 victory was set up by Folkins' interception on the Vandals' 37. On the sixth play of the drive, Borders cruised five yards around end for the final tally.

The final game of the freshmen season was played in Eugene against the Oregon Ducklings. The Pups crushed Oregon 33-0, scoring twice in the second and third periods and once in the final stanza. Washington rolled up 336 yards on offense and gave up only 183. Several long pass plays -- one a 19-yard scoring play and another a 29-yard touchdown strike -- keyed the victory. One of the spectators was Tim Bullard who came to see his older brother's team completely dominate the Ducklings. "Beating the shit out of Oregon" was one of the key factors in Tim's choosing Washington over Oregon and joining the class of 1962. He liked what he saw.

What was clear from the short season was that the conditioning drills, the execution of a simple offensive system -- players recalled there were eight running plays and three passing plays -- and the tenacious defensive play were paying off. Some of the players who turned out at the start of the season didn't want to pay the price and left the program. Some who stayed had moments of unhappiness and frustration. Wooten talked to his dad about quitting. "Dad told me that after you quit once, from then on, it's a lot easier to quit in other areas of your life."

The coaches had instilled in the players of the Class of 1961 the attitudes they wanted. They didn't have to wash some out with drills like the Death March. If a player did not buy into the program, he washed himself out. The coaches molded the players. If they didn't have the talent, coaches would work to develop it once they committed to the program.

The Pups ended the season way ahead of the other Northwest schools in the conference. They were ready for the varsity.

CHAPTER 5

A Lively Contest with an Oval Pigskin

College football in the 1950's was much different from the sport that begin in the 19th century. Football historians place the game's origins with rugby, an English game similar, in many ways, to football. Rugby began in 1823 at the famous Rugby Boy's School in central England on the River Avon. Another cousin of football is soccer. It's beginnings can be traced to 11th century England.

Soon after the Civil War in the United States, colleges began organizing football games. In 1867, Princeton led the way in establishing some rudimentary rules and, in that same year, the football was patented. Rutgers College, some sixteen miles from Princeton, also established a few rules. With the relatively short distance between the two schools, a game was set up on at New Brunswick, NJ, between Rutgers and Princeton on November 6, 1869. That contest, won by Rutgers 6-4, was played with an oval-sized rugby ball and no forward passes were permitted. Point values were assigned to different scoring plays and there were severe limitations on the number of players on a team and substitutions during the game.

In 1873, representatives from Columbia, Rutgers, Princeton, and Yale met in New York City to formulate the first collegiate football rules for the increasingly popular game. These four teams established the Intercollegiate Football Association and set 15 as the number of players to be on the field at the same time for each team.

Yale coach, Walter Camp, wanted to have 11 men on the field. Since he chaired the IFA's rules committee, he soon was able to cut the number of players from 15 to 11. The committee also decided to establish the size of the playing field at 110 yards. In 1882, Camp also initiated the system of downs. After first allowing three attempts to advance the ball five yards for a first down, the rule was changed to ten yards in 1896. The fourth down was added in 1912.

At the turn of the century, concern over the increasing brutality of the game led to its ban by some colleges. In the ten years beginning in 1895, nearly 180 players had suffered serious injuries and 18 deaths had been reported from the brutal mass plays that had been common. In 1905, President Theodore Roosevelt called upon Harvard, Princeton, and Yale to help save the game from its demise.

The institutions invited other schools to discuss the issues and agree on reform. The group appointed a seven-member Rules Committee and established what would later become known as the National Collegiate Athletic Association. This committee legalized the forward pass and prohibited mass plays like the flying wedge and locking the arms of teammates to clear the way for their ball carriers. The length of the game was shortened from 70 to 60 minutes and the length of the field was reduced to 100 yards (in 1912).

Soon athletic conferences were established throughout the country. The Rose Bowl was established in 1902 to provide post-season play as well as a civic celebration on New Year's Day. The Orange and Sugar Bowls started in 1935 followed by the Cotton

Bowl in 1937. The Sun (1936), Gator (1946), Citrus (1947) and Hula (1947) bowls rounded out the eight bowls that featured the major conference winners and outstanding independent football teams in a festive holiday package.

In the 1950's the major conferences were the Atlantic Coast, the Big Eight, the Big Ten, the Border Conference, the Ivy League, the Missouri Valley, the Pacific Coast, the Skyline Conference, the Southeastern, Southern and Southwest. Independent schools with major football programs included Army, Boston College, Navy, Notre Dame, Penn State, Pittsburgh, Rutgers, and Syracuse.

Before the 1940's, many leading teams featured single-wing attacks with nary a forward pass thrown. Clark Shaughnessy began to have great success at Stanford with the T-formation in the late 1930's. With Frankie Albert at quarterback and Norm Standlee at fullback, Shaughnessy's 1940 Stanford team won the Pacific Coast Conference title, finished second in the nation and beat seventh-ranked Nebraska 21-13 in the 1941 Rose Bowl.

Many college teams began to implement the T-formation because of its enhanced speed and deception. Also, it was easier to teach, especially with regard to blocking assignments.

During World War II, some major colleges dropped football during the war-time period. Others continued to operate, albeit with many coaches and players off to military service. Many teams played a limited schedule, including service team opponents, and restricted their travel distance to play games. The Pacific Coast Conference limited football rosters to 28 players. In 1943, the Huskies played five games including the 1944 Rose Bowl against Southern California. The Trojans shut out Washington 29-0. Three of the four Husky regular games in 1943 were played against service teams. In 1944, Washington played eight regular season games -- California, USC, two service teams, and home and home contests with Whitman and Willamette.

Some universities were selected for the Navy V-12 program that was started in 1943. This was a program for developing officer candidates. Recruits went through an accelerated college education curriculum along with naval science courses. The Navy encouraged the recruits to participate in intercollegiate athletic activities. Notre Dame, Northwestern, Michigan, and Washington were among the schools with such programs, and they ended up with student-athletes from other major football programs.

Also, many military facilities around the country organized football teams. Some of the approximately 130 service teams played top college teams. The best of these teams -- Great Lakes and Iowa Pre-Flight -- were included in the top ten in the 1943 Associated Press Poll that combined the best college and service teams.

One of the major offensive football innovations during the war-time period was the split-T formation. Don Faurot, the head coach at Iowa Pre-Flight introduced the formation in 1943. One of his assistants was Bud Wilkinson who implemented the split-T at Oklahoma when he became head coach in 1947. Because of Wilkinson's success, many major programs started to install the split-T including Bear Bryant's Texas A&M teams.

With 13 million young men in service during World War II, attendance at college football games drastically declined. However, there were several outstanding teams during the period. Coach Earl Blaik's Army teams of 1944, 1945, and 1946 had a record of 27-0-1. Led by All-Americans and Heisman Trophy winners Doc Blanchard and Glenn Davis, Army won national championships in 1944 and 1945 and finished second to Notre Dame in 1946. The only blemish on the Cadets' record in 1946 was a scoreless tie with Notre Dame in Yankee Stadium.

Coach Frank Leahy's Notre Dame teams earned national titles in 1946, 1947, and 1949. Irish quarterback, John Lujack, won the Heisman Trophy in 1947 and end Leon Hart was the Heisman winner in 1949. Hart is the only lineman ever to receive the Heisman Trophy in the history of college football.

After the war ended, college football had a huge resurgence with record attendance levels set at many schools. The sale of television rights provided a new source of revenue to major football programs. The additional revenue helped to offset the significant increase in expenses for football programs as teams began to play two platoon football in 1947 and 1948. As a result, many smaller schools simply dropped their football programs. In 1953, college football returned to one platoon football until 1965. Rules were changed to limit substitutions.

When college teams returned to one platoon football, players had to develop all-around skills -- offensively and defensively and in the punting and kicking phases of the game. In the one platoon era, teams typically consisted of about 50 players.

In 1955, the substitution rules were marginally liberalized to allow a player who started a quarter to be taken out and return only one more time in the same quarter. This change resulted in a legion of bookkeepers parading the sidelines.

The "wild card" rule was implemented in 1959 which permitted coaches to substitute one player into the lineup any time the clock stopped. A year later, the rule was changed to allow a single player to enter the game at any time, even if the clock was running. This enabled coaches to send in plays from the sidelines, a process that had been illegal since 1953.

In 1965, free substitution was permitted leading to the return of two platoon football. The impetus behind the rule change was, in part, the growth and popularity of professional football. The pro's used two platoons and a more wide-open game featuring offensive and defensive specialists.

In the 1950's, the football powerhouses were in the Mid-West and in the South. Oklahoma (Big Eight) won national titles in

1950, 1955, and 1956. Big Ten schools Michigan State and Ohio State won in 1952 and 1954; the Buckeyes shared the title with Auburn in 1957. Maryland (Atlantic Coast) won in 1953 and Syracuse in 1959. Southeastern Conference schools -- Tennessee, Auburn, and Louisiana State -- won in 1951, 1957, and 1958. Only three Pacific Coast Conference schools were ranked in the top ten in the country during the early and middle fifties -- California was fifth in 1950; UCLA was sixth in 1952, fifth in 1953, shared the national championship with Ohio State in 1954, and was fourth in 1955.

The California schools dominated the Pacific Coast Conference through the mid 50's. Cal won the title in 1950, Stanford in 1951, USC in 1952, and UCLA from 1953-1955. Oregon State won in 1956 and tied Oregon for the conference crown in 1957.

The Fifties also saw the beginning of the civil rights movement. Among the many benefits of the new social and political order was the admission of blacks and other racial minorities to private and public universities. In the early history of college football, there were only a handful of black players. Almost all of the major southern schools had all-white student bodies and an all-white football team. Segregated football in that part of the country continued well into the 1960's. That was particularly noticeable in Southeastern and Southwestern Conference schools such as Alabama, Clemson, Kentucky, Mississippi, and Southern Methodist. The first black player to win the Heisman Trophy was Ernie Davis of Syracuse in 1961. As desegregation finally took place in all major conferences and black players had opportunities to compete, almost sixty percent of the Heisman winners since Davis' recognition would be black.

In the 1950's, there were no formal divisions separating major football powers from those not so powerful. In 1937, all National Collegiate Athletic Association member schools were officially designated as a major program or a college program. Major football programs were those institutions that played most of their games against other major schools. Size of the school was not the determining factor. Classifying schools into the current three NCAA divisions did not take place until 1973.

In the mid-fifties some schools -- most notably in the Ivy League -- started to de-emphasize football. In 1956, five years after Princeton, led by Heisman Trophy winner, Dick Kazmaier, finished sixth in the nation, the Ivy schools went to a round-robin format. Each team played the other seven schools and a few other neighboring non-Ivy opponents. They also decided to provide scholarships on the basis of need rather than for athletic prowess. Bowl games and spring practices were banned.

Many faculty members of other major conferences throughout the country also wished to see their schools follow the Ivys' direction. In 1959, after the demise of the Pacific Coast Conference, the faculty representatives of five of the Big Ten Conference institutions voted to eliminate participation in the post-season bowl games.

In 1957, the University of Washington supported nine major sports -- all were men's teams -- and a few minor ones. The major sports were baseball, basketball, crew, football, golf, skiing, swimming, tennis, and track and field. The Intercollegiate Athletic Department had revenue of $681,700 and expenses of $679,400. Football revenue of $470,400 generated net income of $221,900. By 2005, the Department would have 23 sports (11 men and 12 women) with over 650 student athletes. The revenue generated would be $43,200,000 and expenses (excluding extraordinary one-time expenses) would be over $41,800,000. Football revenue would be in excess of $27.1 million, including over $7.4 million in contributions, and generate net income of $13.6 which was used to support the sports that generated low revenue.

Football has been the major sport at Washington since its first game in 1889 -- 20 years after football began in America. The origins of Husky football and its glorious stadium are humble, as might be expected of a game imported to the West. The early history of the Washington football program -- for the 30 years before the construction of Husky Stadium -- was a nomadic journey through a variety of Seattle-area parks and fields. Those first teams, however, attracted the attention of the region's citizens at the very time the city began a remarkable transformation from a small logging community to a diversified metropolis.

Originally founded as the Territorial University in September 1861, the University of Washington opened for classes on November 4th on a knoll overlooking Elliott Bay in downtown Seattle. The first public university on the West Coast, it had few students and no athletic field. Asa Mercer, the school's first president and only instructor, taught in the school's main building, a stately, two-story structure. The Territorial University became the University of Washington in November 1889, when the region gained statehood.

That same year the school fielded its first football team. The migration of the sport of football to the Pacific Northwest was inadvertently sparked by the great Seattle fire of June 1889. After the blaze leveled 25 city blocks comprising some 60 acres of waterfront property south of University Street, stories heralding the rebuilding of Seattle and its "boom town" nature began circulating through the country. Tales of frontier life lured fortune hunters and adventurers, including recent graduates from eastern colleges. Some of these hearty souls had played football during their collegiate careers.

Accounts of Washington's first game describe it as a match-up of the Eastern College Alumni and a team of University of Washington students who, under the direction of a student named

Frank Griffith, raised enough money to send to Philadelphia for an oval pigskin and a copy of the sport's rulebook. The game was held Thanksgiving Day, November 28, 1889, at Jackson Street Baseball Park. The field was located south of Jackson Street in a large, open area bounded by 16th Avenue on the west and Florence on the east. The game was not sanctioned by the University and was generally frowned upon by its administration. In lieu of uniforms, which they didn't have, Washington players wore woolen undershirts and baggy pants made of tent canvas. Helmets had not yet been introduced to the sport. The Alumni won the lively contest with the oval pigskin, 20-0. A newspaper report failed to mention that Washington might have fared better if Griffith, Washington's captain, had played the entire game. Unfortunately, he departed with 15 minutes left, a sartorial wreck, with nothing to wear. An Eastern brute had torn his clothes completely off.

The following year the school scheduled a single game, again on Thanksgiving, and this time in Tacoma. While the team did not score, the result was an improvement as Washington battled the College of Tacoma to a scoreless tie. With no victories, and no points, in two years, the University curtailed football when only eight men turned out for practice in 1891. At the same time, momentum was building for a greater venue for all university activities: a new campus. Leading the effort to relocate the school was Edmund Meany. One of the first University of Washington graduates, he sponsored a bill in the Washington legislature that authorized the purchase of 580 acres of land at what was known as the Interlaken site: an area between Lake Union and Lake Washington. The total cost of the land was $28,313.75, backed by a $150,000 construction appropriation.

As the campus population grew, student organizations emerged including the Athletic Association, which would later be renamed the Associated Students of the University of Washington (ASUW).

In an effort to emulate the traditions of more established college athletic programs, a student assembly was called in 1892 to adopt school colors. Factions debated to a stalemate the use of the nation's colors, red, white and blue, as school colors in honor of George Washington, the University's namesake. Some regarded the choice as a patriotic tribute; others considered it an inappropriate gesture. The discussion ended when a young English instructor, Miss Louise Frazyer, stood and recited from the first stanza of Lord Byron's "Destruction of Sennacherib" these lines:

The Assyrian came down like a wolf on the fold,

And his cohorts were gleaming in purple and gold;

And the sheen of their spears was like stars on the sea,

When the blue wave rolls nightly on deep Galilee.

The students quickly agreed: purple and gold, the colors of royalty, would become the first great tradition of Washington athletics, one that has stood the test of time.

Washington named its first coach, William "Billy" Goodwin, for the two-game 1892 season. After losing to the Seattle Athletic Club in mid-October, Goodwin's gridders won the rematch on December 17 at the Madison Street Athletic Park, claiming the school's first victory. Fullback Frank Atkins, who had played in Washington's first game as a pre-collegiate student, ran five yards for the school's first touchdown in the 14-0 win. To celebrate the victory, students paraded through downtown streets. At the offices of the Seattle Post-Intelligencer, the University lads gave three cheers as the score was chalked on a large bulletin board. Washington played five games in 1893, including its first intercollegiate contest. Stanford visited on December 29 and won 40-0 before 600 spectators in West Seattle. The Stanford travel party included a manager named Herbert Hoover, who would become the nation's 31st President (1929-33).

In 1895, when the new University campus became a reality, the football team found an on-campus practice site, soon named the University Athletic Field, on the north end of campus, while playing games at a variety of off-campus locations. The practice field paid immediate dividends as Washington enjoyed its first unbeaten season, outscoring opponents 98-8 in compiling a 4-0-1 record. With only a handful of West Coast colleges fielding teams and with funds for travel to out-of-town schools limited, Washington's first decade of football was played primarily against Seattle athletic clubs, YMCA teams and small local colleges. That began changing in 1900 when Idaho, Washington State and Oregon first appeared on the schedule.

Two years later, more stability came to the sport when the Northwest Intercollegiate Athletic Association (NIAA) was formed. Washington could finally compete for a championship. Washington's greatest rivalry got its start in 1900 when the school faced Washington Agricultural College (later named Washington State University) on Thanksgiving Day at Seattle's Athletic Park. Washington tied its unbeaten, cross-state opponent, 5-5.

The UW program took another major step in 1902 when it hired its first full-time coach, James Knight, who also launched the school's rowing program. His first football team went 5-1 and the following season improved to 6-1, winning the school's first NIAA championship, and defeating Nevada 2-0 at Athletic Park. The game was considered the Pacific Coast championship since Washington had defeated all its Northwest rivals and Nevada had defeated California and Stanford. The defensive struggle featured Enoch Bagshaw, who made a game-saving tackle near the end of the contest. Bagshaw would later return to his alma mater to coach Washington to its first Rose Bowl appearance.

In April 1906, the ASUW recommended that bleachers be erected at University Athletic Field (later renamed Denny Field) to encourage holding athletic events on campus rather than in the city. On October 26, 1906, the eve of the team's first on-campus game, The Pacific Wave, the student weekly newspaper, reported that every carpenter available had helped complete covered grandstands with seating for 1,200 people, all sheltered from the rain and sleet by a roof of "good and fat boards." The newspaper also noted: "For the benefit of the players, it would be best to add that little stones which are now so much in evidence on the field will be removed, so there will be no danger of one of the contestants falling thereon and thereby breeding a scab on the end of the nose or marring his beauty in any manner."

When Gil Dobie arrived on the Washington campus in 1908, he hardly presented the appearance of a football coach. The tall, lanky Scotsman let his demeanor speak for him. A group of entering freshmen was among the first to meet the new coach and, as one of them recalled, "No smile, no handshakes, no slap on the back ... nothing but a pair of eyes peering coldly out of a dark face that was hidden partially by a slouch hat drawn loosely over a head of mussed black hair." After a brief introduction, Dobie, in a rasping voice, stated, "Remember, all you fellows, practice Monday starts at 2 p.m. One thing I demand is promptness." His concern for promptness, his preparation for games, and his psychological skills paid off handsomely.

During his nine years at Washington, Dobie's teams never lost a game, winning 58 times and playing to a tie on three occasions. Dobie's players outscored opponents by a remarkably lopsided 1,930 to 118 margin. From 1907 to 1917 Washington's teams built an incredible streak of 63 games without a defeat. The achievement, that includes a tie with Idaho in 1907, remains an NCAA record for consecutive games without a loss. In the midst of the football program's successes, one of Washington's greatest traditions was born. In 1915, Lester J. Wilson, a 1913 UW graduate, wrote words and music for "Bow Down to Washington," the school's "Prize Song." His original lyrics included a second chorus intended solely for the California game. It declared, in part: "See the Golden Bear, From his mighty lair, For we're goin' to hang his carcass in the Northland." Dobie's teams were loaded with players who were Washington's first stars.

Toward the end of Dobie's amazing run at Washington, the Pacific Coast Conference (PCC) -- predecessor to the Big Five, the PAC-8 and later the PAC-10 -- was formed. In 1916, Dobie's last season in Seattle, Washington won the inaugural PCC championship. The final game of the season proved to be another milestone for the growing program. More than 9,000 fans jammed Denny Field to watch Washington beat California 14-7. It was the largest crowd to ever see the team play. Despite the championship, the season ended on a sour note when Dobie decided to leave Washington. He lost the backing of the faculty and University President Henry Suzzallo when he sided with a player in a dispute over an academic suspension.

Surprisingly, Dobie's teams never received a bowl game invitation. Washington State was selected to face Brown in the 1916 Rose Bowl on the basis of comparative scores. A year later Oregon was presented the invitation because railroad fare from Eugene to Pasadena for the entire team was $250 cheaper than from Seattle.

Thanks to the success of the Washington program, however, Denny Field underwent several upgrades to accommodate the growing crowds. A large grandstand was built on the south side of the field in 1911. Five years later the area was re-graded and a larger north grandstand was added to increase capacity.

The first nickname for Washington's athletic teams was adopted in November 1919. As a protest to the banning of the popular campus magazine, Sun Dodger, students applied the name to school teams. As a negative reference to the Northwest's climate, however, Sun Dodgers was deemed less than inspiring, and in 1921 a student committee was formed to find a more suitable moniker. Frustrated by the committee's progress, athletic officials, acting while students were away on a holiday break in December 1921, decided to refer to Washington teams as Vikings. Students protested the choice and, within two months, settled on Huskies — a name considered appropriate because of the University's proximity to the Alaskan frontier and because the Husky stands for "fight and tenacity, character and courage, endurance and willingness."

In 1919, a crowd of 16,000 watched Washington stun highly regarded California 7-0 at Denny Field. While the record crowd cheered wildly, thousands of other fans were turned away at the gates for lack of seating. It was clear that a larger facility was needed.

The move to replace Denny Field began in November 1919 when Darwin Meisnest, the 24-year-old graduate manager of the ASUW student organization, proposed a new stadium at the first student assembly of the year. When Meisnest took his post earlier in the year, two large projects were before the ASUW: a new athletic stadium and a new student union. He persuaded students that a stadium, not a student union, should be built first because it would receive the financial support of the business community, while the student union would not. Meisnest was right. Most of the $260,000 raised prior to completion resulted from the sale of 3,500 seat plaques, many of them to enthusiastic businesses.

University President Henry Suzzallo and the Board of Regents quickly approved the ASUW's recommendation, and a Stadium Committee was established. The Committee recommended a stadium be built in two phases of 30,000 seats each. with an ultimate seating capacity of 60,000,. The structure would be an open-ended bowl to preserve the site's scenic views of Lake

Washington and the Cascade Mountains in the distance. Though never completed, the design called for two great Collegiate Gothic towers surmounting the main entrance on the west. Four smaller towers were planned, two each on the north and south sides of the stadium. A colonnade would provide space for memorials, inscription of records and a covered practice track. The field would be encircled by a full quarter-mile track with a 220-yard straight-away on the north side.

A statewide fund-raising campaign, launched in the spring of 1920, was supported by the Washington State Chamber of Commerce, its affiliated commercial bodies and the alumni and students of the University. Loyal Washingtonians visited virtually every firm in Seattle seeking contributions. Five-hundred student salespersons sold small bronze plaques to supporters who bought season tickets. The price of a plaque was $50 for two years and $100 for five years, reduced to $25 and $50 for purchasers living more than 50 miles from the city. Plaque sales eventually resulted in more than $240,000 for stadium construction.

Students aided the cause by approving an ASUW recommendation to raise student fees from $5 to $10 and allocate $4 of the fee to pay a portion of the initial stadium costs and help retire bonds issued to pay the contractor's fee. The fees provided almost $124,000 for construction.

The stadium's groundbreaking ceremony was held April 16, 1920. Suzzallo and Seattle Mayor Hugh Campbell were joined by students, faculty and prominent stadium supporters. Three weeks later Puget Sound Bridge and Dredging Company signed a contract with the ASUW and work began. The entire excavation of the field and the filling of the side embankments was accomplished with hydraulic sluices and pumps. Great pressurized streams of water – 687-million gallons taken from the nearby lakes – gouged the earth and washed it away into directed channels. In this way, 230,000-

cubic-yards of dirt and silt were removed, leaving a drainable base of sand and gravel.

The project was completed in little more than a year from the time of Meisnest's proposal. On November 27, 1920, 24,500 fans cheered as the Dartmouth and Washington teams emerged from a tunnel on the southwest side of the stadium -- the present tunnel on the northwest side was not in place until 1927 when the Washington Pavilion (later renamed Hec Edmundson Pavilion) was completed . The match-up marked the first intersectional game for Washington. Bob Abel, Washington's quarterback and the ASUW president, scored the first touchdown in the new stadium on the game's opening drive. When Dartmouth was forced to attempt a field goal, Abel broke through the line and blocked the kick. The ball bounced into his hands, and he rambled 63 yards for the historic score. Abel's return, however, would be the only highlight for Washington. Sporting a solid passing game, Dartmouth scored four times to defeat Washington 28-7.

After one season of play in the new stadium, Enoch Bagshaw, a former Washington football captain, joined the program as coach. During nine years at the helm, he helped the Huskies compile a 63-22-6 record. The stadium did not record its first capacity crowd until 1922 when 30,075 filled the stadium after the team started the season with five consecutive victories. Purple and Gold patrons left disappointed, however, as California overpowered the Huskies 45-7. Washington played Southern California for the first time in 1923. The game drew so much interest that the first radio broadcast of a Husky game was arranged. The Post-Intelligencer's station KFJC provided "instantaneous radiophone coverage of all the action."

Just sophomores at the time, future Washington stars Elmer Tesreau and George Wilson both scored touchdowns in a 22-0 rout. "The Huskies swarmed over the touted Trojans like ants on a picnic pie," wrote well-known Seattle sportswriter Royal

Brougham. The game was a turning point in rebuilding the Husky program. Washington proceeded to win every game of the season except for a 9-0 loss to California, as the Golden Bears played a final time on their historic California Field. Despite winning their fourth consecutive PCC title, the Bears declined the 1924 Rose Bowl invitation, and Washington made the trip, tying Navy 14-14 in the University's first bowl appearance.

In 1925, when Bagshaw guided the Huskies to the conference title, another crowd of 35,000 jammed the stadium to see the Huskies shutout Stanford 13-0, a team led by All-America fullback, Ernie Nevers. The next week Washington beat California 7-0 in Berkeley before 80,000 fans and ended the season two weeks later with a 15-14 win over Oregon. With a 10-0-1 overall record and a 5-0 conference mark, Washington won the Pacific Coast Conference championship while leading the nation in scoring for a second consecutive season. The Huskies went on to face Alabama in the Rose Bowl, losing 20-19 in one of the greatest games ever played in Pasadena on New Year's Day.

George Wilson, Washington's first consensus All-American, was sensational in leading the Huskies to a 12-0 half-time lead. Midway through the second quarter, Wilson was knocked unconscious and was carried off the field on a stretcher. Alabama scored three touchdowns in the third quarter with Wilson on the bench. He entered the game at the end of the third quarter and engineered an 88-yard scoring drive to get the Huskies within one point, the margin of victory for the Crimson Tide. With Wilson in the lineup, Washington gained over 300 yards and scored all its points. During his 22 minutes off the field, Washington gained 17 yards and was held scoreless, and gave up 20 points. Wilson was voted the game's Most Valuable Player, along with Alabama's Johnny Mack Brown.

Led by coach Jim Phelan and consensus All-American guard

Max Starcevich and All-Coast running back Jim Cain and tackle Vic Markov, the 1936 Husky team recovered to record six shutouts and a 7-1-1 overall record. In conference play, Washington's only blemish was a 14-14 tie with Stanford. Washington had risen to sixth in the national rankings when it faced 20th-ranked Washington State in the final regular-season game. With a Rose Bowl bid on the line, a crowd of 40,735 turned out for the Thanksgiving Day affair. They watched Washington play what some observers called the "Perfect Game" routing the Cougars 40-0.

The mighty Huskies, though, fell short in the 1937 Rose Bowl. Allowed to select their opponent, they passed on LSU, the popular choice, and selected Pittsburgh instead. Coach Jock Sutherland's Panthers proved to be too much, and the Huskies fell 21-0.

The growing popularity of Husky football led to the first major expansion of the stadium. In 1937, 14 rows of seats in 20 sections were added above the original bowl. The additional 10,000 seats increased capacity to 40,000.

World War II had an interesting impact on the Husky roster and schedule. Players who were transferred to Washington because of its campus military training program joined the team, while others left the team when called into service. Eight Washington State players suited up for the Huskies at some point during the war years when the Cougar program was suspended. In 1943, Washington played only four regular-season games, three against military teams that included older, more experienced players. The best of these teams was the Fourth Air Force Flyers of March Field, California. With a roster of collegiate standouts, the Flyers were heavily favored when they faced Washington on October 23, 1943. Husky Coach Welch devised a special defense to thwart the Flyers spread offense. Washington's Sammy Robinson scored twice and Al Akins, a Washington State transfer, returned a punt 68 yards for a score to lead the Huskies to a 27-7 upset.

Wartime travel restrictions turned the 1944 Rose Bowl into a match-up between the PCC Northern and Southern Division champions. Not having played a game since October 30, the Huskies faced a USC team that had been soundly defeated by March Field. But Washington's roster no longer included two of its key backs, Pete Susick and Jay Stoves, who were pressed into military service. The Trojans won easily, 29-0.

The war ended at the same time that Harvey Cassill became Washington's athletic director. In 1948, he replaced Coach Welch with Howie Odell. During Odell's five years, the Pacific Coast Conference was dominated by the California schools. Cal won in 1948, 1949, and 1950, compiling a 29-3-1 record. Stanford won in 1951 and USC in 1952. During those five years, Washington was 23-25-2. Cassill had ambitious plans for the football program. He envisioned the Seattle community and the campus population growing and Husky Stadium expanding to meet the demand. He also realized that to draw prominent opponents, he needed more seats to enlarge gate receipts to cover the guaranteed payout. Since Washington was not drawing capacity crowds, however, critics of Cassill's expansion plan considered it a waste of resources.

As Cassill pursued his plans for the stadium, the arrival of running back Hugh McElhenny and quarterback Don Heinrich fanned new hope in Husky fans for a conference title. While McElhenny and Heinrich would finish their careers as two of the most productive offensive players in Washington's history, injuries kept them from playing together in two of their three seasons at Washington. McElhenny missed most of 1949, and a shoulder injury in 1951 sidelined Heinrich. In 1950, the only full year they appeared together in the backfield, the team finished 8-2, losing only to California and Illinois.

Despite some criticism of Cassill's plan, the 1950 season opened with the addition of a towering upper deck to the stadium, adding

15,000 seats to its capacity. To combat the Northwest's rainy climate, a cantilevered steel roof partially covered all seats in the upper deck and approximately 6,000 in the lower sections. A two-level press box and camera deck was part of the project. Seating for about 75 members of the press provided a view 165 feet above the stadium floor. The project, dubbed "Cassill's Castle," cost $1.7 million and was financed by ASUW funds.

Kansas State headlined the "Castle's" opening, but only 30,245 fans attended the game. No one, presumably, wanted to test the new, upper-stand seats. Those who stayed away missed a show. McElhenny set a school record by gaining 177 rushing yards on 16 carries, including a 91-yard scoring run. Heinrich threw four touchdown passes for another Husky record, including a 65-yarder to Roland Kirkby, as the Huskies breezed to a 33-7 victory.

Another Husky tradition, the annual Band Day, traces its origin to the Kansas State game. Conceived as a means to promote tickets sales in communities across the state, the event was originally called Western Washington Band Day. In 1952 the name changed to High School Band Day, as invitations were extended to schools in central as well as western Washington.

While the football stadium was classic because of its alignment to the lake and mountains and its new upper deck, the coaching facilities were quite different. Just north of the Husky swimming pool, stood an old wooden shack-like structure. It housed the football and basketball coaches. One entered it up a ramp that extended from a parking lot adjacent to the Edmundson Pavilion.

On a breezy day, the odors from the nearby Montlake garbage dump drifted into the shack. The upper floors of the two-story building included the coaches' offices and the lower half was a "meeting room" big enough for about 40 players. The floor of the room was dirt and during the rainy season it turned to mud. "It was like going into a coal mine, and with the smell from the dump,"

Coach Owens laughingly recalled, "it gave us a hell of a recruiting advantage." He would add, "Every time I walked by that shack, I shuttered."

John Cherberg became the Husky football coach in 1953. He ended a three-year stint with a 10-18-2 record, a team mutiny, his own firing and Cassill's resignation. Darrell Royal coached the Huskies to a 5-5 record in 1956 before moving to the University of Texas. Without a conference title since 1936 and a Rose Bowl appearance involving non-conference opponents since 1937, Washington fans had patiently waited for someone to lead them to a championship season. They pinned their hopes squarely on the broad shoulders of Jim Owens.

CHAPTER 6

The Youngest Team in America

Jim Owens and his staff greeted 70 men for the start of spring practice and 20 scheduled workouts. It was a marked contrast from 1957. The coaches had the players sorted into working units right from the start -- the purple unit (first team), the gold squad (alternate unit), and then the red, green, black and white jerseyed groups.

Twenty-eight sophomores-to-be, many of whom had played on the unbeaten freshmen team, were among the aspirants trying to make the varsity. Other first-year varsity prospects included tackle Kurt Gegner and quarterback Bob Hivner. Both had red-shirted in 1957. Running backs George Fleming and Don McKeta were junior college transfers who would provide many needed skills. Only seven seniors were among the varsity candidates. It was a very young and inexperienced group.

Most of the sophomores started their Washington football career under Owens and his assistants and were largely recruited for their ability to fit into the Owens system -- handling the conditioning, the mental and physical toughness drills, and paying the price the coaches exacted.

Unlike 1957, when he had very little depth at the quarterback position, Owens could choose from five hopefuls -- all sophomores. Owens was convinced that any of them could provide the passing skill which the Huskies has lacked the season before.

During the spring, Hivner and fellow sophomore Bob Schloredt began to emerge as the most promising candidates to lead the offense. In the line, five sophomores looked like potential starters in the fall -- Chuck Allen, Barry Bullard, Gegner, Bill Kinnune, and Roy McKasson.

Bullard, a scholarly engineering student, felt that the coaches were still developing a playbook. It would be based on the strengths of the young players. "The upcoming freshmen were really the focus of what became the Washington offense. Owens knew what he wanted to do. He knew where he wanted to set his offensive line. But he needed to determine our ability to execute certain blocking angles before a play got into the play book." Bullard continued. "By the time we were seniors, the coaches had their play book. They were extremely innovative."

Near the end of the spring sessions, Owens was pleased with the team's progress, particularly in the passing game. "We've got a couple of quarterbacks who can throw long. They may not hit them long, but at least they will keep the defense honest. Last year, the other club's deep backs were coming up to make most of the tackles on us."

Owens still felt the emphasis would be on a sound running game, strengthened with passing. "If you notice, a good running team usually is right up among the leaders in touchdown passes. And those are the passes that count."

During the spring, the coaches started to develop a strategy for using the new two-point conversion which was one of the rule changes for the 1958 season. When asked about his strategy, Owens said, "I haven't given the extra point business much attention yet. Our problem is to get the first six." Recognizing that the two or one-point decision was going to create a second guesser's Shangri-La, Owens quipped, "Maybe I'll follow (California's head coach) Pete Elliott's advice. When we score and line up for the conversion, I'll ask for a show of hands from the crowd."

During the spring, a new ticket plan was announced. It targeted the "man in the gray flannel suit." Seats in the northwest section of the stadium could be bundled into a family plan for the 1958 season's five home games for $27 -- two adult and two children's tickets. Season tickets on the south side would cost $18 per seat.

In late spring, Keith Jackson, KOMO's sports director, would join the Husky crew in what Jackson would call his greatest sporting venture in over 50 years of sports broadcasting. "The mess created by Coach Cherberg and Torchy Torrance created one of the greatest sports stories of all time," Jackson reflected. It was the Husky crew upsetting the world's best eight, the Trud Club of Leningrad, in a race near Moscow. The victory was one of the greatest upsets in the annals of collegiate rowing.

On September 1, the football team moved into the Conibear Crew House to eat, sleep and focus on pre-season two-a day practices. Fifty-three men were invited to report including 17 lettermen and 30 sophomores with no varsity game experience. Owens and his staff were raring to go. "In the first few sessions, we'll find out who's in shape and who wants to play and go from there," Owens exclaimed.

Before the practices started, the oracles had spoken. The Official NCAA Football Guide asserted that UCLA would be the Pacific Coast's most feared team in 1958 with Ohio State as the Big Ten favorite. Because of the Huskies' relatively young and inexperienced roster, the sports writers covering the Pacific Coast Conference schools predicted Washington to be near the bottom with Oregon State and Washington State most likely to join the Bruins at the top of the conference.

Early in the pre-season, Ray Jackson, another sophomore, visited the team workouts. Jackson, an accomplished fullback, attended Bakersfield Community College in California and played there during the 1957 season. Bakersfield coach and former USC player, Howard Beatty, squawked in all four directions and all the languages he knew when he heard Jackson had come to Seattle. Because of his coach's behavior and some personal problems -- including a wife and children -- Jackson returned to Bakersfield for the 1958 season. He would return to Washington in the spring of 1959.

In the season opener at home before 28,000 fans, Washington beat the San Jose Spartans 14-6. Hivner and Schloredt engineered the two Husky scores. Hivner scored at the end of a 62-yard drive with a quarterback keeper from the four. Early in the fourth quarter, the Spartans drove 58 yards to pull within one. Late in the final stanza, Schloredt intercepted a pass to set up Mike McCluskey's short touchdown run with less than two minutes to go.

On September 27, the Huskies met Minnesota in Husky Stadium. 38,000 showed up to see the Huskies beat the Big Ten opponent 24-21. Washington took the opening kickoff and ripped the Gophers to pieces on a 73-yard touchdown drive. It featured a new formation -- an unbalanced line, strong to the right or left with the left halfback spread wide -- which puzzled Minnesota most of the afternoon. The fans were in disbelief when Washington opened the drive with five straight passes -- the big one a 35-yard strike to Luther Carr.

The Husky offense turned defense didn't have time to take a deep breath as the Gophers churned 66 yards in 15 plays to even the score. Early in the second stanza, Minnesota marched 83 yards to take the lead 14-7. But not for long.

Carr took the ensuing kickoff and returned it 44 yards to the Gopher 32. With fourth and one on the three, Hivner dove over right guard to balance the board. The Huskies stayed in command for the rest of the half. Carr teed off another touchdown drive by returning a punt 13 yards to the Gopher 37. Then it was the Hivner show -- a pass to Carr for 10; again to Carr for 11; a fake pass and run over tackle for nine. Finally, a four-yard throw to McCluskey for the score. Fleming's third extra point put the Huskies up 21-14.

With the clock winding down, Phil Borders, another Husky quarterback, punted and the coaches and players witnessed the payoff of all the punishing punting drills. McCluskey sped downfield. The Gopher safety elected to catch the ball on his nine, blissfully unaware that McCluskey had just launched himself with his helmet aimed at his opponent's chest. He separated the football from the helpless Gopher and Bob Echols recovered on the nine. The Huskies stalled. On fourth down, Owens rushed Bruce Claridge into the game not with a special touchdown play but the kicking tee.

With seconds ticking away like a countdown at Cape Canaveral, fans began to scream at the Huskies to hurry thinking that the coaches were not aware of the situation. As usual, the coaches were well aware of what was going on. With two seconds remaining, Fleming calmly drilled the ball from the 16-yard line through the uprights and Washington led 24-14. "I didn't see the ball go through. Every time I look up, I miss. I just kick it and turn around and trot off. I let the crowd tell me if I made it," reported Fleming. The Husky fans, frantic a few seconds ago, cheered loudly and joyously. The field goal would be the margin of victory. Washington supporters left the stadium thinking maybe this Husky team would be the one to turn the losing situation around.

Next up in Columbus, Ohio were the Buckeyes of Ohio State coached by Woody Hayes. In the 1957 season, his team was the National Champion and the 1958 Rose Bowl victor over Oregon 10-7. Ohio State, ranked third behind Oklahoma and Michigan

State, featured the simplest and most punishing attack in college football. Its backs merely lined up behind a massive front line and ran the ball down the opponent's throat. Hayes had three of the finest backs in collegiate football and a line that averaged 233 pounds. The Huskies averaged 197 and were 20 point underdogs.

Washington gave the Buckeyes all they could handle. In Thursday's practice, the day before the team flew to Columbus, Owens came over to Schloredt and said, "Bob, you know that we have our fullbacks pretty well beat up. I want you to practice a few things at that position. Schloredt recounted, "In those days, quarterbacks knew the assignments of everyone. We didn't have that many plays so it wasn't such a big deal. As a fullback, you were also a linebacker. So in practice, I ran about six plays on offense and defense. About ten minutes before the game started, Coach Owens walks up to me and says 'you are starting at fullback.' "

With a quarterback turned fullback and linebacker, the Huskies took charge. Their line play crackled as they repeatedly beat the giants in red and white with their savage blocking and tackling. The Buckeyes looked sluggish and often befuddled and outfought. What shocked the 82,000 spectators was the manner in which the young, spirited Huskies stood up on their hind legs and clawed and scrapped. They outgained the Buckeyes 276 to 196.

The Huskies scored on their second possession, taking over on the Ohio State 31 after a bad Buckeye punt. McKeta plowed for 14 and a few plays later for 12 more up the middle for the touchdown. Fleming kicked the point and the Huskies led 7-0 and the partisan crowd was stunned.

The Buckeyes scored with 52 seconds remaining in the first quarter after Bob White, Ohio State's powerful fullback and linebacker, intercepted a pitchout and took the ball to the Husky 28. Seven plays later, Ohio State scored but failed in its two-point conversion attempt -- 7-6 Huskies.

In a game that had 31 exchanges of the ball, the Huskies repeatedly thwarted the Buckeyes on fourth and short situations. It seemed like Ohio State was playing its typical conservative brand of football and waiting for a break to happen. It did. Schloredt, back to punt on the Ohio 46, had trouble handling a bad center snap, juggled the ball and then kicked a split-second too late to avert the wave of red-shirted defenders who swarmed in to block the punt. Right tackle Jim Marshall picked up the loose ball and chugged to the Husky 27 as the third quarter ended. It was the same Jim Marshall who would become a member of the Minnesota Vikings' feared "Purple People Eaters." Despite his enormous success as an NFL player, Marshall would become famous for an incident in 1964. Against the San Francisco 49ers, Marshall recovered a fumble, but ran 66 yards with it the wrong way and into his end zone. He spiked the ball, it went out of bounds, and the 49ers had two points. Fortunately for Marshall, the Vikings won, 27-22.

After Marshall's recovery for Ohio State, the table was set and the Buckeyes dug right in. They scored in seven plays to go on top 12-7, failing again on the two-point conversion. The Huskies threatened one more time late in the fourth quarter only to see their hopes die on the Ohio 22.

Owens and Hayes met at midfield after the game. Hayes could have said a lot of things such as "You are a young coach with a young team. You outplayed us and we were lucky to win. Congratulations to your players," or several other positive comments. Instead, he said, "Coach, I think you're going to have to work real hard on your offense." In 1966, Washington would again face the Buckeyes in Columbus. Donnie Moore rushed for 221 yards as the Huskies pasted Hayes' charges 38-22. Owens said it took all his discipline and biting of his tongue to not say, "Coach, you have to work on your offense."

During the week between the Ohio State game and the Stanford game, the NCAA informed the University of Washington that all the rights and privileges of NCAA membership that had been taken away in 1956 had been restored. Washington was no longer on probation with the Pacific Coast Conference and the NCAA. Accordingly, all Husky athletic teams were eligible to compete in post-season play.

After a defeat like the one in Columbus, good teams don't let down. They figure a way to get ready for the next opponent with the drive, intensity, and execution that is necessary to play well week after week.

The Stanford game in Palo Alto indicated Washington was not yet a good team. The Indians had the Huskies groveling on the ground and recorded their first win of the season 22-12. Stanford, who had lost their first three games by the combined score of 98-13, outgained Washington 378 to 207.

At the start of Monday's practice, Owens told his players, "The Stanford loss is on the coaches. We didn't make the necessary adjustments during the game. We apologize."

For many players, it was a special moment. It never occurred to them that any coach would apologize for anything.

Husky mediocrity continued the next week when the UCLA Bruins came to Seattle and left with 20-0 victory. Maybe Coach Hayes was right. The Huskies did have to work on their offense. Three lost fumbles, five intercepted passes, and poor pass defense keep the homecoming crowd cheerless for most of the game. The weather was awful. The game's television announcer, a California resident, muttered, "This is the worst rain and wind I've ever seen." The game ended with a radiant rainbow stretching from north to south across the east side of Lake Washington. It wasn't for Washington.

Husky fortunes didn't improve on October 25 in Portland's Multnomah Stadium as the Oregon State Beavers downed

Washington 14-12. The Beavers dominated the first half. With their single-wing attack, they piled up 231 yards to the Huskies' 62. Surprisingly, they led by only two points, 8-6, at the intermission.

Schloredt's punting was a big factor in keeping the game close. In the first half, his two punts went 62 and 70 yards. The second one set up the Huskies' score. Beaver wingback John Horillo fumbled the punt and Jack Walters smothered it. On the first play of the series, Schloredt hit Carver Gayton out of the backfield for the touchdown. His pass to Fleming for two points hit the halfback's finger tips and he couldn't bring in the ball.

One of the plays that could have given the Huskies the victory was the punt coverage of McCluskey. Horillo gathered in another one of Schloredt's booming punts and was absolutely leveled by the Husky marauder. In those days, there was no three-yard radius to protect the punt returner from being punished. The ball was jarred loose and recovered by Duane Lowell on the Beaver 20. Four plays later, Fleming attempted a 46-yard field goal. It skidded off his foot and died out of bounds on the Beaver three.

Shortly thereafter, Oregon State scored on a 89-yard drive, failed on the two-point try and led 14-6. The Huskies had two good scoring chances in the fourth quarter. One ended on the Beaver 14. The other came late in the quarter after Kurt Gegner's vicious tackle resulted in a fumble. Sam Hurworth recovered on the Beaver 23. Schloredt scored from the six but his run for the tie failed.

One thing was becoming very clear. Owens' tough punting drills were paying off. Opponents were being held to very little return yardage and sometimes were fumbling deep in their territory and giving Washington great field position. With Schloredt, the Huskies had a punter who could kick the ball high and deep. The coaches were also developing punt return schemes featuring the smooth gliding and shifty running style of Fleming and the vicious come-back blocks of the linemen. In 1958, the Huskies held their opponents to 3.2 yards a return and gained 6.8 yards on their returns. In 1959, the results would be 2.9 for the opposition compared to 8.7. In 1960, the results would be even better -- 3.8 against versus 14.2 for the Huskies.

Frustrated by four straight losses, Owens announced at the Monday practice -- normally a comparatively light one -- that he was sending the team back to first grade. "All eleven positions are wide open." He then proceeded to send his charges through the roughest, toughest drills since early September. Owens told the squad that during the week, there would be a decided emphasis on the fundamentals of blocking and tackling and the basics that win football games.

On the next day, the practice ended with an all-out scrimmage and a donnybrook with everybody socking every body else. After the practice, Owens vowed "there would be more earthy-type football in preparation for Oregon. In addition to weekly challenge drills, he matched the first and second units to fight it out -- head to head -- for starting positions. He and the other coaches were mad. The Ducks had better be ready when they came to Husky Stadium.

Thirty-two thousand fans witnessed a tough defensive struggle. The Ducks, seemingly, had all the offense in the world at their command as they marched up and down the field. However, when they got into scoring territory, the Huskies shut them down. The lone touchdown was scored in the second quarter, primarily by the exploits of two backs who had been demoted to the bench during the week. It was Hivner throwing and Carr running.

With about six minutes gone in the quarter, Hivner woke up the Husky faithful. From his own 20, he hit Carr for 13. Next he threw to Lowell for 8. Again to Carr for 12. From the Oregon 47,

Hivner swept left end for 10 yards and another first down. Then the Huskies landed the haymaker -- a perfectly executed screen play to Carr. He stomped, danced, twisted and turned through the Oregon linebackers and a cluster of defensive backs to complete the 37-yard scoring gem. Fleming's kick went awry and the score stood at 6-0.

The Ducks threatened many times -- once from the Husky 12. At this juncture, they were hit with a 15-yard penalty for an illegal substitution. One of their players came back into the third quarter one too many times. With fourth and five, Oregon sent in Alden Kimbrough, a rangy pass receiver and one of quarterback Dave Grosz' favorite targets. The complex substitution rules had turned coaches into bookkeepers. The rules allowed a player who started a quarter to return only once that quarter. "Kimbrough forgot he'd been in (twice) already," Oregon coach Les Casanova replied to a question in the post-game press conference. "Our student managers forgot to check Kimbrough's substitution record in the third quarter. We even have a special place on the bench for guys who are ineligible to return." So fourth and five turned into fourth and 20. A screen pass fell incomplete and the Ducks were still scoreless.

The Ducks had one more chance. From their own 24, they drove to the Husky seven. On third down, Schloredt, the all-stater from Oregon, intercepted a pass from Grosz, the all-stater from Washington, in the end zone.

It was Owens' first shutout at Washington and the first Husky shutout in 33 games -- back to 1955 when they beat USC 7-0. Owens expressed delight with another statistic. "No fumbles, no fumbles...(that) one must go clear back to Bagshaw (Husky coach from 1921-1929)."

The Oregon win would be the Huskies third and last one for the season. The Huskies committed several critical mistakes in the

Los Angeles Coliseum a week later, and USC shutout Washington 21-0.

The next Saturday, November 16, Quarterback Joe Kapp led his Rose Bowl bound California Bears into Husky Stadium. The Huskies led at half-time 7-6. The Bears drove 65 yards to go ahead 12-7 late in the third quarter after being denied several times deep in Washington's end of the field. Owens had a deep, abiding passion about losses. However, after the game, he admitted to mixed feelings about the loss to Cal. "I don't feel as down about this one as I have before. I'm down on myself, because the kids did everything we asked them to do, and we still didn't win." Owens continued. "We're the youngest team in the United States. Nobody comes close to us. Today we had eight sophomores, one junior, and two seniors in our first unit. We had seven sophomores and four juniors on our second unit. I was real proud of the way those kids hung in there and hit back. That was a top team effort, and I'm not down a bit over the way they played."

Kapp also felt the Huskies had played very well. "Washington has a real tough team. They hit as hard as any team we've played. I can't understand how Washington ever loses, the way they hit. And they're all young guys. In another year, that bunch is going to be hard to beat."

On November 19, the NCAA approved 11 post-season bowl games. The four traditional games -- the Rose, Cotton, Orange, and Sugar Bowls -- were to be played on January 1. Some of the others were the Mineral Water Bowl, the Blue Grass Bowl, the Gator Bowl, the Tangerine Bowl, and the Sun Bowl -- all to be played before New Year's Day.

The Huskies closed out the season in Spokane with its traditional Governor's Cup game -- the Apple Cup did not come into existence until 1962 -- against the Cougars. The Washington State fans cheered with their voices but listened for the final result from Berkeley. The Bears edged Stanford 16-15 to finish one game ahead of the Cougars in the conference standings.

The Huskies fumbled five times bringing their season total to 37. Two of the four lost fumbles gave the home team possession on the Washington 13 and 27. Both led to Cougars' scores and with less than seven minutes elapsed in the first quarter, Washington State led 12-0.

The Huskies clawed back. They scored late in the first quarter and just before half-time to take a 14-12 lead. The Cougars scored midway in the third quarter to seal the victory 18-14. Owens was disappointed but proud of his defense. "We gave them two easy ones and then we fought them down to the wire."

With its 7-3 record, Washington State was prominently mentioned for both the Sugar Bowl and Gator Bowl. The Pacific Coast Conference had a policy which banned member schools from any post-season play except in the Rose Bowl. The policy did permit a school to ask for a waiver of the policy. Washington State requested a waiver on November 25. A few days later, faculty representatives from six of the eight other schools voted to deny the waiver.

Late in November, in a much more far-reaching ruling, a Federal Court knocked out a Louisiana law barring competition between white and black athletes. The law passed by the state legislature in 1956 "prevented mixed boxing matches and teams with Negro players meeting all-white squads in events such as the Sugar Bowl (played in New Orleans)."

Presumably, the chief beneficiary of the ruling was the Sugar Bowl because segregation against teams with black players narrowed the field to a handful of teams mainly located in the Southeast. The ruling provided an opportunity for the bowl committee to consider a much larger list of teams. However, based on the teams invited to play in the Sugar Bowl for several years after the Federal Court's decision, it appeared that the Sugar Bowl's committee still had its own segregation policy.

Louisiana State, a segregated team, captured the national championship title. Pete Dawkins, Army's All-American running back, received the Heisman Trophy as the most outstanding football player in the land. In the 1959 Rose Bowl, Iowa romped over California 38-12.

At the annual post-season football banquet, all seven seniors spoke. Reese Lindquist ended his remarks with comments about the next season. He thought the talent level would be better. He felt the young players had bought into Owens' system and knew what the coaches wanted. They were gung-ho and admired and respected the coaches and each other. He ended by predicting that 1959 was going to be a winning year. As Lindquist walked away from the podium, he heard Athletic Director George Briggs say, "God, I certainly hope so." Owens, going into his last year of his three year contract, might have said the same thing.

CHAPTER 7

A Band of Brothers

In the fall of 1959, West Coast football was entering a new phase. The Pacific Coast Conference went out of existence in the summer. The Athletic Association of Western Universities -- dubbed the Big Five -- was formed to replace the PCC. However, its exclusive hold on the Rose Bowl bid did not become effective until the 1960 season. The 1959 western representative to the Rose Bowl would be the team with the best record among the nine schools in the defunct PCC. One of the favorites for the conference title was USC who was put on a two year probation effective January 7, 1959, thereby eliminating its chance to go to Pasadena. California could not go either because a PCC rule did not allow its teams to have repeat appearances in the Rose Bowl.

The Big Ten conference, after humiliating PCC contenders in 12 of the 13 games played after a pact was formed in 1946, decided in the summer of 1959 not to renew its part of the contract with the Rose Bowl. It authorized individual members of the conference to accept, at their discretion, any Rose Bowl invitation. Thus, the AAWU could decide to invite an opponent from anywhere in the land including the Big Ten.

The University of Washington was also starting a new phase in its journey as the "university of a thousand years" to become one of the nation's leading universities. Founded in 1861, it was the oldest public institution of higher learning on the West Coast. In the late 1950's, it was mostly a local-regional university. In the fall of 1959, about 60 percent of the 16,100 students enrolled, came from King County in which the university was located. Many were commuters. Only 1,800 students came from states other than Washington and less than 500 came from foreign countries.

The most far reaching University development after World War II was the establishment of the Health Sciences School incorporating medical and dental instruction. In 1945, the State Legislature appropriated $3,750,000 for buildings and $450,000 for operations. University President Lee Sieg reached retirement age during the war but continued in office until the Board of Regents could appoint a successor. The Board wanted a person to lead the university in the post war era who had a knowledge of the health sciences. It found Dr. Raymond Allen, the head of the University of Illinois' Chicago campus and Dean of its Medical School. He became Washington's President in 1946.

By the late 1950's, the construction investment in the Health Sciences exceeded $30 million. The funds were used to construct the schools of medicine, dentistry, and nursing; a three-hundred bed teaching hospital; specialized laboratories, classrooms, support facilities, and administrative offices. It was well on its way to the top ranks of health sciences programs in the world.

Another very significant event was the appointment of Charles Odegaard as the new University President in 1958. His talents were enormous and his scholarly and administrative leadership influenced all phases of University life. His tenure from 1958-1973 would be a period of explosive student growth. As college enrollments rapidly increased, Odegaard initiated the tri-part system of higher education in the state. The first tier included the two research-oriented universities in the state -- Washington and Washington State. The next tier included the four-year schools such as Eastern, Central, and Western Washington and Evergreen College. The third tier was the state's community college system. Odegaard wanted the University of Washington's primary focus to be on the education of students who had the academic capability to not only complete a rigorous four-year undergraduate program but also be interested in graduate study. He established targets to have the majority of the university's students be upper class undergraduates and graduate students.

Such a structure meant the university would accept an increasing number of community college transfers at the junior year -- students who had demonstrated in their community college work that they could successfully handle the requirements of the University. He changed the mission of the various professional schools and individual departments on campus to concentrate on their majors and graduate students. The community colleges would then focus on educating students who, for whatever reason, chose to start their general undergraduate education in such colleges.

Odegaard also promoted research of the highest quality -- especially in engineering, science, and medicine. He pushed such disciplines to obtain federal government funds. When he retired, the University ranked among schools such as M.I.T. and Johns Hopkins in its level of research funds. The University's teaching and research space more than doubled on his watch. The more focused research environment would result in many interdisciplinary innovations such as the kidney machine and several Nobel Prize winners.

The University was on its way to being widely recognized as a world leader in research and graduate education, but Husky fans wanted a more modest result -- a winning season and a conference title.

Bill Kinnune remarked, "We were now a group of players who just didn't want to lose. Before our period, visiting teams would laugh and joke in their locker room about how they beat Washington. In 1958, the visiting team had players bleeding and hurt and they were very quiet. They knew when they played Washington, they were going to get beat up. It was going to be a miserable, rough, rotten game. We were a bunch of street fighters. It wasn't dirty. It was hard clean football."

Royal Brougham, the veteran sports columnist for the Seattle Post-Intelligencer, commented, after the 1958 season, about the toughness of the Huskies and the pain they inflicted on their opponents. His analysis indicated that no team that played the Huskies beat the point spread in the week following its game with Washington because of the injuries suffered at the hands of the Huskies.

The 1959 Husky football team was loaded with juniors who had gained significant experience in 1958. They had acquired confidence from close games with Ohio State, Oregon State, and California and wins over Minnesota and Oregon. Fundamentally, few teams could match the Huskies. Although most of their 1958 opponents beat them in the scoring column, they never beat them physically. Washington had won the respect of their opponents for its hard-hitting, crisp tackling, and aggressive play.

The Owens-Tipps doctrine of rough, physical, hard-nosed football was paying off. By the start of Owens third season, Washington football was on solid ground. Players who were not willing to play a sometimes painful price had been drummed out or quit. The survivors were coming together as a team. There were no names on the jerseys, no big stars. They were a bunch of guys who liked to play football, who liked to knock their opponents down, and who supported and cared for each other.

The players recognized that the coaches' philosophy and methods of teaching were paying off. They understood the personalities of the various coaches and how each worked to develop individual and team skills to reach outstanding performance. Every coach brought something special to the task.

Owens was the leader, the overall strategist, and the one who stressed the mental and physical toughness required to succeed. The players were somewhat in awe of him. He looked like he could beat anybody at any phase of football. Dick Dunn remarked, "He basically was God. He was the kind of guy you were proud to have as your head coach." Ray Jackson likened him to a general. "He was always in the ball game on the sidelines. You could depend on him and his word." He expected each player to succeed in the classroom and have good character both on and off the field. Owens started a study table for the players because he understood that for most of them, professional football was not going to be an option. "When we were at Washington, he stressed that we needed to get a good education for some other professional career," Mike Crawford exclaimed.

He was also intense. He hated to lose. "When the Huskies lost games in the 1957 and 1958 seasons, you would go into the locker room and it was just like there was going to be an execution. Players didn't dare smile or become too loquacious with the press," John Thompson recalled.

In order to have success, a head coach needs good assistants. Tom Tipps and Chesty Walker were two of the very best.

Tipps stressed mental and physical toughness. He did everything in his power to instill it in the minds and actions of all the players, especially the linemen. He was the driving force behind the way Washington punished their opponents. "Tipps was like General Patton," said Chuck Allen. "He had the notion that toughness was the quality of the mind." He brought about discipline, timeliness, and doing all the things -- big and small -- that players were supposed to do to win. He always stressed the right way of doing things. He knew how to drive people up to their breaking point. He made everybody better. He brought out the best in the players.

Players sometimes hated him and then loved him. "He would give you hell and then give you a hug," said George Pitt. He earned the respect of the players because he was so dedicated to making them better. He was a magnificent teacher. Bill Kinnune said, "If I had a son, I would want him to play for someone like Tom. He would grab you by the helmet and scream at you and have tears in his eyes because he felt you hadn't played as well as you were capable of."

He was a great pre-game motivator. He had the ability to succinctly stress what the players had learned and the sacrifices they had made and get them focused on what they had to do to succeed against their opponent. He lifted the players' confidence and pride and made them believe they could do anything. "All of us would have gone to war with him," Tim Bullard remarked.

Chesty Walker was the "Silver Fox." He was more friendly with the players than the other coaches. He would put his arm around a player's shoulder and whisper something inspirational to him. He would get the most out of a player by his encouraging style. He was a counter balance to Owens and Tipps. He was an offensive genius. Dan Wheatley admired him. "He pretty much designed the offense and put in all the new wrinkles that would exploit the opponent's defensive weaknesses. In the secondary, he was sharp at picking up defensive coverages and designing special plays to beat them."

Football has often been compared to war. Tipps told the players that football is the closest thing to combat they would experience. It is a series of skirmishes in which squad-sized units fight each other. The action begins in the "trenches." The quarterback is the "field general." He throws "bombs" into the "enemy" territory. The linebackers "blitz" him to prevent his throwing "bombs." The defense tries to protect its "flanks." The battle is fought in all kinds of weather. A football team, like an army or marine corps squad, functions best when each team member is ready to sacrifice for the success of the unit without any thought of personal gain or loss.

The Huskies who had made it through the grueling practices, challenge drills, and punishing conditioning exercises got through because of an intense determination and commitment to the goals of the coaches and to each other. Like all elite units, they had their unique badges and symbols -- the stronger and bigger necks from isometric exercises, the scars on the nose and forehead from punishing opponents with their helmets.

The result of their shared experience, both on the practice field and in games with tough opponents, was a closeness unknown to all outsiders. Their trust in, and knowledge of, each other was total -- from the first unit to the fourth unit. They knew each other's background, where they came from, and what their capabilities were. The linemen knew each other's assignments and their blocking and tackling skills. The backs understood their offensive schemes and defensive responsibilities and how they complemented each other.

Football also comes closest to war in evoking comradeship. Football players are true comrades when each is ready to give up part of his individualism and quest for glory for the good of the team. The coaches are the officers and the drill sergeants. They are at times hated by the players for pushing them to the limits of exhaustion, for humiliating them, and for other forms of harassment. They are admired and even loved for what they are teaching and for demanding sacrifices that would pay off in the enjoyment of competition and winning.

Eventually, the players realized that the coaches were driving them to become a group of warriors and a band of brothers committed to do whatever it takes to win battles on the football field. Their success didn't lay so much in having the best talent. The difference was their resolve. They had gone through a lot together.

They believed in themselves. They never believed they could lose. Tipps would say, "We had boys that grew up to be men pretty damn fast. You can't win games with boys. Each player laid it on the line for the guy next to him. That unity was all up and down the team. They cared for each other."

They also had a mix of older players and many married players that provided maturity. Some had been in the service. They gave stability and leadership to the younger players. They all wanted to win as a team. They didn't want anybody around that wasn't pulling their weight. Individual statistics didn't mean anything. Ray Jackson said, "We did what we were supposed to do. We didn't have free-lance ball players. You hit the hole you were supposed to hit and you hit it quick. You didn't do a lot of improvising."

Teammates enjoyed the success of their other brothers. There were no petty jealousies, no bickering. They didn't showboat. There was no sense of ego. Before each game, they picked co-captains in recognition of their team contributions. It was another act of team unity. Carver Gayton summed up. "There was no one incident that created the unity that brought us together. There were a series of things that took place that bolstered a sense of team. If you take any element out, we would not have been successful. What we had doesn't come along very often."

John Meyers, a sophomore lineman in 1959, said, "We had pride. We had pride that we wouldn't be laying on the field. We never called a time out because of an injury unless the guy was knocked out...was unconscious...It was something the coaches instilled in us. If you laid down on the field, it meant that you were out cold or your back was broken or you were dead. For anything other than that you got yourself off the field. I saw Barry Bullard walk off the field when the cartilage in his knee was gone. His knee was wobbling around. But he made it off the field."

Meyers continued on about the spirit of violence that was

developed on the practice field. "We had fights. I mean fights. One unit against another unit, not one player against another player -- although that went on as well. If the green unit was scrimmaging the gold unit and somebody on the green unit gave a cheap shot, a fight would start. Unit versus unit -- 22 guys. And it was neat. The coaches used to get right in and fight too. And afterwards we'd all laugh about it."

What had emerged at the beginning of the 1959 season was a team with unshakable self-confidence and absolute unselfishness. "There wasn't any Rose Bowl talk before the season opened. I told them they had the ability to become a fine team. They had learned to pay the price for greatness, in work and practice," Owens said.

Coach Tom Tipps cut through all the rhetoric and reminded the players that "the only thing that wins games is players. Players that want to play and want to win." The Huskies had some very good players who wanted to win. They constituted two teams -- the first team and the alternate team -- to fit into the coaches' philosophy of playing two units and substituting backup players when required.

One of the backup guards was Mike Crawford. "Things started to click. We had a hell of a good starting unit and a hell of good backup group. We had a lot of depth. We were pretty much three deep."

Right halfback Don McKeta -- 5'10", 185 pounds -- was a very intense guy and the player most responsible for team unity and spirit. At 24, he was the "old man" on the team, having spent four years in the Navy. After his discharge, he spent a year at San Jose Junior College and transferred to Washington in 1958. He was the team's leader and would earn the Flaherty Award in 1959 and 1960 as the team's most inspirational player -- only the second player in Husky history to twice receive that award. Tim Bullard commented that he never did anything at half speed. Dick Dunn observed that

"McKeta was everything the coaches wanted. He bought into their system completely. He was a big cheerleader and one of the guys who led by example. He was older and he had all the gung ho stuff. McKeta was tougher than nails." He was an aggressive quick-reacting defender and with his sheer determination, he gained many yards after initially being hit.

Barry Bullard commented on his leadership. "He was the one who always got up when he was hurt, shake his fist, and say 'Come on, let's go.' The players looked up to him more than anyone else."

Backing up McKeta were Don Millich and Brent Wooten. Millich was a senior who, after lettering in 1957, sat out 1958. He was the Huskies' top running back at the tail end of the 1957 campaign. Wooten, who lettered as a sophomore in 1958, was an all-state selection in baseball, basketball, and football at Walla Walla High School. He was a hard-nosed tackler and pass defender.

Left halfback George Fleming was considered by many as the most gifted athlete on the team. From Dallas, Texas, he transferred to Washington in 1958 after one year as a quarterback and halfback at East Los Angeles Junior College. He was Washington's most all-around offensive player. He was the team's best pass receiver and biggest breakaway threat. Fleming ranked as one of the top place kickers in the nation and excelled at punt and kickoff returns. As a defensive safety, he led the team in interceptions in 1958.

Gayton was the backup at left half. A senior and two-year letterman, he attended Seattle's Garfield High School. He had good speed and was tough for his size at 160 pounds.

Fullback Ray Jackson -- 5'9", 180 -- was one of the team's best runners. He made the belly series and trap plays in the split-T option work very well. Quarterback Bob Schloredt felt that Jackson was the quickest starter among the backs. "He could get off the mark and move laterally with one little step. He couldn't run the 40 as fast as the other guys but he could run 10 yards faster than anybody." Another teammate marveled at his ability to run through a hole the size of a "gnat's ass." Halfback Charlie Mitchell said Jackson was short and would hide behind the lineman. "We would start an option play and the defense would react and then the quarterback would tuck the ball into Ray's belly and you would look up and he would already have 15 yards." Jackson drew high praise from quarterback Bob Hivner. "Ray was fantastic. I remember one time I gave him a hand-off and I turned around and he's still banging around like a bowling ball and going through guys and making 5 or 6 yards. On another play I remember, we ran a trap. Somebody missed the block and the guy came flying in and hit Ray smack in the mouth. He bounced back and went another six yards up the field. I said, 'Holy shit.' "

Jackson transferred to Washington in the spring of 1959 after two outstanding years at Bakersfield Junior College where he was a Junior College All-America selection. He was a teen age parent and after graduating from an all-black high school in Waco Texas, he joined the US Army. He earned All-European honors in 1955 and 1956.

When he arrived at Washington, he had a wife and two children. With financial needs greater than the support he was receiving from Washington, he worked for the sheriff's department from 10 PM until 6 AM during the 1959 pre-season practices. "I had to be on the field early in the morning for the two-a-day workouts. Then I would get off the field for breakfast, meetings, and lunch and then I could sleep for a couple of hours before the afternoon practice. Sometimes I would oversleep and get to practice late. The way the coaches would punish me was -- we would have our scrimmages and they would make me stay with the second unit after the first unit was done for the day, then with the third unit. They would make me scrimmage with every unit. Then, they would make me run."

Jackson continued. "Then I would go to dinner and a team meeting. I would sleep a little and then go back to work at night. We lived in the crew house in the first few weeks of pre-season practices. Some of the guys who knew I was working would look out for me. They would put stuff in my bed so that when somebody came around for bed check, it looked like I was there. When school started, I stopped the job."

Fullback Joe Jones at 6'0" and 195 pounds, transferred from Vallejo Junior College in the spring of 1959. He was probably the best conditioned athlete on the team. Being in top condition was a major motivator for him. With his quick reactions and speed, he excelled as a linebacker on defense. The fullback played linebacker and the other three backs played in the defensive secondary. "Jackson and I fed on each other. On wind sprints, I could never seem to beat him. We drove each other because we both wanted that purple jersey. There was no question in my mind that I was better on defense. He had special qualities on offense -- lower profile, quicker steps."

Senior Dan Wheatley and junior Sam Hurworth provided strong support to Jackson and Jones at fullback.

Washington had two very good quarterbacks who were instrumental to the team's success in 1959 and 1960. The quarterbacks called the plays. In fact, it was against the rules for coaches to call any plays. Quarterbacks had to take command without much help from the sidelines or upstairs in the coaches' box.

Hivner had led the Huskies in total offense in 1958 with 834 yards, second in the conference to California's Joe Kapp. A very smart field general, he completed 42 percent of his passes in 1958. A graduate of Southgate High School in Los Angeles County, he played at Compton Junior College in 1956. He led Compton to the junior college national championship in the Junior Rose Bowl game played in Pasadena and made the junior college All-America second team that year. Owens and Coach Clark paid a visit to Hivner shortly thereafter and the 5'10" 170 pounder transferred to Washington in the winter quarter of 1957. Hivner redshirted in the 1957 season.

Bob Schloredt shared the quarterbacking duties with Hivner. In 1958, he had established himself as one of the Huskies' most versatile players. His booming punts contributed significantly to Washington's opponents being held to only 3.2 yards per return. In 1958, he set a school record for the most punts over 60 yards in a season including a Husky record 70-yard punt in the Oregon State game. A rugged defender, he had the mindset of a linebacker, a position he played in the 1958 game against Ohio State. At 6 feet and 190 pounds, he was a tough runner well suited for the option plays in the split-T offense.

When he was seven years old, he lost most of the vision in his left eyeball when it was seared by a piece of hot, flying glass from an exploding firecracker in a coke bottle. He came to Washington from Gresham High School where he was an Oregon all-state quarterback.

When comparing the two quarterbacks, their teammates observed that Hivner was the better passer and Schloredt was the better runner. He was a great option runner and opponents looked to him to run the ball rather than pass. As a result, defenders were frequently fooled on a pass play. The team had faith in both of them. Both took command in the huddle. Both were cocky.

Another quarterback that would get significant playing time was sophomore Kermit Jorgensen from Renton High School. At 6'1 and 195, he was a strong, powerful runner and exceptionally good on option run-pass plays.

Bear Bryant once said, "Football games are won in the trenches."

Washington had some great players up front. In 1959, the linemen were tabbed the "Sturdy Seven." They would hold opponents to 65 points in the ten regular season games during 1959 and record four shutouts. They held their opponents to 216.5 yards per game. They were disciples of Owen's philosophy that the game of football started with defense.

Meyers, Bullard, and Kinnune were on the strong side of the line on offense. Their primary role was to do on-line blocking and open up the holes for the running backs. There was no disguising the fact that these linemen -- the biggest and strongest of the front wall -- were coming at their defensive counterparts. On the snap of the ball, they would hit the opponents at the same blocking angles and grind them back and inside to open up the sweep and quarterback option plays.

Meyers was a sophomore tight end. He was an all-state selection in both basketball and football at Richland High School. He did not turn out for football in his freshman year. He reported for spring practice in 1959 to join some fraternity brothers who were turning out. "I went out as kind of a lark." At 6'6" and 225 pounds, Meyers quickly attracted the attention of the coaches. He also was interested in helping others.

Tim Bullard, another sophomore lineman, remembers a cold rainy evening during the 1959 season when he, John, and Jim Williams (Meyers friend from Richland) were downtown for a few beers and were walking toward the 5th Avenue Theatre. At that moment, people were exiting after the movie was over. Many were college students. There was a poor guy standing in the rain outside the theatre selling newspapers. "The college guys were kind of blowing him off. Meyers looked at us and said, 'Jim, Tim, come on, we are going to help this guy out.' So he took the bowler hat that Jim was wearing, tucked it under his arm, grabbed all the papers and gave some to me and Jim. We went shoulder-to-shoulder up the street toward the exiting movie-goers. John went up to the first college student. 'You want to buy a paper?' 'No, I don't want the paper.' John then looked down at the student and said, 'You cheap son-of-a-bitch, the paper is only a dime.' The guy just about ripped out the bottom of his pants' pocket to get the dime. You could just look at the others following and see them reaching for their coins. Finally, John took all the money for the papers, threw it in the bowler, took off the newspaper seller's rain hat and dumped all the money in it. The guy took off gleefully running down the avenue."

Six feet, four inches and 225 pounds, Bullard, an all-stater from Coos Bay, Oregon, played in only one losing game from eighth grade through his freshman year at Washington -- that was Oregon's annual Shrine All-Star contest when his team was upended by the Metro team quarterbacked by Schloredt. Bullard played on three straight state championship teams at Marshfield High School. An excellent engineering student, he carried out his football assignments with almost precision-like perfection. He logged 192 minutes in 1958 as a tackle.

Kinnune was another sophomore standout in 1958. He had great natural ability at tackle or guard and was an outstanding blocker with his speed, agility, and toughness. At 6'2" and 215 pounds, Kinnune lettered in four sports at Everett High School -- football, basketball, track and field, and wrestling. He earned all-state and All-America honors in football. He played 378 minutes in the 1958 season.

Roy McKasson, another Washington all-stater at Clover Park High School, was the center. He was undersized for the position at 6'0" and 195 pounds, but he was extremely aggressive. He started several games as a sophomore in 1958. His teammates marveled at his quickness and agility. Some called him the finest linebacker on the team. He seemed to be always in the right spot on defense and understood how to play his positions very well. Dick Dunn, his backup, remarked, "He was just so nice. To have him be the guy who played ahead of you and be as nice as he was sort of pissed you off."

On the weak side of the offensive line were Chuck Allen, Kurt Gegner, and Lee Folkins. They did most of the down-field blocking. They were smaller and faster than the strong side players.

Many teammates called Allen the most complete lineman on the team. At 6'1" and 205, an all-stater from Cle Elum High School, he was praised by opposing linemen and coaches as "one of the toughest men" they faced. With his tremendous football savvy and desire, he rarely made a mistake and seemed to always be in the right place. He was a player who could get knocked down and then bounce up and make the tackle. Some of his teammates would say, "It was like he swallowed a gyro when he was a child." He played 398 minutes in 1958, his sophomore season.

Gegner never played football until 1954. He got a late start in the game because he was born and raised in Yugoslavia. Because of his German nationality, Kurt's father was conscripted in the German Army shortly after the Nazi invasion. In 1943, he was captured by the British. Kurt and his family lived in various displaced persons camps after World War II ended. Because of the Gegner's German status, the family had to elude the invading Russians. After fleeing to Chicago to join relatives in 1953, they came to Seattle.

While attending Seattle's Roosevelt High School, Kurt was asked to join the football team. His parents were curt with Kurt. They just said "No." Finally the coach prevailed and Gegner suited up in his senior year.

After graduating from Roosevelt High School, he played on the 1956 freshmen team as a walk-on and red shirted in 1957. In 1958, he played 448 minutes. "He had the God-given ability to stay on his feet which is everything in football. He had a body like a logger (at 6'2", 205)." Kinnune called him "one tough son-of -a -bitch. He was not anybody you liked to turn out against in scrimmage because he only had one speed and that was full-speed all the time. He was very intense. His initial charge resembled the crack of a whip and he usually got a jump on the opposition."

At left end was Folkins. Another graduate of Roosevelt High School, Folkins played 184 minutes as a sophomore in 1958. At 6'5" and 195, his size and good hands provided a great target for Hivner and Schloredt. His height and speed made him particularly effective at putting the rush on opposing passers, often forcing them to throw high. He was the first player recruited by Owens' staff.

Key backups in the line were seniors Mike Crawford, Bob Echols, George Pitt, Jack Walters, and Bob White; juniors Ben Davidson, Dick Dunn, Dave Enslow, and sophomores Tim Bullard, Ron Quincy, and Jim Skaggs. Senior Ed Peasley and juniors Stan Chapple and Pat Claridge provided depth at the end position.

Claridge was the team's headhunter. "I became a ferocious player. I roamed downfield with my helmet. I didn't need any other gear. I never blocked at the ankles or legs. I hit from the chest up." For Claridge, the helmet was a weapon. "Where it was devastating was on a short pass route. All of a sudden you would have three or four of us downfield coming back and picking off the poor bastards trying to get to the receiver. We tried to get them in the head." His favorite was the come-back block on punt returns. "When we came back we just creamed the opposing player. We never wanted to hurt anybody. We just wanted to take them out of the play. It was devastating." Because of Claridge and others, some opposing players who had suited up against Washington in prior seasons used to tell the new players about Husky head-hunting. Craig Fertig, a USC quarterback and a good friend of Hivner said he would tell

USC players to "have your head on a swivel. Look around because a Husky will be coming to nail you."

In 1959, Owens' first unit would be an all-junior squad except for Meyers who was a sophomore. His alternate unit would usually consist of four seniors, five juniors, and two sophomores.

During pre-season practice, Owens continued to refine his playbook. He mixed in some elements of the single-wing and the pro-T formations. He established a "swing man" left end who would play on either wing and the left halfback as a "wingback." He planned to use the unbalanced line formation more. He also added former Husky Whitey Core to his staff. Core was an All-Coast guard and co-captain in 1957, his senior season.

During the pre-season practices, the players lived in the Conibear Shellhouse. Built in 1949 and overlooking Lake Washington and the Cascade Mountains, it was one of the finest facilities for student-athletes in America. During the two-a-day sessions, the routine was rigorous.

6 AM	Out of bed, a glass of juice, and over to the locker room in Hec Edmundson Pavilion to dress for practice
6:45 - 8:45	Practice
9:00	Breakfast of eggs, bacon or ham, fruit juice, cereal, toast and honey, non-fat milk
10:00	Skull practice, blackboard diagrams, and discussion of plays, defensive schemes, etc.
12:45 PM	Lunch of thick soup, sandwich, juice, milk, and fresh fruit
1:45	Nap time

3:15	Report to practice for a two-hour scrimmage and drills
7:00	Dinner of steak, roast or fish, large salad, vegetables, ice cream, milk, hot tea
8:30	Review of film of the day's scrimmage; quarterback drill on strategy, study of play book
10:30	Lights out

The shell house provided a climate for bonding, the creation of team unity, and the cementing of friendships that would last a lifetime. It was a unique environment.

Several things happened before the season started that would bring the team even closer together. One was the loss of one of their brothers. Brian Stapp, a small, hard-hitting halfback from Chehalis, Washington, lost his life in a swimming accident early in the fall. Although Stapp did not get much playing time in 1958, his sophomore year, he displayed fearlessness in the way he played and devotion to teammates.

Owens established a weight training program in 1958. He enlisted the aid of Harry Svetnam, a noted Seattle physical culturist, to design a set of body-building exercises that coincided with movements of the players on the field. The program wasn't compulsory but the team's leaders got together to promote it. Soon many of the players were lifting. In many instances, they increased their body weights 10 to 15 pounds, without adding any fat. The weight room was on the second floor of Hec Edmundson Pavilion and was about the size of a moderate size living room.

Once two-a-day practices started, it was hard for the players to keep their newly added bulk. One reason was the hard practices;

the other was hunger. Owens had the players on a lean diet. Players would supplement it any way they could. Junior lineman, Ben Davidson, remembers that his parents sent him $60 per month for food. "I would get a hamburger every night." Others recall midnight raids. In the crew house kitchen, there were food lockers that were locked each night by the cooks after they cleaned up after dinner. Dave Enslow said he and a few teammates could force one of the locker doors open and get some food. After they were finished eating, they would slam the locker door shut. The raids irritated the cooks and they complained to Owens who said it would never happen again. Well, it did. So Owens called a team meeting. He said that "somebody has stolen food from the food lockers and I want to know who did it. If I find out who did it, I will take away his scholarship." Nobody said a word. Nobody was going to rat on their brothers. The show of silence brought the team together in another way.

In the pre-season polls, the scribes didn't give the Huskies much of a chance for a title in the new conference. Southern California was the overwhelming favorite followed by Cal and UCLA. Washington was listed to finish only above Stanford. Even the Seattle writers didn't see much hope for success. Emmett Watson wrote. "Frankly, I don't think they'll win more than five games, and those, they will have to win on toughness; they won't fool anybody."

The Huskies were ready for the opener on Folsom Field in Boulder, Colorado. Before the game, McKeta rallied his band of brothers around and said, "The only way for us to win is to reach down and play it from the heart." The slogan, "Play it from the Heart," became the rallying cry and the Huskies' intangible ingredient throughout the season.

Playing its first opening game away in 12 years, Washington scored late in the first quarter. The touchdown was set up with

Jackson's darts up the middle and off tackle for big yards. The payoff was a 19-yard pass play from Hivner to Fleming. In the second quarter, Colorado's quarterback, Dale Weidner picked off a Hivner pass and returned it 94 yards for the score. The Buffalo's two-point try failed and the half ended with Washington up by one.

In the third quarter, Owens decided to switch to the unbalanced single-wing-like offense. The Huskies liked it. They marched 53 yards with Gayton taking a pitchout to the right side for six yards and the score. The conversion put the Huskies up 14-6. The lead would increase on the next play. Jerry Steffen, the Buffalo's veteran junior halfback was back to receive the kickoff. Incomprehensibly, he watched the ball come to a stop in the end zone and Allen pounced on it for another Husky score. That touchdown sealed a 21-12 Husky victory.

Taking advantage of Boulder's high altitude, Schloredt averaged 57 yards on six punts. His longest was 66. More than 27,000 fans sat in awe of his booming high kicks and the deadly manner in which the Huskies covered punt returns.

A visitor to the locker room was Owens' father, James Evan Owens. His father and mother, Eloise, had flown in from Oklahoma City to watch the game. They had a great time basking in the joy of victory and meeting many of the happy Huskies. And the players saw Owens as a proud and loving son, a much different role than a tough, hard-nosed coach. Respect and admiration for Owens went up a notch.

Monday's practice started with bad news. The team learned that Hivner had broken a finger on his right (throwing) hand in the Colorado game. Schloredt would take command of the purple team. Kermit Jorgensen and Jim Everett would step up to the alternate unit.

On September 26, over 24,000 fans sat in rain-swept Husky

Stadium to watch the Huskies blank the Idaho Vandals 20-0. The wet conditions hurt both teams. Washington lost four of five fumbles. Fumbling had been a Husky problem for the last two years and prompted Emmett Watson to devote a whole newspaper column on the art of fumbling.

"To clear up any misapprehensions, it must be pointed out that the Washington Huskies do not practice fumbling. You might get that impression since they fumble so frequently, and do it with such poise. But actually they don't practice the art. It just seems to come so naturally."

Part of the issue seemed to be the intricacies of the split-T formation. Watson went on to write about a conversation he had with Frank Leahy, the former head coach of Notre Dame. After Leahy had discussed the advantages of adopting the split-T, he finished by saying, "I will tell you one thing about the split-T. Any team that uses it is likely to lead its league in fumbles."

At home the next week, the Huskies started off by fumbling. From the Washington 37, Utah drove quickly for a score. For the next 50 minutes, the Utes were battered like a shuttlecock in a badminton game. The Huskies showed a balanced attack -- passing for 214 yards and rushing for 203. They introduced a new pass play, dubbed the "Utah Special," one which they would use in critical situations during the season. It was basically a post pattern with the left end running left to right and the right halfback swinging left out of the backfield and down the far sideline. Against Utah, the new play worked to produce two touchdowns in the 51-6 win.

No word shined brighter in the Owens' lexicon of football than the word "shutout." He was ecstatic the next week after Washington recorded its second shutout -- this time over conference foe, Stanford, 10-0. It was the Huskies' first victory over the Indians in Seattle since 1947. The Husky defense held Stanford runners to just 88 yards and constantly frustrated Stanford's receivers and its great passer, Dick Norman. The Huskies intercepted four of his passes. McKeta led the Husky offense with 98 yards in 11 carries including a 30-yard touchdown scamper in the first quarter. A Fleming field goal late in the third quarter finished the scoring. Schloredt played the entire game. For his performance, McKeta was named the Big Five "Back of the Week."

Sixth-ranked USC was next. The Trojans had opened the season with shutout victories over Pitt and Ohio State and a 27-6 win over Oregon State. The Huskies were convinced that if they played their best game, they would produce one of the major upsets of the week, maybe the season. "The club has jelled," Owens said during the week. "Nearly all of these boys were recruited by my staff and are playing their third season together. They've matured." He added the club had no sensational breakaway runner, no outstanding backfield or line speed. But, he felt the team carried out their assignments well after being together for three years. And, the team had improved its pass defense and implemented a more sophisticated offense.

The Trojans featured the McKeever twins -- Marlin, an end, and Mike, a guard -- tackle Ron Mix, and halfback Jerry Traynham. Willie Wood, USC's co-captain and one of the few black quarterbacks in college football, had been sidelined with a shoulder separation and was only available for limited action. The team had a unique regime for visiting teams. After arriving by a United Airlines charter from Los Angeles the day before the game, they went directly to Lake Wilderness, southeast of Seattle, and worked out on the resort's golf course. The first time they would see Husky Stadium was game day, October 16.

The contest was widely anticipated. The victor would have the best shot at the conference title. Many observers felt that USC would field the best team to play in the stadium since national champion Notre Dame came to town in 1949. A few Los Angeles columnists opined that the three best teams on the Coast were the Trojan's first, second, and third teams. Washington was a two touchdown underdog.

Over 54,500 crowded into Husky Stadium on Homecoming Day. Some had pre-game jitters but none as much as Jack Ehrig, the Homecoming Chairman. His wife said that he was so nervous when he awoke on game day that he shaved with Pepsodent and brushed his teeth with Burma Shave.

On a bright, crisp fall day, the contest had everything to make it a classic one -- power plays, stirring defense, momentum shifts, great strategy, artfully executed plays, a minimum of errors, and victory in the balance until the final seconds.

For many a long turn of the clock, it appeared that the Huskies would be overrun by the invaders from Troy. Pulling their fast guards and ends ahead of the ball carriers, USC swung the Husky flanks and powered up through the tackles. The Trojans scored the second time they had the ball and again in the second stanza to lead 14-0.

After Kinnune recovered a USC fumble on the Trojan 47, the Huskies unveiled a new offensive formation -- the "Bug Eye." They set the line strong to the left with the swing end split left and the left wingback set in the slot between the end and the rest of the line. It was essentially a "flood pass" formation. Immediately Schloredt hit Folkins, the swing end, down to the 35. After several runs got the ball to the Trojan 12, Fleming, running wide around left end, fumbled. Allen saved the drive by recovering on the enemy's 14. Schloredt hit McKeta on a short pass to the nine-yard line. On the next play, Schloredt faked a pass, tucked the ball firmly away, and charged between two defenders right into the end zone.

The Trojans were penalized 15 yards on the successful extra point play. Fleming tried an onside kick from the USC 45. McKasson dove on the ball just inches short of the required 10 yards. USC failed to muster any threat before the end of the half.

The Huskies got an extra boost when they ran out of the tunnel from Hec Edmundson Pavilion onto the field after the intermission. In a Homecoming tradition, former Husky letter winners, with their Big W blankets held high, formed two lines through which the team ran. However buoyed the Huskies might have been by the lusty cheers of the former athletes to start the second half, it did not do them much good in the third quarter. USC was not very good either until it recovered a botched Husky hand-off on the Washington 19. The threat died when Wood's field goal attempt from the 23 fell woefully short.

On Washington' next possession, Schloredt punted the ball high and long -- 47 yards -- and as it came down, it drifted away from Traynham, the Trojan receiver. Unable to get his hands squarely on the ball, he fumbled and Millich smothered the pigskin on the USC 20. Then a little razzle-dazzle unleashed a crowd roar that was heard across the lake and into the eastern foothills.

Schloredt pitched to Millich who handed it back to Schloredt going back to the right. The Husky quarterback hit Meyers, his tight end, for a first down on the six. On second down, Schloredt went to the spread offense again. After rolling to his left, he slanted back and into the end zone to pull within one point. Owens detested ties and so there was no question about going for two. Schloredt just ran the same play and the Huskies were on top 15-14 with ten and a half minutes to go. The crowd sent shock waves that rattled the windows in nearby communities and throughout the campus. The Husky faithful were talking about one of the biggest upsets in Husky history.

Wood and his teammates were thinking "Not this day." In nine plays they drove 80 yards. It was Traynham and Wood doing the most damage. The alternate unit was on the field for the Huskies. Why? They were fresh and Owens believed that the second unit was almost as good as the first team. Traynham broke loose for a 42-yard race down the north sideline. Crawford had Traynham trapped on the USC 35-yard line. "I should have nailed him but he got loose. God, I was discouraged." Jorgensen playing defensive back on the opposite side ran across the field and tackled Traynham to prevent a touchdown.

Five plays later, USC was in a second and goal situation on the Husky six. Wood ran a bootleg to the left and danced into the west end zone. Then he passed for the two extra points and the Trojans regained the lead 22-15.

The Huskies fought back and nearly pulled the game out in the final eight minutes. On their first series, Schloredt's long pass to McKeta in the clear was just beyond his finger tips. After Schloredt's 52-yard punt rolled dead on the Trojan 18, the Huskies forced a quick kick and took over on their own 49. Washington drove to the USC 17. Schloredt lost four and then his pass to Dick Aguirre fell incomplete. Jim Everett came in to replace Schloredt. His throw was intercepted by Ron Mix.

Owens praised his players. "I'm real proud of them. USC is the best team we've played since I've been here. And a comeback like these kids made is really tremendous. We knew before the game that we might have to bounce back against a good outfit like this. And we did bounce back, and were going toward another touchdown right at the end. I can't say enough for their spirit."

Owens' wife, Martha. when interviewed, was more terse. "I'm sick." Then she went on to say, "I don't think any game has affected me like this one did. I feel so sorry for the kids when they played so hard and came so close to winning."

For Washington to stay in the race for the Rose Bowl, the players had to cast aside the "what ifs" in the USC game and look squarely ahead to the game in Portland's Multnomah Stadium against undefeated Oregon. Nobody was thinking more about what might have happened in the USC game than Fleming. After being hit high and low by the McKeever twins, Fleming fumbled and the miscue led to the Trojans' first score. "The Sunday morning after the game, I was sitting in the dining room with my head between my legs still feeling bad. Bert Clark walked in and said, 'Georgie Boy, get your head up. Yes, that was a bad one. That one's behind us. We need you against Oregon.' "

Washington had to curtail its fumbles. They had coughed up the oval 23 times and lost 15. The Ducks had lost the ball only twice in five games and were ranked eleventh in the nation. Oregon planned to rack up the Huskies with a Washington native at quarterback. Dave Grosz, from Kent, a town south of Seattle, was a cool and cagey passer and a resourceful field general. Ducks' fans bellowed, "We will beat the Huskies with one of their own guys." Of course, they were overlooking the fact that one of *their own guys* -- Husky star Schloredt -- was from a Portland suburb. It would be a battle flamed by the fact that Washington had joined the Big Five leaving Oregon as an independent. It was "Hate the Huskies" week.

Before a turn-away crowd of about 37,000 in Portland, the Huskies staged a great come-from-behind triumph to shoot the Ducks 13-12. Through the mud and mist, Washington erased a 12-point deficit. The Ducks dominated the early stages of the game. They drove 78 yards for a touchdown after receiving the opening kickoff. Roger Daniels, a reserve quarterback, was sent in to kick the extra point. Grosz, the holder, fumbled the snap from center and flipped the ball to Daniels who started to run around the left corner. Schloredt rushed up and struck him down on the two-yard line.

Oregon scored again early in the second stanza and the two-point conversion try failed. McKeta then started to inject some fire into the Huskies. He led by example. First, he intercepted a Grosz pass and returned it to the Oregon 41. His 15-yard scamper keyed a nine play touchdown drive. Husky fans were shocked as Fleming missed the extra point try. And they were getting very wet as the torrential rains poured down.

Midway in the third quarter, Washington let an Oregon punt die on its 36. Schloredt then opened up the throttle and took his club all the way to victory. He hit Fleming for 29 yards down to the Oregon 27. Fleming went off right guard for nine. Schloredt hit McKeta for ten and a first down on the Ducks eight. McKeta again for four and then over left guard for the score. The margin of difference was Fleming who calmly kicked Oregon out of the ranks of the unbeaten. But not without some late Duck drives that tested the resolve of the Husky defense.

Schloredt recovered a fumble to stop one drive. Folkins intercepted a pass for another stop. A third drive put the ball on the Husky 22. Grosz fired what appeared to be a bullseye to Dave Grayson. Like a phantom, a leeping figure catapulted through the air, and left Grayson groping in the wind. Schloredt had sunk the hopes of the Oregon faithful by intercepting the pass in the end zone. On the final Duck drive, Millich intercepted Grosz' last pass, the Huskies' fourth interception of the day.

Owens praised his entire purple unit but Tipps directed his praise at McKeta. "It was that tough son-of-a bitch Don McKeta who won the ball game for us. He picked us up when we were getting whipped in the first quarter, and (he) pulled us together and brought us back."

In Los Angeles on Halloween, the Bruins saw ghosts and goblins as the Huskies tricked UCLA for a 23-7 treat. Schloredt passed for two touchdowns and scored another. Fleming added a 37-yard field goal. In the post-game interview, the press focused on the race for the Rose Bowl. While they asked questions that showed their lack of knowledge or experience as a coach or as a player, Owens sat quietly at first and then abruptly ended the interview by saying all he was thinking about was Oregon State at home next week. "I wish you'd lay off that kind of talk. Right now, Oregon has a better chance (of going to the Rose Bowl) than we have."

Against the Beavers, McKeta and Schloredt again led the Husky forces. Schloredt hit eight of 14 passes for 162 of Washington's 264 yards of total offense. He scored in the second period and teamed up with McKeta on a 45-yard scoring pass in the third quarter. By beating Oregon State 13-7, the Huskies remained tied for the Rose Bowl bid with Oregon at 7-1. Washington State was at 5-2. USC, ineligible for the Rose Bowl because of NCAA violations, was on top of the Big Five conference. Washington had California in Berkeley and the Cougars at home to finish the regular season. Oregon traveled to Pullman to face Washington State and then ended its season with its traditional foe, Oregon State. It would be an exciting two weeks.

The players had come closer together. Barry Bullard said, "We had played together as freshmen and had banded together to survive and stand up to the coaches. It was a tough coaching staff. They expected a lot from us. I will never say they punished us or were unfair to us but they expected a lot from us."

The coaches' expectations didn't get much higher than in Berkeley, California on November 14. The day before, the coaches sensed that the players were pretty cocky and perhaps overconfident. As they rode through the campus, they opened the windows and started singing. "The California Bears are losing all their hairs." Bullard again. "We were just smart asses and really ripe for getting knocked off the next day."

Tipps knew how to get the players' attention. Not only was he gruff and tough, he knew how to get under a player's skin. In practice, he would call the players names like "Shirley" and "Lollygagger." When he called someone a "Lollygagger," it was after the player got beat on a play or had a lousy attitude, or didn't hustle. "Shirley" was the worst name to be called. It usually was directed at a player that Tipps thought was blocking poorly -- a "titty blocker." The player didn't fire straight out at the opponent but instead came up in his stance or took a step inside to get a better angle for the block. Players who were frequently called "Shirley" dropped out. They didn't want to put up with that abuse.

After the game-day breakfast, the coaches waved everybody out of the room except the players. They started off on the linemen. They picked out something that was very personal to each one. Bullard again. "In my case, it was my brother Tim. Tipps said, 'Come on Barry. You've got to cut the apron strings. You can't mother Tim all the time. He has to stand on his own.' And they hit on each lineman. Well, we were so mad. By the time that I stepped on the field I was livid."

On Sunday morning, a Seattle newspaper headline read "Washington Blasts Cal 20-0. Bowl Bound Huskies Hit by Penalties." As is frequently the case, the headlines did not tell the full story. First, Oregon eked out a 7-6 win in Pullman in the last ten seconds. So, the Rose Bowl race would not be decided until the next week and the completion of the last game of the regular season. And second, the game account said the officials were calling an especially tight game. Bullard had another explanation. "On the first play, I knocked the Cal lineman all the way back to where the fullback was. I grabbed the quarterback and the fullback and just tackled both of them. If the ball carrier was crossing the end zone 35 yards away, we would still be knocking people down. We were still very mad from the pre-game tactics of Tipps. If there was any Cal player on the field still standing, we would try to take him down. We were totally out of control. In fact, they (the coaches) prepared us so well, they lost control of us. It was the best job of coaching I have ever seen. After the game, I was still so furious that I didn't want to talk to anybody."

Coach Tipps remembers as well. "I think I got to the linemen. Coaches sometimes have to deal with each person with a little bit of a lie. You have to come up with something that the player resents. They resented me all right. They were sure ready for Cal that day."

The Huskies were penalized 163 yards -- still a Washington single-game record. The defense held the Bears to 72 yards on the ground and 17 in the air. Cal players returned eight Washington punts a total of five yards. Cal's coach, Pete Elliott, called Schloredt "the best kicker I ever saw. Every boot was 40 to 45 yards. But not only that. The kicks were so high that they were impossible to return."

There was one game left to decide the Pasadena bid. The Seattle newspapers carried stories about the various possibilities for the outcomes of the remaining conference games and who would go to the Rose Bowl under each scenario. From Washington's perspective, to get the bid was quite simple -- beat the Cougars.

Before the then largest crowd ever to see a Husky home football game -- 55,782 -- Washington recorded their fourth shutout of the season, downing the Cougars 20-0. With the Beavers beating the Ducks and UCLA upsetting USC, Washington finished in a tie with the Trojans for the Big Five title and ahead of all the old Pacific Coast Conference teams eligible to be selected for the Rose Bowl.

It may have been Washington's finest overall game. The Huskies outgained the Cougars 348 to 175. Schloredt ran for 111 yards and threw for 72. Washington cut down the Cougars on the flanks, jammed them in the middle, and blunted their air assaults. As one reporter summed it up, "It was a perfect November day for the Husky rooters. The stakes could not have been higher. The teams were determined. The game became something very much like a distilled and symbolic version of life itself."

Owens was hoisted on the shoulders of some players, grinning from ear to ear. He said, "They didn't have to carry me. I was just floating. Nobody left. The fans were sitting in the stands. The game was over and they didn't want to leave. It was unbelievable." Then he added, "I knew we were going to get there (the Rose Bowl) but not that quickly -- and I didn't know it would be that exciting."

There was only one sign which had stayed in place in the locker room since Owens brought it to Washington three years earlier. "Toughness is a Quality of Mind. Without it, Physical Condition Is a Mockery." His team was mentally and physically tough. They were good players that bonded together to become a great team. "We might not have any All-Americans, publicity-wise," said Schloredt, "but this team is great, simply great." McKasson, the Huskies center and linebacker, chimed in. "It's what the coaches taught us, that's what made this team good. All season, we've had a chance to apply what they taught us. We saw other teams make mistakes that shouldn't be made, and we had the chance to see the value of our coaching."

It was an afternoon for the players. There was no need to talk about next week's opponent. "Next week" would be January 1, 1960 in Pasadena, California. "I've been planning on going to the Rose Bowl with this year's team ever since I was at Roosevelt High School (Seattle)," said Folkins. Chesty Walker (who recruited me) took me to breakfast one morning and asked me if I wanted to come to Washington. I said 'I wasn't sure' and then he said, 'Well, Lee, we'd sure like to have you come to Washington. If you go anywhere else, we'll beat you.' I've never been able to forget that -- and that's why I knew we had a winner all along."

Eventually, the locker room thinned out and became more quiet. McKeta, the toughest of the tough, sat on a bench, still wearing some of his battle gear. He was tired and beat up. His elbows rested on his knees and his head was down. In one hand was a red rose.

Coach Jim Owens is carried off the field after the Huskies beat the Cougars 20-0 to win the 1959 conference title and a trip to the 1960 Rose Bowl. The players in the foreground (left to right) are George Pitt (50), Jim Skaggs (70), and Roy McKasson (55). At the far left, in the white sweater, is Don Nielsen, the ASUW President.

Photo Credit: Museum of History and Industry Seattle Post-Intelligencer Collection

CHAPTER 8

Close to Perfection

With the dissolution of the Pacific Coast Conference, the Big Ten Conference faculty representatives, in May 1959, failed to renew the 1946 agreement between the Big Ten and PCC for Rose Bowl participation. However, they did not exempt any Big Ten team receiving a bid to play in Pasadena from accepting. Shortly after the regular season ended, the athletic directors of Washington and Wisconsin -- George Briggs and Ivan Williamson -- accepted the bid for the 1960 Rose Bowl, the 46th in its glorious history.

The Badgers were ranked sixth in the nation, the Huskies eighth, in the final regular season Associated Press poll. Syracuse was crowned the National Champion. Running back Billy Cannon of third-ranked Louisiana State, received the Heisman Trophy.

Team success begets individual awards. Bob Schloredt was selected as the first-team All-America quarterback by the AP. He was selected over Penn State's Richie Lucas and Don Meredith of Southern Methodist. Schloredt was also picked on the All-Coast first team and was named the West Coast Back of the Year by the AP, the UPI's West Coast Player of the Year, and received the W.J. Voit Trophy for the Player of the Year on the West Coast. Chuck Allen was also selected to the AP and UPI All-Coast first unit. Kurt Gegner and Roy McKasson were on AP's All-Coast second team. United Press International put Schloredt, Allen, and Gegner on its first team and George Fleming on its second unit. Don McKeta would join Allen and Schloredt on the Big Five All-Conference team. McKasson was a second team selection. Jim Owens was selected as the Coach of the Year on the West Coast and finished sixth in the balloting for the AP's National Coach of the Year.

At the team banquet held shortly after the regular season ended, McKeta received the Flaherty Award as the team's most inspirational player and he and Schloredt were selected as the season's co-captains. Game co-captains were selected throughout the season. Dick Dunn received the first Brian Stapp Award, given to the most outstanding non-letter winner.

Schloredt led the Huskies in total offense with 988 yards. Only two of his 75 passes were intercepted. He was responsible for 13 of his team's 29 touchdowns. He averaged 40 yards on 52 punts. He tied teammate, George Fleming, for the most interceptions -- six for the season -- and led the team in scoring with 54 points, two ahead of Fleming. He was also a defensive stalwart who hit like a linebacker. He played 488 minutes of the 600 in the season -- 60 against Stanford and 58 against USC.

He was the sixth Washington back to receive All-America honors -- George Wilson in 1925 and Chuck Carroll in 1928 were consensus selections. Don Heinrich was the AP's selection in 1950 and 1952 and Hugh McElhenny in 1951. Dick Sprague was the Football Writers" Association pick in 1950.

In the NCAA football season statistics, Washington ranked high in several categories. The team led the nation in punt return yardage allowed, giving up only 2.9 yards per return. The Huskies were fifth in interceptions and eighth in points allowed -- 65 in ten games.

The teams were set. Both were looking to reverse their fortunes in previous Rose Bowl games. The Huskies had not won in four previous appearances and had not scored since the Coolidge administration. The 7-2 Badgers had appeared in the 1953 affair and lost to USC 7-0. It was the only loss by a Big Ten representative in the thirteen years of Rose Bowl games played between Big Ten and PCC teams after World War II.

Wisconsin won the Big Ten title on the last day of the regular season. In Minneapolis, the Badgers beat Minnesota 11-7 on a fourth quarter touchdown followed by a two-point conversion. They lost to Purdue 21-0 on a dreary rainy afternoon in early October. Illinois inflicted the other loss when it capped an 82-yard drive to score as the clock ran out to gain an upset victory 9-6. With three games left in the season, Wisconsin traveled to Evanston to meet undefeated Northwestern, then atop the conference. In one of the great games in Dyche Stadium, the Badgers prevailed 24-19. Despite its two conference losses, Wisconsin bested Michigan State who had a 4-2 conference mark and a 5-4 overall report card.

The Badgers would start a mostly senior team in the Rose Bowl. Their offense was built around Dale Hackbart, a 6-4, 200 pounder, who also lettered in baseball and basketball. The defense was led by All-American tackle, Dan Lanphear, and co-captain and All-Big Ten guard, Jerry Stalcup.

The men from Madison fielded a typical Big Ten team, huge in the line and heavy in the backfield. The line averaged fifteen pounds more than the Husky front wall. Oddsmakers quickly established the Huskies as a six-and-a-half point underdog.

Owens, Athletic Director George Briggs, John Thompson (Sports Publicity Director) and Ivan Travis (Events and Ticket Manager) soon headed south to evaluate facilities. They selected Long Beach City College for practices. The Husky party would stay at the nearby Lafayette Hotel in downtown Long Beach. "Staying in Long Beach was probably the smartest decision George and Jim made. It was away from all the distractions. They still had official activities to go to but they were focused on winning the Rose Bowl," related Thompson.

During their stay in the Los Angeles area, they dined in Pasadena one evening. The group was seated in a half circle booth with Owens in the middle. Salad had just been served and water and drinks were also on the table. From across the room, an inebriated Husky fan spotted Owens. He staggered over to the table and yelled "You're Jim Owens!" Then, in his attempt to shake the coach's hand, he lurched right on top of the table. The food and drink splattered all over but mostly on Owens. Thompson recalls, "A Caesar salad was all down his shirt and wine and scotch ran down his pants." Oh, the joy of being the head man and having to put up with some of the boosters.

Owens gave the Huskies almost two weeks off to prepare for final exams and to heal the wounds from the regular season. All players continued individual workouts to be ready to resume team workouts.

On the December 18, forty-seven players joined their coaches for the trip to Long Beach. At 11 AM, an hour before the flight's departure time, Greater Seattle, Inc. staged a giant rally at the airport. Dignitaries included Governor Albert Rosellini and Seattle Mayor Gordon Clinton.

Tournament of Roses officials, the Rose Bowl queen and her princesses, and Long Beach officials and townsfolk enthusiastically heralded the Huskies as they arrived in Long Beach. The Huskies joined police escorts and three marching bands in a parade through the city. They were given a formal welcome at the Lafayette Hotel and entertained at a civic dinner that evening. The Huskies were celebrities in this city of 325,000 residents whose civic leaders had begged Rose Bowl teams for years to train and stay in their place along the Pacific.

In the parade, Coach Owens got in the lead car with the Mayor of Long Beach, Raymond Kealey. To open the conversation, Kealey asked, "Where are you from young man?" "Oklahoma City." "Fine, fine," said the Mayor, "and what position do you play on the Washington team?" "Right end -- when they let me get in there," answered the slightly amused mentor.

Kurt Gegner reflected on the trip. "It just occurred to me that if I wrote a letter to my aunt and uncle in Germany that I was leaving today to play in the Rose Bowl, they wouldn't have any idea what I was talking about. It's a humbling thought, isn't it?" Gegner didn't know what the Rose Bowl was until his freshman year at Washington. "Oh, I heard of it. But I certainly didn't associate it with anything that would happen to me," remarked the Husky tackle whose route to the New Year's classic was by way of displaced persons' camps and fleeing Yugoslavia with his German family after World War II.

On the Huskies' bus return from their first workout in Long Beach, the engine went dead. While waiting what seemed an endless period of time, sophomore tight end, John Meyers, looked into the matter. He had the reputation of being able to fix anything. His reputation remained intact after he fiddled around with the engine until it started. Dr. Geehan, the team physician, kept the team's morale up by quipping, "Heck, this isn't bad. It could have happened in the airplane."

Soon, the greatest mass movement to California since the Gold Rush of 1849 would begin. Twenty thousand Northwest fans would journey to the game. Greyhound scheduled 17 chartered busses from Seattle to Los Angeles. United Airlines added 13 additional flights to the Los Angeles area. Bowl officials indicated the contingent would break all records for out-of-state attendees at the Rose Bowl. The game had been sold out by the time the Huskies left.

This game was a big, big deal. The Rose Bowl game was the oldest in the nation. It started in 1902 with Michigan stomping Stanford 49-0 and was called the "granddaddy of them all" when referring to the nation's bowl games. Owens felt it was the biggest bowl game by far. Not only was it the oldest, it attracted the greatest attention because of its community involvement, the Tournament of Roses Parade, and the pageantry. "I remember listening to the 1936 Rose Bowl as a young boy," Owens said, "hearing Stanford beat SMU 7-0 and thinking it would be great to be in the Rose Bowl. None of the games in which I played -- the 1947 Gator Bowl, the 1949 and 1950 Sugar Bowls -- matched my experience in the Rose Bowl."

Owens and his staff were clearly focused on beating Wisconsin. They chose Long Beach to get away from the entertainment and attractions of Los Angeles. Owens would let the players go to the functions required by Tournament hosts -- Disneyland and Lawry's Prime Rib House, and a few others -- but they were in Long Beach to work. "We were really concentrating. There was an overarching concern for winning this game," Joe Jones said.

And work they did. In the few practices that were open, sports writers viewed the drills and scrimmages as far tougher than they had seen and even rougher than many games they witnessed. "Those Husky kids were like hungry tigers in practice," one columnist remarked.

Owens agreed. "We practiced very hard. We were a young team and we wanted to try to advance a little bit further and just continue our conditioning. The press was real surprised that we had as much contact work as we did."

All the players attested to the toughness of the practices. Mike Crawford recalls, "We immediately started some serious workouts -- closed ones that nobody could visit. Owens toughened us up again. There was no question that we were going to play a ball game and we were going to win. It rained a few days and we worked through that. One of our schemes was that we were going to double and triple team Lanphear. It didn't matter where we ran the play, we were on him, we were going to block the hell out of him, and stay after him until the whistle blew."

Backup quarterback Kermit Jorgensen said, "Practices were tougher than spring and pre-season practices. We worked on some misdirection plays and the Utah special but, other than that, we didn't do a whole lot different on our offense. I think the coaches felt pretty confident of our speed and that we could handle their big guys."

Owens wanted the practices to be tough and focused. "The

purpose of my secret practices isn't necessarily to experiment with new plays. I just like to keep my players' minds on the practice, not the spectators. We can accomplish much more behind closed gates than we ever could with people hanging around."

Most of the columnists didn't give the Huskies much of a chance. Husky lineman Ben Davidson read many articles building up to the game. "I remember the newspapers making fun of us. One newspaper reported, 'The Huskies are small and they are slow too.' It was going to be a mismatch of the century -- the mighty Wisconsin Badgers against the lowly University of Washington. There were just a lot of articles maligning the poor Huskies."

The coaches felt differently and spent lengthy periods in preparing the Huskies. Tom Tipps recalled, "Chesty Walker and I spent two weeks breaking down every play Wisconsin ever ran. I don't want to brag about it, but I think we knew what they were going to run before they did. We stayed up late lots of nights in Long Beach. We were serious about our preparation."

After the morning practice two days before Christmas, the players joined the Wisconsin team at Disneyland. As the Huskies were milling around on arrival, Mickey Mouse came running through the crowd headed straight for the team. He was yelling, "Where's Keith Cordes, where is Keith Cordes?" The beloved Disney character and Cordes had gone to high school together in Long Beach. At that moment, Cordes was the Huskies' most famous player.

That evening, the Badgers and the Huskies attended dinner together. At the outset, some of the Badgers didn't exactly endear themselves to their opponents. Some of the Wisconsin players were already seated before the Huskies arrived. The Huskies had been taught that nobody sits down until the whole team was together. Some of the first Huskies to arrive stood waiting for their teammates. The Badger players kept saying, "Boys, you can sit down. Wisconsin has arrived." The word "Boys" was emphasized. Some other Badgers called the Huskies "Loggers." McKeta would remember that moment. "It is so important for teams to realize how words can change the complexion of the game before it starts. Their words certainly fueled our fire."

Dick Dunn remembers having great disdain for Wisconsin. "They looked like buffoons. At Lawry's, there was a prime rib eating contest. One of their guys ate three or four large pieces and our guy ate about one and a half. Owens had us on a diet all through the season. Lunch for us was soup and a sandwich and a cookie. His idea was to have everybody as slim as they could be. Our body fat was low. A big gut was not good. I was proud that my teammate didn't each much."

Thompson, working on public relations activities for the Huskies, also had a chance to observe the Badgers. "Wisconsin was at the Huntington-Sheraton Hotel in Pasadena. Right opposite the the hotel is where I spent many nights working. The Badgers were so sure of winning the ball game. They were definitely cocky."

On the day before Christmas, the Huskies got back to full contact and worked very hard in practice. The coaches made some adjustments to the defense which they had introduced three days before. Owens declared, "Now we'll ease up over the holiday and by Sunday (the 27th), I hope, we will be able to settle down and do the best we can of getting tuned up to beat Wisconsin."

It was a good Christmas for everybody in the Husky family. The coaches' wives and those of the 16 married players had arrived a few days before. The training table was off. At breakfast and lunch, they ate what they wanted. Some bought tiny Christmas trees and contested with their teammates to see who had the most decorated rooms. The "no swimming" rule was lifted and despite a gale blowing in from the Pacific, some ventured into the swimming pool in the lanai section of the hotel.

The biggest hit was Dunn's entry into the pool off the diving board. He took several bounces on the board and on the last one, it snapped like a stick of kindling. Dunn apparently had a little too much food during the Christmas break.

Both teams were together again a few days before the game. To acknowledge the presence of Wisconsin's Lanphear that evening, one of the crooneers sang "Danny Boy." About two-thirds through the song, Coach Norm Pollom's voice could be heard loud enough so every Husky around him could hear. "That son-of-a-bitch better screw on his helmet tight. We're coming right after him."

In the remaining practices leading up to the game, the Huskies worked on speed, precision, ball handling routines, the kicking game, pass offense and defense, and physical fitness. On December 31, they journeyed to Pasadena for a tour of the Rose Bowl. They were impressed with its size and shape and the condition of the field. Fullback Ray Jackson gushed, "Oh, I am going to do well. This is the first time my feet have been warm on a football field this whole season." His feet would get much warmer the following day.

Up to now the Huskies had worked very hard and had been entertained at several popular places and by many people. In 24 hours, *they* would be the entertainers. Over 100,000 spectators would fill the bowl and many more would view them on national television. They were ready, they were confident. McKeta, their inspirational leader, voiced the team's feeling, "We ain't here to lose and we ain't gonna lose."

Early New Year's morning, the Huskies awoke to do battle. They ate, mostly in silence, as they focused on the biggest day of their lives. Some stared ahead, some talked in hushed tones. There wasn't any laughter or raucous banter. They were preparing to be assassins.

▶ *The 1959 Husky team on its visit to the Rose Bowl the day before the 1960 game against Wisconsin. This team was the first Washington football team to be admitted to the Husky Hall of Fame.*

Photo Credit: From the personal collection of Dick Dunn, a member of that team.

They boarded a bus for the 30-minute ride to the most famous bowl in the land. Motorized policemen, with their engines purring, were ready to escort the Washington team to Pasadena. Owens and Walker sat in a front seat completing substitutes' seats for the sideline and reviewing mimeographed diagrams of Husky plays. Bob Hivner and Schloredt sat beside each other. Hivner stared out the window. Schloredt was soon dozing.

Off the freeway and into Pasadena, the traffic thickened. Spectators walked by toting blankets for cover on this brisk day. At 20 minutes to noon, the bus threaded through cars already parked around the stadium. The driver was directed to back into a tunnel on the south side of the huge bowl. Silently and with determined faces, the young men filed off the bus and into the locker room for their final preparation.

When the Huskies entered the field for their pre-game warm-up, the frost on the grass was glistening as it slowly disappeared under the rays of California sunshine. The contest would be played under bright sunshine but cold winds from the north would blow bitterly throughout.

Wisconsin was already on the field. Some players had their tongues hanging out from the pre-game drills; some had sacks for stomachs. Jorgensen observed, "They may outweigh us. But we are trim, light weight guys in much better shape than they are. We are going to kick the shit out of them."

Fleming had other thoughts. "Playing in the Rose Bowl was a childhood dream of mine. I had watched Rose Bowl games growing up in Dallas. I wanted to go to UCLA or USC to play in the game. It was the granddaddy of them all." A few days earlier, Fleming had suffered a knee injury when he banged into McKeta in practice. The decision to play him was going to be made right before the game. He was heavily taped. As the Huskies trotted off the field for the locker room, Owens asked, "Can you go?" Fleming replied, "Try and keep me off the field!"

Owens spoke briefly to the players before they returned to the battle ground. He told them they were faster and quicker than Wisconsin. He told them that they had paid the price all season. This game was the payoff. Joe Jones thought, "We are in better shape than they are. I believe the price is right."

Co-captains McKeta and Schloredt met Wisconsin's Jerry Stalcup and Bob Zeman in the middle of the field. The Badgers won the toss and elected to kick off and defend the north side. When asked "why?" Coach Bruhn replied, "We've got a good kicker and there was a strong wind blowing (from the Wisconsin players' backs)." For the next few minutes, Bruhn's decision seemed sound. Fleming stood near the ten-yard line waiting to cradle the ball into his chest and return up field. He was hit on the 27, fumbled, and recovered his own miscue. After getting a first down, the Huskies were stopped. Schloredt arched a 42-yard punt down to the Badger 12 where sophomore quarterback, Jim Bakken, fielded the bouncing ball and was immediately knocked out of bounds.

The defense had stopped the Huskies and now the Wisconsin offense thought it would push the lighter foe down the field. But Washington just stuffed them on three plays. Fleming returned Hackbart's punt 14 yards to the Wisconsin 49. Already, Washington's punting advantage was paying off.

On fourth and one, Schloredt ran a keeper to the right for six yards and a first down on the Badger 34. On third and nine, Schloredt lobbed a short pass to Jackson sliding out the backfield for seven. Schloredt rolled left for a first down on the 23. Gegner was already beginning to think that Lanphear was not that good. "He tries to run around my blocks instead of hitting me head on. Our line is getting off the ball very quickly and opening some huge holes. We are sticking our helmets on their chests and driving through." Tipps added, "Lanphear was part of our scouting process.

He was the backbone of their whole defensive philosophy. We went right over where he was playing. And that depressed him."

On the next play, Schloredt faked to McKeta, rolled right and weaved 17 yards to the Badger 6. On the tenth play of the drive, the entire right side of the Husky line sealed off Wisconsin's left side by driving their opponents back and inside. Left guard Chuck Allen pulled to the right and hit the cornerback on a perfect block. Jim Skaggs fired out from the left tackle spot and drove the left outside linebacker almost into the end zone. McKeta cut up inside Allen and raced untouched into the end zone. McKeta thought "this is too easy." Fleming's kick put the Huskies up 7-0.

Schloredt's strategy was simple -- get Wisconsin off balance and keep them there. "We hit them with plays forcing them to adjust to our strong side. Then we hit them on the weak side."

The Huskies were attacking aggressively on every play. The linemen were ramming the Wisconsin front wall with their helmets. The Badgers were back on their heels. On the Badgers' first play from scrimmage after returning the kickoff to their 23, they met the Huskies' alternate unit. They got a rude welcome. Halfback Billy Hobbs fumbled after colliding with end Stan Chapple and Brent Wooten recovered for the Huskies on the 29. A double reverse, Hivner to Don Millich to Wooten, gave the Huskies a first down on the 19. On fourth down on the 18, Fleming kicked a 36-yard field goal into the wind to put Washington ahead 10-0.

Four plays later, the Huskies were on the scoreboard again. On Wisconsin's next series, Bakken set up to punt on third down from the 16. At dinner, several days before the game, the athletic director's wife, Beth Briggs, was seated next to Tipps and Walker. The Husky coaches told her that they planned to block a punt because they saw something on film that suggested they could do it. Mrs. Briggs watched the next play with some anticipation. With a vicious charge, Kinnune knocked his opponent into the backfield and stretched out and blocked the ball. Bakken recovered and was hit by Meyers on the four-yard line. Mrs. Briggs was out of her seat leading the cheers. On fourth and 17, Bakken punted again, this time booming it 49 yards. Fleming took it on the second bounce on his 47, raced laterally to the far side and cut inside the first would-be tackler. He then picked up some initial blocks to clear a lane. He sped through the next wave of defenders and kept his eye on Gegner. The German immigrant was blocking Bakken inside and Fleming darted outside and cruised the last 15 yards into the end zone.

Husky Quarterback Bob Schloredt on a rollout in Washington's smashing victory over Wisconsin in the 1960 Rose Bowl.

Photo Credit: University of Washington Athletic Communications Department / Collegiate Images.

No celebration. He had been in the promised land before and didn't need any high fives or hugs or to spike the pigskin. He calmly tossed the ball to the official and trotted back to get the kicking tee. After the 53-yard play, the Huskies had really popped the Badgers' balloon. The score was 17-0 and Wisconsin didn't have a first down. Husky fans were giddy with delight.

In the middle of the second quarter, after Hivner's punt went out of bounds on the Wisconsin 31, the Badgers mounted a nine-play drive to score and add a two-point conversion to close the lead to nine.

On Wisconsin's next possession, Hackbart sent Fleming back to his 18 to field a 44-yard punt. The ball bounced high and Fleming leaped to grab it. He started right toward the far hash mark and cut inside the first Wisconsin defender. Folkins' block to the inside opened up a lane near the sideline. Just as a Badger was ready to stop the Dallas Dodger, Gegner was coming back on the inside and stretched his 6'2" frame out to strike the surprised Badger down. Now at full speed, Fleming did the rest on his own. He bowled over several defenders at the 32, stiff-armed another at midfield, and was finally caught from behind by Tom Wiesner, the last Wisconsin defender, on the Badger 27. Schloredt was annoyed at himself on the play. "I could have broke him loose, but I loafed a little. I saw three Wisconsin guys pin him against the sideline and I gave up, and all of a sudden, he got free again. I could have blocked that last guy out." Schloredt, with a grin on his face, added, "It's lucky that didn't happen during the regular season. I'd really get chewed out. Why if Coach Owens saw those pictures, he'd make me pay my way into the next game."

On third and six, with a little more than two minutes to go in the half, Schloredt teamed up with Folkins on the most spectacular play of the game. Schloredt rolled right. "What I was taught was that when I came to the corner, I am coming to run and unless the defensive back leaves somebody open, I'm running the football. I would run with the ball high most of the time and throw the baby right at the last moment. I ran on two-thirds of the pass plays I called. So the coaches designed a play where the right halfback would roll left and I would drop back and semi-roll to about the tight end spot on the right side of the line. We would have several pass routes. One was a post -- usually the split left end. The right halfback would swerve the other direction and go down the far sideline. The tight end would look like he was going the other direction from the roll-out." It was the Utah Special.

"As I rolled right, I was looking to see where the safety was and the safety gave me room down the middle. I saw Lee and he was pretty even with the safety and I just led him into the post." Folkins raced left to right between two defenders. The Husky quarterback threw it up high and Folkins launched his 6'5" frame and long arms as far as he could and caught the ball on his finger tips. "I threw the ball where he had a chance of getting it and the defensive backs didn't. Lee goes up and makes one of those damn finger tip catches." Folkins deftly brought the ball into his chest as his outstretched body landed in the end zone to complete one of the most amazing touchdown catches in Rose Bowl history .

"It was the same pass Schloredt threw to me in the last game of the season against Washington State but not in the end zone. It was a well thrown ball between two defenders. I will never forget Roy McKasson getting up from his blocking position and running full tilt into the end zone and hugging me. It was a special moment." It was also a catch that put Folkins in professional football. Folkins told Schloredt many times after they graduated, "that if it wasn't for that catch in the Rose Bowl, I would never have played pro football. I had never been contacted before, and I didn't know anything about the pros."

Wisconsin threatened on their next series. A 43-yard field goal attempt by Karl Holzwarth, the Badgers' 245-pound tackle and Hackbart's brother-in-law, was straight but it sailed under the crossbar. The Huskies went into the dressing room ahead 24-8. The Badgers had outgained the Huskies -- 145 to 124 -- but had lost three fumbles and had given up almost 121 yards on punt returns to Washington's none.

Keith Jackson said the press corps was buzzing during the intermission They were asking "Who are these jackrabbits? Who is this guy Fleming?"

Washington would receive the kickoff to open the second half. As the players returned to the field, Owens took Schloredt aside and stressed the importance of the Huskies' first possession. "This is a very important time. We have to go down and drive and let them know they are not going to get back in this ball game." He told Schloredt if the Huskies' scored, it would break the Badgers' hearts and souls.

Fleming got the Huskies in good field position by returning the kickoff 29 yards to the Washington 34. The Huskies executed Owens' directions perfectly. In just over four minutes, Washington ran 11 plays, most of which were just smash-mouth football. Barry Bullard and Meyers cleared the way over the right side and Jackson followed. He ran the football five times through that side for 47 of the 66 yards. After Jackson's first carry over right guard where Lanphear was defending, Bullard and Meyers came back to the huddle and told Schloredt, "We think we hurt Lanphear on that last play." Schloredt decided to take advantage. "I was calling the plays and we ran the next three over Lanphear's side." Lanphear eventually went out of the game.

On his third straight carry, Jackson's 25-yard rumble put the ball on the Wisconsin 16. Schloredt then threw the only pass of the drive to Folkins in the end zone. This time it fell incomplete. So he went back to Jackson for six to the 10. Then the drive appeared doomed. Schloredt rolled right down to the four where he was hit. The ball popped loose back to the 11. But there was Fleming. Trailing the option play, he recovered the football. Again, Schloredt faked the pitch, kept the ball, and muscled his way around end down to the six. After the play was dead, Hackbart came up out of his defensive back position and tried to level Fleming who was standing out of bounds. The referee threw his flag and the Badgers were penalized for a personal foul down to the two -- half the distance to the goal from the spot of the transgression. Jackson shook off Stalcup, Wisconsin's all-conference guard, with ridiculous ease to score standing up. Fleming again for the conversion. The modest Jackson commented on the drive. "When they called my number, I just ran. I never remember individual plays." At the end of the game, Tipps went over to Jackson and gave him a little kiss on the forehead.

The Huskies were leading 31-8 with less than 26 minutes to play. But the game was over for the Badgers at that point. They were being annihilated and they knew it. Rick Redman, a Husky two-time consensus All-American in 1963 and 1964 was sitting in the stands that day with his parents. He was a high school junior. "The Huskies were looking forward so much to showing people how they played. They had the system perfected, they had the intimidation factor down. They couldn't wait to get out there. And when they got off to the fast start, it just mushroomed. They were killing Wisconsin. The Badgers didn't know what hit them. Huskies were going out of their way to crush guys on roll-back blocks. Wisconsin players were dropping like flies out there."

The Huskies scored two more times in the fourth quarter. But not before Wisconsin mounted one more effort to score. Late in the third stanza, Wisconsin started a drive from the Washington 42 which took the Badgers down to the seven. There, Hackbart threw four passes. One went off the fingers of Henry Derleth in the end zone. Fleming nearly intercepted the next one intended for Wiesner on the goal line. Allen knocked down the third fling on the one. On fourth down, Jackson, from his outside linebacker position, put great pressure on Hackbart. His pass fell incomplete in the right corner of the end zone with McKeta providing great coverage. It was the first time, in their whole season, that the Badgers had failed to score after getting inside the opponent's 20-yard line.

On fourth and inches on the Washington 16, Schloredt boldly called a quarterback sneak up the middle and got two to keep the drive alive. High in the press box, a sports writer had his binoculars on Owens. He put the glasses down and said, "This is the damnedest thing I've ever seen; they run on fourth down on their own 16 and Owens never changed expression."

McKeta charged 15 yards on a cutback run. The officials called the play back when they saw Kinnune block Hackbart downfield with his helmet a little less gently than the umpire thought was appropriate. So Schloredt faked right and threw left 34 yards toward the far sideline. It was a perfectly thrown ball, just over the outstretched hands of a Badger defender. Fleming, under a full head of steam, looked the ball into his hands and continued down the sideline. Slanting from the left side, Hackbart dragged the gimpy Husky down on the 17, ending a 65-yard pass play.

On the next play, Schloredt spun to his left, faked a pitch to Fleming running left, and then reversed to the right side. After faking a pass, he turned up field. Fighting off two defenders, he then dragged two more for another four yards down to the seven. After Jackson gained one over center, Schloredt picked up three tough yards over left tackle and ran over the same spot for the score. Washington 38 to 8.

With less than 11 minutes to go, Wisconsin was desperate and went to the air on almost every play. Owens began clearing the bench. All nine seniors got some playing time. One of them, Carver Gayton, hobbled into action on a troublesome knee in the waning moments. Former student manager Artie Buerk was on the sidelines as "manager for a day." "Third stringers were coming off the field saying Wisconsin players were praying to get the game over with. They were moaning on the field about getting the thing over."

On Wisconsin's next-to-last possession, Bakken's fourth-down pass was knocked away by third-string end Ed Peasley. The Huskies started one more scoring drive on the Badger 45. Hivner hit Peasley for 22 yards and a first down on the Badger 23. This combination had scored touchdowns on the same field for Compton College in the Junior College Rose Bowl a few years before. After Sam Hurworth bolted for six over center, Hivner again hit Peasley for 13. Hurworth trailing the play, circled around to the side of Gerald Kulcinski and delivered a mighty blow with his helmet to the side of the head gear of the unsuspecting Wisconsin guard. The officials had to keep the frustrated and angry Badgers from retaliating. Hurworth's act was typical of the way the Huskies played football.

After play resumed, Hivner rolled over right tackle to the one. Millich then sliced left out of the backfield and into the corner of the end zone. Hivner found him all alone for the touchdown. Nobody was within ten yards of the Husky senior running back. "I had a smile on my face two yards wide. I was all alone and I knew it. All I had to do was reach up to the ball and say 'Hi, Baby.' " He mildly celebrated, tossing the ball about ten feet in the air to the official. On the conversion, Hivner tried to send Millich out in even grander style with a two-point conversion attempt. He tried to hit Millich in the right corner but his pass was intercepted. The final score -- 44 to 8.

In the post-game analysis, Wisconsin's coach. Milt Bruhn, paid tribute to Washington's overall speed. "...this team had more speed than any we met all year...Their line speed was most impressive and was about the only thing -- except for the final score -- that surprised us." He would praise many Huskies. "The turning point was Fleming's punt return for their second touchdown. We found out right there that our second unit wasn't going to be much help. In addition, it took some fire out of us. From the start, Washington was higher than we were. Their quick scores gave them even more incentive. We knew they had fine pursuit and were aggressive, but we weren't prepared for all that speed."

People in the press box were very impressed with Washington's tremendous pursuit. They observed that a Husky player might have been knocked to the ground, but he never stayed there. Wisconsin's Hackbart sighed and said, "It was discouraging to see our guys put some good blocks on the Washington players and then have them get up and run back to the play. We've never seen tigers like that in the Big Ten -- NEVER!"

Newspapers reports were full of praise for the Huskies -- none more so than Lloyd Larson's column in the Milwaukee, Wisconsin, Sentinel. "What an unhappy New Year's afternoon. Really unhappy and just as shocking. Yup. It's true what they say about Bob Schloredt. And George Fleming. The same can be said about all those Huskies from Washington. As a group, they were quick, alert, poised, aggressive, and razor sharp. Man, O Man, were they ever ready." He finished his column. "At no time during the regular season did our Wisconsin Badgers run into an outfit like that. In fact, I doubt seriously that any college team in the country had that misfortune."

The Huskies ran 68 plays to Wisconsin's 31. They gained 352 yards to the Badgers' 276. Thanks to Mr. Fleming, they returned punts 130 yards to Wisconsin's 10 -- an average of 32.5 to 3.3. Wisconsin fumbled four times and lost all four; Washington fumbled twice and recovered both times.

Jokingly, McKeta remembers the game as a disappointing win. "Think about it. You play all season to get to the Rose Bowl. I played less time in the Rose Bowl than in any other game in the season. It was such a rout. You were happy for the team but you wanted a lot closer game. But you saw all your brothers having a good time. You see them score, running all over the field, just kicking Wisconsin's butts. That part was fantastic. But as to competition, it was a dud." He also cited Folkins' catch. "I was wide open (down the left sideline). Schloredt threw the ball and when I saw where it was going, I said 'what the hell are you doing?' "

Keith Jackson had this perspective. "The score shocked the country, particularly the middle of the country . The 'big dogs' back east thought they ruled the world back in those days, and they did. Remember in those days, you were talking about Seattle which was geographically isolated. The whole Northwest was isolated from the rest of the country because of the mountains and the population. Not a hell of a lot of people on the East Coast paid any attention to what was going on in Seattle."

Emmett Watson wrote in his column in the Seattle Post-Intelligencer the day after the game. "One remembered the bad years of Owens' beginning at Washington -- when material was thin; when he put the squad through its 'Death March' to separate the tough ones from the letter-seekers; the little smoke signals of dissent. It was easy then to remember that Owens was called a coach 'with no imagination.' And the times he was criticized for 'working the boys too hard.' "

When asked about his muscle building program. Owens said, "That was part of it, but the real work was done on the practice field. Everybody saw the fun our kids were having in front of that big crowd. But the real work is done in practice where it gets boring and monotonous. Real tiresome and no fun at all. But in the fourth quarter, when you look up and see the guy across from you -- and you see that he's tired and you feel good... well, that's when the fun begins."

Fleming and Schloredt were named Co-Most Valuable Players for their outstanding performances. The Husky halfback gained only five yards on three carries. But he racked up 122 yards on punt returns, including one for a touchdown, and 80 yards on kick-off returns. He caught one pass for 65 yards. His place-kicking was perfect -- one field goal for 36 yards and five conversions. He had 272 all-purpose yards.

His teammate passed and rushed for 183 yards, completing four of seven passes. He scored one touchdown and averaged almost 40 yards on four punts.

A distant observer of the game on national network television called Owens after it was over. It was Owens' former coach, Bud Wilkinson. After congratulating his pupil on the stunning victory, he said, "It would be hard to find a club anywhere, anytime, that played a 60-minute period any better than that team that day."

The reaction to the Huskies' victory took many forms. George Briggs attended an athletic directors' meeting a few days after the Rose Bowl game and Ivan Williamson, the Wisconsin AD, got down on his knees in front of Briggs while all the other AD's in attendance stood up and applauded the Washington delegation. Then Briggs, Owens, and some of the other coaches went to New York to attend an NCAA meeting. On their way back to Seattle, Briggs was opening mail that had accumulated over the past few days. One was a letter from the conference office with a check for one million dollars. It was the first payment from NBC Sports to the host team. Owens quipped, "George, why don't we just go to Mexico?"

Coach Pollom went to Santa Anita Raceway and he and his friends ran up a pretty large bar bill. He saw Washington Governor Rosellini in the crowd and said, "We did a great thing for the State of Washington, so would you mind paying the bar bill?" Rosellini said he couldn't do that, so Pollom signed the bar bill "Ivan Williamson, Athletic Director of the University of Wisconsin." Neither Pollom nor anybody else from the Husky party ever heard a word about the bill.

Meyers, the sophomore tight end, went to another Husky locker room a few days later to join the Washington basketball team for its game against UCLA in the Los Angeles Sports Arena. Meyers said, "They weren't going to let me in the place. I had to borrow a press pass from (Seattle Times sports columnist) Georg Meyers to get past the gate." He got into the game for 19 seconds and hauled down one rebound.

Co-Most Valuable Players of the 1960 Rose Bowl, George Fleming and Bob Schloredt, receive the Key to the City from Seattle Mayor Gordon Clinton at a huge rally upon the Huskies' return from Pasadena.

Photo Credit: University of Washington Athletic Communications Department / Collegiate Images.

The Huskies spent three days celebrating in the Los Angeles area and arrived home on the evening of January 4. A large crowd greeted them at the airport and Seattle Mayor Clinton gave a symbolic key to the city to Fleming and Schloredt. Giant searchlights pierced the sky and illuminated the airport arrival area. A "presidential-style" motorcade, led by the police motorcycles from the city and county police departments, gave escort to busses filled with Husky players and their wives as they wound their way from the airstrip and north onto Highway 99. They proceeded through the city and the University District, and down to the University of Washington crew house. All along the route, people lined both sides of the route waving and cheering the victorious band of brothers.

Keith Jackson said the reception was "like we won the war. It was the first time in my life that I fully realized how a college football team could pick up an entire state and region and revitalize it."

CHAPTER 9

The Cardiac Kids

In 1960, the Huskies returned the entire starting lineup from the Rose Bowl victory plus ten other lettermen who saw considerable action as part of the alternate unit. Because of their success in 1959, they would have a bullseye on their backs. Owens reminded the team in the spring that it would get special attention from all its opponents. He also reminded the players about what they had been through, what they had accomplished, and what they could achieve in the upcoming season.

The team would be buoyed by several sophomores up from the 1959 freshmen squad and upperclassmen who had significantly developed their skills and were ready to play key roles in 1960. The sophomores included linemen Duane Locknane, Ray Mansfield, Dave Phillips, and Rod Scheyer, and running backs Charlie Mitchell and Bob Monroe.

Locknane -- 190 and 6'0" -- was a guard who earned all-state honors at Seattle's Roosevelt High School. Mansfield at 220 and 6'3" was clearly ready for significant playing time at strong tackle. All-state at Kennewick High School, he averaged 24 tackles a game in his senior year. He also won letters in baseball, basketball, track and field, and wrestling. He had four brothers and three sisters. "When we are all home, we drink four gallons of milk a day."

Phillips, at 5'9" and 190 pounds, was one of the smallest

169

linemen on the West Coast. A graduate of Lincoln High School in Seattle, he had many of the characteristics of Locknane - - quickness, toughness, desire, and intelligence. Scheyer was a backup to Gegner. 6'2" and 210, he had good speed and excellent football sense. He played at East High School in Bremerton across Puget Sound.

Mitchell was the fastest back Owens had since taking over in 1957. A great break-away threat, Mitchell would see considerable action at left halfback along with senior George Fleming. He was an all-state and All-America selection from Seattle's Garfield High School.

Monroe, another all-state selection from Roosevelt, was voted the most valuable player of the 1959 East-West All-State football game. He would provide depth at right halfback behind seniors Don McKeta and Brent Wooten.

Several senior linemen who had played backup roles in 1959 had to step up in 1960 because of injuries to the Rose Bowl starters. They included senior ends Stan Chapple, Pat Claridge, senior interior linemen Ben Davidson, Dick Dunn, Dave Enslow, and Sam Hurworth, and juniors Tim Bullard and Jim Skaggs.

Chapple, hampered by a knee injury in 1959, was a great pass rusher at 210 and 6'4". Claridge was the team's head hunter. From Canada, he was very physical at 6'2" and 195.

Davidson was a work-in-progress. He played no high school football and took up the game at East Los Angeles Junior College. "I played well enough to get some scholarship offers. I had lunch with Jim Owens. I was very impressed with him. The most impressive thing was that he paid for my lunch. That was pretty big time." Owens was impressed because Davidson was 6'7" and 250.

He arrived in Seattle in January 1959. "I never called anybody to tell them when I was coming. Washington had sent me an airline ticket to look at the campus. I took that ticket, cashed it in, and bought a one-way bus ticket. I packed up my clothes in cardboard boxes with a rope around them and got on the bus. I stopped in San Francisco and spent a couple of days there. I finally arrived at the bus station in downtown Seattle and got a room at the Virginia Street Hotel at five bucks a night. The next day I called someone in the athletic department. "Where are you? How come you didn't tell someone you were coming?"

"They got me a job before I started attending classes in the spring quarter. I started in a ship repair yard in Winslow (Bainbridge Island). They moved me to the YMCA in downtown and I lived there a couple of days. Then, I was joined by another recruit, Keith Cordes, from Long Beach. We finally moved to a boarding house near St. James Cathedral."

One of Davidson's friends was 6'1" 210 pound guard Dave Enslow. Nicknamed the "Bear," he had great lateral speed. From Lake Washington High School, he was also a top heavyweight wrestler in a good Husky wrestling program. Enslow was the football team's free spirit. Teammate Chuck Allen recalls Enslow's rain dances. During spring practice, the team had thirty days in which they could have the twenty practices allowed by the NCAA. Enslow would do his dances hoping the rain would come and the practice would be postponed. "Dave would grab a garbage can, put beads on it, and start dancing around it. And it would soon start raining and we would not practice."

If it rained during the fall, the Huskies would sometimes go into Hec Edmundson Pavilion. There they faced rats that lived under the basketball floor that was laid on the Pavilion's dirt floor. Allen said, "To make room for our practice, we would take out sections of the basketball floor and turn into a rat patrol." The linemen hated the practices in the Pavilion. It had a dust powder floor and the dust would get on their faces and in their eyes. They looked like owls when the practice was over.

Dunn backed up Roy McKasson at center. An all-state selection from Olympia High School, Dunn was very popular with his teammates. Coach Tipps described Dunn as "the scrappiest old piece of furniture you ever saw."

Hurworth was one of those players who wanted nothing more than to play as much as possible. To do so, he switched from fullback, where he played in 1958 and 1959, to guard in 1960. Hurworth hailed from Port Angeles.

Barry Bullard's younger brother, Tim, was a versatile lineman who could play both center and guard. Six feet and 210, he was a standout for Marshfield High (Coos Bay, Oregon) on state championship teams.

At 215 and 6'2", Skaggs was a lineman who logged 215 minutes and played several positions in 1959. He had been an outstanding lineman at Arroyo Grande High School in California.

Owens felt the 1960 team wasn't as strong as the 1959 squad because the alternate unit was not as capable as the previous version. The Huskies would not creep up on any of the powerful teams they would face in 1960. All opponents would have ample incentive to knock off the Rose Bowl champion. The Northwest schools particularly pointed for Washington given that they had not been invited to join the Big Five conference. Also, the new conference was strong. The staff would have to have the players charged up for every game.

Seventy four turned out for spring practice. McKeta thought the coaches did a great job deflating the Rose Bowl balloon. "They said the starting eleven has been told that they are the greatest team ever to hit Washington. They said you guys hardly even have to practice. So we will work with these other guys to get them up to your caliber."

There was healthy competition at all positions. In the intra-squad game at the end of spring practice, the Gold unit whipped the Purple unit 33-0. The Purples -- essentially the Rose Bowl starting unit -- were so embarrassed by their lethargic and haphazard play that they challenged the second team to an extra quarter. The Purple unit capitalized on two Gold fumbles and won the additional stanza 13-0 to gain some solace.

Owens announced at the end of spring practice that the days of the 1960 Rose Bowl starting unit were history. "We won't have the Rose Bowl team next season. Next fall, you'll find several -- or even many -- new faces on our first unit."

Owens gave the "Rose Bowl team" something to think about during the summer when he wrote on the locker room chalkboard:

Purple | 48 plays | 177 total yards | Gold | 76 plays | 414 total yards

He also told the Purple players and others that they had better get in shape during the summer because "you will have a hell of a lot of competition coming in this fall."

Several off the field changes took place during the spring. Owens took on the additional job of Athletic Director after George Briggs resigned, early in 1960, to take an executive position in banking. Assistant Coach Norm Pollom left for a similar role at USC. He was replaced by Don White.

White graduated from Seattle Prep in 1946 and played end at Santa Clara for four years under coach Len Casanova. In 1952, White joined the coaching staff at Oregon where Casanova had become the head man in 1951. White took on the head coaching job at Burns (Oregon) High School for two years, starting in 1954. He then moved on to become the head coach at Aberdeen (Washington) High School and compiled an outstanding record over his three year tenure. Before joining Owens' staff, he spent a year as head coach at Highline High School.

KOMO-TV won the bid for the televison rights to replay Husky games on the Monday evening following each game. The program went head-to-head with the Chet Huntley-David Brinkley Report on KING-TV. The ratings on the Husky show, anchored by Keith Jackson, presumably got higher ratings than the renowned newscasters.

The Big Ten voted to reverse its previous decision of barring member schools to compete in post season play. The Big Five conference continued its policy of picking the best team in the country, not just from one league, as its opponent in the Rose Bowl.

When fall practice commenced on September 1, the coaches were very focused on achieving as much, if not more, success in 1960 than in 1959. They recognized many pieces had to come together to win another conference championship and repeat as Rose Bowl champions.

In 1959, few key players were injured. Would that be the case in 1960? Sophomores would have to step up and contribute in key positions. Who would they be? The players would have to recommit to "playing it from the heart" with lots of emotion and tenacity. Who would fuel the emotional fires? The coaches would have to determine how to keep the players from being overconfident given their lofty achievements in 1959.

One of the coaches concerns became evident after the first week of two-a-days. Many players were not in good condition. Owens called them "fat and out of shape." Fleming recalled, "Several of us came back out of shape. I had a summer job with Rainier Brewery covering the African-American markets. It was the first year I came back to the pre-season over 200 pounds -- about 15 pounds more than my playing weight."

Bill Kinnune said, "The coaches worked us very hard. Many of us had come back out of shape. They put us on two meals a day during the two-a-days." Challenge drills were intense. At the end of the first week, very few of the Rose Bowl starters were on the Purple unit.

The 1960 Husky coaching staff. Top row: Tom Tipps, Jim Owens, Bert Clark, Chesty Walker, Kneeling: Dick Heatly, Don White, Whitey Core.

Photo Credit: University of Washington Athletic Communications Department / Collegiate Images.

Slowly, as the Rose Bowl heroes got the message, the more familiar names from the 1959 team emerged on the first unit. At the end of the pre-season, nine of the Purple unit for the season opener had started in the Rose Bowl. Lee Folkins and John Meyers, the two other starters, had been edged out by Pat Claridge and Jim Skaggs. Meyers had suffered an ankle injury.

Third-ranked in the pre-season polls, Washington rolled over its first two opponents with ease. The Huskies simply crushed the College of Pacific 55-6. It was the highest point total for a Washington team since it scored 120 points in a shut out of Whitman College in 1919. The following week, Washington stomped Idaho 41-12. One of the sophomores that clearly showed the ability to significantly contribute was Charlie Mitchell. He led the Husky ground game in the College of Pacific game with 100 yards in eight carries. He had another dazzling performance against the Vandals. He gained 71 yards on eight runs in the first half, scoring Washington's first touchdown by racing nine yards around left end. After he returned the second-half kickoff 85 yards for another touchdown, Owens put the smiling sophomore into mothballs.

One of the opponents' scouts in the high perches of the stadium during the Idaho game was Navy's assistant coach, Steve Belicheck, whose son Bill was cavorting as a youngster at Navy practices and beginning to accumulate his football knowledge. As the New England Patriots' head coach, Bill would lead the Patriots to three Super Bowl victories in 2001, 2002, and 2004. Father Belicheck felt the Huskies had played the game "under wraps." He added, "Last year we played Syracuse (the national champion) and this year we got Washington. I'd rather play Syracuse. You know what they're going to do. You don't know what this team (Washington) is going to do." His Navy team would find out.

The easy games were over. The 17th-ranked Midshipmen from Annapolis, Maryland, were next. The Huskies would not see a finer running back all season than Navy's Joe Bellino. Although this was a non-conference contest, it had a greater build up than one to decide the conference title.

Navy, along with Army, were perennial top-ranked teams in the 1950's and 1960's. The service academies -- Army, Navy, and the Air Force Academy, which opened in 1955 -- were respected and admired for their mission and for the commitment and discipline of their students. The teams and their supporters always seemed to do things with a measure of class and elan. The service academies teams had to get a lot out its student-athletes to be competitive. The athletes usually were not as big, nor as fast, as their opponents.

For example, Harry Dietz was the Navy backup quarterback. In 1959, he was behind two larger Navy signal callers in the depth charts. So he shifted over to 150-pound football -- where no player could weigh more than 150 pounds -- and led the Navy lightweights to the Eastern title.

Early in the week, it was announced that Navy had secured a goat from Bainbridge Island to stand in for the Navy mascot. The "real" goat was an old and ailing animal who could not fly to Seattle because of his health. The Navy contingent that had secured "Sandy", the stand-in, announced that he had a definite air about him but assured the fans that only those in the lower stands would be aware of it.

Next, it was announced that the game would be piped in to most of the corps of 3,100 midshipmen back in Annapolis. They had taken a collection to pay for the lease of a direct phone line from Seattle to a field house on the Navy campus. There, a battery of microphones were set up. With special loud speakers set up behind the Middies' bench, the players would hear the cheering and singing of their fellow students.

The only time the two teams had faced off was in the 1924 Rose Bowl when they played to a 14-14 tie. The Huskies evened the score late in the fourth quarter. On fourth and goal from the 12, Washington executed a special play. The Huskies lined up in an unbalanced line with a running back up on the line and the left end in the backfield. The formation made weak side guard, Jim Bryan, an eligible receiver on the left side. The Middies put eight men on the line and nobody covered Bryan, who, after a brief engagement with a Navy lineman, slipped into the end zone and caught Fred Abel's pass for the touchdown. Les Sherman, hobbled on the field favoring his broken toe, and calmly kicked his second extra point of the game to tie the score.

In 1960, at the Sand Point Naval Air Station, on Lake Washington north of the Washington campus, all hands and cooks were preparing for the arrival of the Midshipmen. The Naval Station had been King County's gift to the Navy in 1922. Growing eventually to 460 acres, Sand Point hosted more than 5,600 Naval personnel, more than 2,400 civilian workers, and hundreds of aircraft at its peak during World War II. Units who trained there fought in some of the most critical battles in the war's Pacific campaign.

Tickets were scalped illegally. Two tickets were going for $100, about ten times the face value of a pair of ducats.

Bill Stern, one of the most famous sportscasters in the land, came to town to broadcast the game over the national Mutual network. "Washington is one of the most-talked-(about) teams in the country," Stern said. "If the Huskies can beat Navy and their great halfback Joe Bellino, it will add a lot to the prestige of Jim Owens' team."

Sports Illustrated, the then fledging sports weekly magazine, whetted the appetites of gridiron followers with a cover photo of Bob Schloredt and a featured story about the All-American quarterback and the success of the Husky program. Schloredt was the first Husky player on the SI cover. The only other one to be similarly shown would be Sonny Sixkiller in 1971.

At a Navy League luncheon the day before the game, Schloredt received a Presidential Citation from Undersecretary of the Navy, Fred Bantz, for the quarterback's efforts to further the employment of physically handicapped people. With only ten percent vision in his left eye, Schloredt had written many letters over the past year to boys and girls who had lost an eye and to parents of such children.

The pre-game excitement reached a level matched by very few prior Washington battles. One of the unusual aspects was that both the Navy and Washington squads stayed at Sand Point Naval Station on the night before the game. For several years, the Huskies had used Sand Point as its pre-game quarters. The Huskies were surprised when they arrived to find their opponents there. Probably the midshipmen were more surprised to see the Huskies. After all, this was Naval property. Many Navy officers and a large number of Navy followers had assembled for dinner when the Huskies arrived for their pre-game preparation. "It was a very strange situation," Dick Dunn recalls. "The night before a game, we would always go to Sand Point. It was a ritual. We go there, have dinner, have a meeting, go to a movie, and then to bed in the Bachelor Officers' Quarters. But, for the Navy game, we get out there and the place is just crawling with Navy brass. And the goddam midshipmen are staying out there too."

Washington was favored by 13 points, largely on the strength of the Huskies' alternate unit, deemed to be far stronger than Navy's second unit.

The then largest crowd to see a Husky home game -- 57, 379 -- got their five dollars worth. Washington's famed first team won the game statistically. They held Navy to 69 yards on the ground -- Bellino got 53 of them -- and 138 in the air. Washington rushed for 193 and completed 6 of 10 passes for 82 yards. The key, as usual, was turnovers. Washington fumbled four times and lost three. On a Husky punting situation late in the final period, a bobbled low pass from center gave Navy field position to kick the winning field goal and to send them back to Annapolis with a 15-14 victory.

Bellino was all he was touted to be. He accounted for 145 all-purpose yards and was a threat every time he touched the ball. Jorgensen remembers his calves. "He had calves you wouldn't believe. He could change directions and he could rip out of a tackle so quickly." His calves were indeed huge -- they measured 18 inches in circumference.

He could run as well laterally as forward. He also seemed to be bottom heavy. When he got knocked up in the air, he invariably landed on his feet.

Keith Jackson remembers the Navy running back getting cramps. "They should have knocked Bob Peterson, the Husky head trainer, in the head and got him off the field. The reason Bellino was getting cramps was his pants were so tight. He wanted his knees protected and wanted the pants below the knee. Peterson went out on the field with a pair of scissors and cut his britches so they would hang over the knee. All of sudden, Bellino tore the Huskies up."

Navy received the opening kick off, ran three plays, and kicked. Washington took over on the Navy 48. The Huskies immediately went into the Bug Eye formation to throw Navy's stunting defenders off. Both the halfbacks set up behind the strong side of the unbalanced line. From the 31, Schloredt threw to McKeta, still favoring his foot injured in the Idaho game, who ran for the score. Fleming's kick was good and the Huskies were up 7-0 with just about four and a half minutes gone in the quarter.

Navy battled right back. Bellino fielded Fleming's kick at the goal line and weaved and darted up field for 30 yards. The Navy all-purpose back was starting to make the Huskies look like they didn't practice tackling very much. Bellino then passed 20 yards to running back Ron McKeown to midfield. Eleven plays later, they were in a position to score. The big play in the drive was a 20 yard pass from Dietz, the "lightweight" quarterback, down to the Washington 15. On the following play, the Huskies were penalized for a personal foul and the ball was marked on the seven. On third and short, Bellino launched himself high over left guard to reach the end zone. Greg Mather's kick was no good.

Early in the second quarter, Washington seemed almost a lead pipe cinch to score again. The Huskies drove from their 30 to the Navy five on the combined efforts of Jackson, Fleming, and Schloredt and a personal foul assessed to Navy. On fourth down, Schloredt hit Claridge for a touchdown. Offsetting penalties nullified the play. Still fourth and five, Schloredt then ran a keeper around right end but came up a yard short.

The Huskies threatened again near the close of the half. McKeta intercepted Bellino's pass on the Washington 20 and returned it 18 yards. On second and 16 on the Navy 36, Schloredt hit McKeta for 14. On the play, Navy's Frank Dattilo became too warlike and was ejected from the game for a wild swing at Husky lineman Jim Skaggs. The ball was moved to the Navy nine -- half the distance to the goal from the spot of the transgression. The coaches had sent Fleming in to try for a field goal after McKeta's catch. They reversed their decision after the penalty and elected to go for six. Schloredt rolled left to the four as time elapsed. Fleming remembers the play. "McKeta was open in the end zone but Schloredt didn't see him." At half-time and well into the weekend, the second guessers had lots to discuss about the play calling.

After an exchange of punts to open the second half, the Huskies took possession on the Navy 43 and struck pay dirt in eight plays. Jackson, Mitchell, and Schloredt did most of the damage to the Midshipmen with Jackson scoring on a three-yard rush up the middle. Fleming's kick made it 14-6.

Bellino bolted forward again on the kickoff returning it 23 yards to the Navy 30. Eschewing the ground game, the Middies went airborne with quarterback Hal Spooner, who was supposed to be in sick bay, directing the aerial assault. He hit Graham for 15, then McKeown for 12, followed by another Husky personal foul penalty. Spooner's last bomb was to W. Allen Hughes (a great name for a future Navy officer) who beat Bob Monroe into the end zone capping a 26-yard play. Navy attempted to rush for the equalizing points but was stopped by the Husky front wall.

The drama reached its climax late in the fourth quarter. On third and four on the Husky 33, Schloredt rolled around left end with a clear field ahead. He stumbled and gained only one yard. He then set up to send a booming punt deep into Navy's territory to put the Middies in poor field position to mount a scoring strike. Dunn's snap was low -- about shoe top high -- and normally Schloredt would handle such snaps. He had injured his thumb earlier in the game and maybe that contributed to his not grasping the ball. It rolled to his left -- the side of his bad eye -- and momentarily he could not find it. Those few seconds allowed the Navy defenders to swarm in and down Schloredt on his 24.

Spooner, on a passing attempt, was chased back to the Husky 35 where he was thrown for an 11-yard loss. Next, he tossed a screen pass to Bellino who weaved his way down to the Husky 16. Captain Joe Matalavage hit over left guard for six and a first down on the Husky ten. Bellino again for one. Spooner then found Navy's floater back, Midshipman Hughes, in the end zone. In the Navy fieldhouse in Annapolis, the Middies were listening to Stern's play-by-play broadcast. When Hughes caught the pass for what seemed to be the winning score, they broke from the stands wildly cheering and shouting odes of joy. The Huskies regained hope when the play was called back for an illegal shift. Everybody -- in the stadium and in the Navy fieldhouse -- was on their feet. 14 seconds showed on the scoreboard.

Mathers trotted on the field for his field goal attempt from the 32. His kick sent the ball skyward. It seemed to hang in the air forever before barely dropping down over the cross bar. An ear splitting naval salvo exploded after each Navy score. This time the exuberant gun crew couldn't resist. It fired two double strength shots. The Huskies were dead.

In Owens' post game interview, he simply said, "Our ball handling was too sloppy to win. Mistakes always beat you and we made more than Navy did." Navy's center, Frank Visted added, "We're supposed to cover after the field goal kick. But I just stopped and prayed. It was all or nothing. The ball cleared the bar by about this much," holding his hands out as if measuring a fair-sized salmon.

Washington players felt that they should have won the game. To this day, they still have vivid memories of that game. McKeta recounted that "Navy was the only team that I ever played that was actually afraid of us at the start of the game. And then we turn around and lose to them. Too many mistakes."

Coach Tipps was concerned about complacency. "We're getting mighty fancy and smart-alecky now. If you want to be cuties, you'll beat yourself. You don't need the other team there to do it for you."

Kinnune remembers the practices the following week. "The first two teams had scheduled a progressive party the night after the Navy game. We had some alcohol. The coaches found out about it. When we came back on Monday, we ran and ran and ran. We had whistle drills on Monday, Tuesday, and Wednesday. During the drills, Coach Tipps would tell me, 'It's 90 percent mental and 10 percent physical.' He would go up and down the field yelling 'Willy, you can do this. You'll pass out before you die.' Hell, we *were* dying." It was a mini- Death March to punish the players who seemed to be more concerned with partying than they were about Navy. The coaches also wanted to remind them that the conference games would be tough and they had to raise their level of play.

In 1959, Washington's seven starting linemen -- Folkins,

Gegner, Allen, McKasson, Kinnune, Bullard, and Meyers -- were named the "Sturdy Seven." None of them played less than 333 minutes out of a total of 600 for the regular season. Folkins had played 436 minutes. In 1960, injuries began to severely impact the line. Meyers suffered an ankle injury early in the season. Allen had a groin injury and Bullard suffered a severe injury in the Navy game. He got hit with a come-back block on his knee. "From then on, I was not able to play much. They would tape my body from my hip to my ankle. They would spray on a substance so the tape would stick to my legs. When the tape stretched, it would pull the skin off and I was bloody from the hip down."

Other teammates would have to step up and get ready for the Huskies first conference game in Palo Alto against Stanford, led by Dick Norman, one of the top quarterbacks in the nation. The game was nationally televised. In those days being televised throughout the land was a much bigger event than it is today. There were a lot fewer channels available and a smaller number of networks interested in collegiate football. Washington received $85,000 from the network covering the game.

Like all great teams and athletes, the Huskies didn't dwell on the Navy loss but focused on their next game and the defense of their conference title. They jumped out to a 10-0 lead in the first six minutes. They took Stanford's kickoff and put together a 67-yard drive that stalled on the Indians' seven. Fleming then kicked a 25-yard field goal. Three plays later, Washington was back in Stanford's end zone. Enslow, filling in for the injured Bullard, hit Skip Face, Stanford's kick-off return man, and jarred the ball loose. McKasson recovered on the 18. On the first play, the Huskies were penalized 15 yards for holding. On the next one, Schloredt found Folkins open on the Stanford ten and the long-legged end strode over the goal line. Fleming's kick was good and the Huskies were flying high.

Stanford brought them down to earth as they mounted a drive that got to the Washington seven before it fizzled. Face's field-goal attempt from the 24 split the uprights to close the gap to seven. On the ensuing kickoff, Washington suffered another blow to one of its starters. Fleming was knocked cold at the end of his return. He suffered a concussion and had to leave the game. Mitchell assumed the duty at the wingback position for the rest of the day. He stepped up quickly.

With just under two minutes remaining in the second stanza, he caught a lofty punt on his own 40 and followed the blocking pattern as it systematically unfolded. He eluded one diving Indian, cut to his right, and found the "alley" formed by his teammates in front of the Stanford bench. He sped for the score that created a buzz among the crowd during the intermission. Mansfield, another sophomore, kicked the extra point, and the Huskies happily trotted off to the visitors' locker room with a 17-3 lead.

Stanford had two opportunities to tie the score in the third period. Mitchell fumbled an exchange from McKeta on a double reverse and Stanford smothered the ball on the Washington 12. On fourth and three, Mitchell redeemed himself by clobbering the Stanford ball carrier two yards short of a first down. Later in the quarter, Norman went to the air and led the Indians 60 yards for a touchdown again narrowing the margin to seven.

Washington's punting game turned the game into a rout. Early in the final period, Schloredt booted the ball to the Stanford 40 where Gary Craig faced four Huskies zeroing in on him. There was no three-yard cushion for the punt returner. The tacklers could just race in near the receiver and blast him right in the chest with the helmet. It was brutal. Craig was either the bravest player on the field or the most foolish when he caught Schloredt's punt. He was instantly bowled over by Dunn, Enslow, Sam Hurworth, and Kermit Jorgensen. The ball bounced loose and Dunn recovered it.

Jorgensen, now playing at running back in place of McKeta, hit left end for one. Schloredt threw to Claridge for 29. Then, the one-eyed wonder rambled straight up the middle for the last ten yards.

The Huskies scored once more with over four minutes remaining to etch the final score at 29-10. Owens wasn't satisfied with the win. "It's nice to win but I'm not happy about the way we played. We've played four games and we haven't turned in a good performance in any of them. We're not consistent like a good team should be." He attributed some of the inconsistency to the number of injuries to key people.

Several of the last six games of the season would put at risk all Husky fans who had heart problems. Some would be admitted to the hospital as the "cardiac kids" won four of the games by a margin of five points -- three of them involving come-from-behind winning drives late in the fourth quarter.

The first heart stopper was against UCLA in Seattle on October 15. The Bruins were playing their first conference game. They had played only two games -- beating Pittsburgh and tying Purdue. They had not played in two weeks and so they were well rested and well prepared to battle the Huskies. UCLA featured Bill Kilmer, the triple threat tailback in the Bruins' single-wing offense. He had excellent receivers including Jim Johnson, the brother of Bruin alumnus Rafer Johnson, the 1960 Olympic gold medalist in the decathlon.

In a mid-week newspaper column, the columnist compared Kilmer and another triple threat star, the Huskies' Schloredt. He felt Schloredt seemed to excel over Kilmer on defense. The Husky All-American was a "bruising tackler. He can smell a forward pass coming."

Another article on Schloredt during the week was entitled "Schloredt Relishes Bruising Grid Combat." He impressed the coaches and players as a blacksmith type of player who couldn't be intimidated. Schloredt was reported to be most articulate and most at ease when discussing the joys of combat. "There's an art to being aggressive. We call it 'head hunting' or 'hunting with the helmet.' The idea is that if you can soften the other guy up, he'll be thinking about you."

Sometimes in football as in war, you lose a skirmish but later win the battle. Before over 54,000 spectators, whose emotions, during the game, ranged from complete enchantment to gut-wrenching misery, Washington's battered band of brothers defeated UCLA 10-8.

The first period was scoreless. In the second quarter, Schloredt was injured when he went head hunting. He took aim at UCLA's Earl Smith as Kilmer's pass fell off the Bruin's finger tips. Schloredt was more than a yard away at the moment. Wanting Smith "to remember me," he lowered his head and attempted to drive his helmet into Smith's chest. Schloredt flew past his mark, caught Smith's legs with a flying hip and toppled over on his side. His elbow struck the ground first, forcing his shoulder back and fracturing his collar bone. So Bob Hivner, who injured his finger in the opening game of the 1959 season, and was replaced by Schloredt, now had to carry the load. On his first offensive series, he directed a 53-yard drive to the Bruin 19. With time running out in the half, Fleming kicked a 38-yard field goal.

Schloredt was in tears on the sidelines not from pain but from bitter disappointment. Gone were the dreams of another All-America season and a possible Heisman Trophy and more importantly, gone was his chance to lead the Huskies to another Rose Bowl. He was out for the rest of his senior season. The only chance for him to play again was if the Huskies won the conference title and got the Rose Bowl bid. The Huskies made a commitment to get him there.

After Schloredt left the game in the second period, many of the players did not know about his injury. He had left the field without saying anything, just like any injured Husky would do. During half-time, all the players realized their warrior was gone for the battles to come. Owens was worried about the team letting down. McKeta had other thoughts. "(Schloredt) going down didn't affect me at all. We had Hivner. We had studs up front. Hivner could hand the ball off as well as anybody."

As the Huskies opened the second half, the coaches were not encouraged. After receiving the kickoff, Washington went three and out and Hivner punted only 29 yards to the Bruin 43 where a fair catch was called. Bill Barnes, the Bruins' head coach, had instructed his punt receivers to make fair catches on every Husky punt after he saw what Washington had done to the Stanford players who tried to run with punts.

After Kilmer kicked out of bounds on the Husky 19, Hivner mixed a ground game with a few short passes as he directed the Huskies to their only touchdown. Jackson went inside, Fleming, McKeta and Mitchell went outside, on an 81-yard assault which included a clutch pass to McKeta for 18. From the one, McKeta bulldozed his way through the enemy line to score. Fleming's kick put the Huskies ahead 10-0 with over five minutes gone in the third quarter.

The Bruins did not go into hibernation. They mounted three drives. The first ended early in the fourth quarter when Claridge snared Rob Smith for a four-yard loss on the Washington ten. After Hivner punted to the Bruin 45, Kilmer directed his forces down to the Husky seven. Enslow wrapped up Kilmer for a six-yard loss on one pass attempt. Kilmer's fourth down pitch into the end zone was far off target. Their third drive was successful but a little too late. Kilmer hit Johnson on a seven yard play to end a 71-yard march. The two-point conversion brought the Bruins within two with less than two minutes to go. UCLA tried a short kick which McKasson brought back five yards to his own 41. The Huskies ran out the clock and off the field with a 10-8 victory.

The Huskies next traveled to Multnomah Stadium in Portland to face the 18th-ranked Oregon State Beavers. The Washington injury list was getting longer with several key starters out. Some of the members of the alternate unit now were starters -- Claridge, Chapple, Hurworth, Phillips, and Enslow across the front. Only two starting linemen -- McKasson and Meyers -- were starters in the 1960 Rose Bowl, an event that seemed so long ago. Allen, Bullard, Gegner, Kinnune and Schloredt were out.

Now McKeta was concerned. "There were guys in the line who went down that I thought would make a difference. You had younger, less experienced guys coming in and we didn't know if they were up to it. But they played like men." Tipps appealed to the injured linemen's inner strength and desire. "You guys have to get well. We cannot finish this season with all of you on the sideline." Because of the number of injuries, Owens planned to send in individual substitutes rather an entire unit. He was trying to keep a nucleus of battle-tested players in the game at all times.

Against Oregon State, the Huskies needed all their courage, determination, guts, and physical toughness. They battled to a 30-29 victory in one of the greatest comebacks in Husky history.

Sophomore Terry Baker, the Beavers' tailback in Coach Tommy Prothro's single-wing formation, scored twice in the first period. His two-point pass attempts failed -- plays that would loom large at the end --and the Huskies trailed 12-0. Baker, showing the brilliance that would earn him the Heisman Trophy in 1962 -- the first awarded to a West Coast player -- set an Oregon State single-game record of 302 total yards.

The Huskies retaliated in the second quarter when Fleming sped 38 yards through a lane formed by his blockers for a touchdown. His perfect kick followed. Oregon State matched that and then some before the intermission. Three points came on a 19-yard field goal; seven came at the end of a 79-yard drive. Baker accounted for almost all of the yards with his running and passing.

At half-time, Mitchell remembers one of the coaches saying, "You completely embarrassed us. You knocked on their dressing room door on the way out to start the game, you challenged them and then you go out and play like wimps."

Mitchell got the message. He returned the kickoff 34 yards. He finished the job on a trap play that gave him room to speed past the Beaver secondary with little more than three minutes gone. The situation called for a two-point attempt to get the Huskies within seven. After a delay-of-game penalty, Hivner set up and found McKeta for the critical two points.

The Huskies gave all of the margin right back several minutes later. Another sophomore, Bob Monroe, coughed the football up and Oregon State took over on the Husky 25. Baker took the Beavers most of the way with Bill Monk scoring from three yards out. The kick was good and the Corvalis crew led 29-15.

With thirty seconds remaining in the third stanza, Washington pulled within six after an 80-yard drive capped off by Fleming's 12-yard scamper. Owens again elected to go for two. This time Hivner hit Folkins for two and Washington trailed 29-23 at the close of the third quarter.

McKeta shut off another Beaver march by intercepting Baker's pass and returning it to the Husky 38. "Baker was rolling out to his left. I am looking and there is no receiver out over on my side -- the left side of the secondary. I see a receiver across the field and I knew Baker was going to throw him the ball," McKeta said. "Vacating my position, I come way across the field and intercept the ball. I ran into Baker, otherwise I would have scored. When they graded the film, I got three errors for leaving my area of responsibility. If they would have scored on that drive, we would have been beat."

After a change of possession, Washington started its last drive at the Husky 36 with less than nine minutes left. Calm and cool, Hivner called a marvelous mix of plays including his own rollout run into the end zone on third and one. One of the key plays was Mitchell's 13-yard sweep around left end down to the Beavers nine. "As I was spinning for extra yards, I got hit in the back and head. I suffered a concussion. I didn't even know who won the game. I stayed overnight in Portland for observations." Two years later in his senior season, Mitchell got cracked ribs in the Oregon game in Multnomah Stadium. He was happy to be done playing in that place.

With the score tied, thousands of Husky fans who had journeyed to Portland, crossed their fingers, held their loved ones and anybody else within reach, and took deep breaths as Fleming zeroed in and kicked Washington's 30th point. Fleming then squelched the Beavers' hopes by stealing Baker's last gasp throw and returning it to the Washington 48.

And so ended a saga of blood, sweat, tears, and triumph. During the Huskies winning drive, they were waging a war of attrition. At one point, three Beavers were prostrate. They wearily pulled themselves to their feet in a vain effort to meet the desperate Washington charge. Owens was proud of his players. "A team has to be great to come back like my team did today. The boys kept their poise. We just seemed to know we could pull it out."

The game provided an interesting contrast in coaching styles. Coach Prothro sat in the coaches' box. He quarterbacked his team by remote control 100 feet above the field. "You can see the patterns much better up here. The bench is an awful place to watch a game from." A dangling participle aside, Prothro wasn't able to give a deserving player a pat on the back or offer words of encouragement. Owens was with his troops and let Hivner make most of the decisions, especially in the second half. The new "wild card" substitution rule that went into effect in 1960 gave coaches the ability to send in all the plays with a substitute player.

The rule change substantially permitted players to enter and leave the game at will. Free substitution would come in 1965 when offensive and defensive platoons could be employed. Owens preferred to have his quarterbacks make the calls and thought college football should be contested with players going both ways.

During the next week, several Huskies suffered from food poisoning. Three regulars -- Chapple, Hurworth, and Phillips -- were hospitalized. "It was an odd one," said Owens. "(Some of the) ones who got sick played the same spots as the ones we had injured. Hurworth was playing in place of the injured Chuck Allen at weak guard; Chapple for Kurt Gegner at weak tackle; and Phillips for Bill Kinnune at strong guard. But each of them played about half the game."

Ben Davidson also had a touch of something because during one of the practices, he suffered diarrhea. The team was practicing outside in white thin practice pants. "I asked Tipps if I could go to the rest room and he said, 'NO.' " So Davidson flushed in his pants. Jorgensen, who was the quarterback of the unit on which Davidson was playing in a scrimmage, said it was awful. "The smell was a lot worse than from the Montlake garbage dump." Davidson finally left the field with his pants a different color. "I found in that situation, that I had a pretty good advantage blocking because everybody shied away from me." Some of the players were not at all amused by the situation. They wondered "How could a coach order someone in Ben's condition to stay on the field?"

On October 29, the five and one Ducks came to Seattle for another slugfest. Senior quarterback Dave Grosz was again at the helm of the Oregon offense. Unlike the Husky quarterbacks, he went to the sidelines on defense to talk with the coaches upstairs and to get a breather. The Ducks were focused on avenging the 13-12 loss in 1959 that took them out of the Rose Bowl race. The Oregon seniors had never beaten Washington. Oregon end Dale Herron summed up the players' feelings. "I'm getting tired hearing about last year's Washington team. I think our team is really ready for this one."

After more than 57 minutes, the Ducks were leading the Huskies 6-0. Oregon had scored in the third quarter when Bruce Snyder, who would later coach at California and Arizona State, reached the end zone on a five-yard run. The Ducks failed to make the extra point attempt but got another chance when the Huskies were offside. The second kick was batted down by Mansfield, the sophomore playing like a veteran, who climbed the backs of interior linemen to swat the ball away.

Don McKeta turns up the field after taking a pitchout from Bob Hivner in the 1960 Oregon Game. McKeta is only the second player in Husky history to twice – 1959 and 1960 – receive the Flaherty Award as the team's most inspirational player. He is the only player in Husky history to twice co-captain Washington teams in the Rose Bowl.

Photo Credit: University of Washington Athletic Communications Department / Collegiate Images.

Late in the fourth quarter, Oregon reached the Husky 20. On third and four, Hivner picked off a deflected pass on the Washington five. And then the "Cardiac Kids" took over. After picking up three first downs, the Huskies faced a fourth and six on the Oregon 47. With less than three minutes to go, the Huskies elected to go for the first down. Hivner threw a short pass to McKeta. Slanting toward the north sideline, the Huskies' spiritual leader appeared to be heading out of bounds. At least that is what Oregon defender, Dave Grayson, and most everyone watching thought. But McKeta had no intention of running out of bounds on his own.

His resolve was born of the UCLA game when he felt he did not give enough effort after being tackled on a critical play. So when he caught Hivner's pass, he thought only of driving upfield or being knocked out of bounds. "I was lucky. I was ready to go out of bounds if Grayson had come after me. I saw I had a step on him and so I turned the corner and ran...I thought sure I would be caught from behind." He wasn't. As McKeta crossed the goal line, he had a great big grin. Georg Meyers, a noted sports writer for the Seattle Times, asked him in the post game interview, " I know you were happy but what was the big grin for?" McKeta, with another big smile, replied, "As I cut back to go up the sidelines, I heard Grayson say 'Oh, shit.' "

With the game again depending on his toe, Fleming kicked the ball squarely between the uprights. He gave a little jump for joy as he heard the thunderous salvo of cheers, picked up by the late October breeze, echo through the stadium and over Lake Washington.

McKeta's touchdown catch and run would go down as one the greatest plays in Washington history. Clearly in sight to any one visiting the Husky equipment room, there was a blazing sign which read: "We issue everything here but guts." Again, the Huskies had supplied the guts.

Oregon coach Len Casanova felt otherwise. "What a way to lose a ball game. Imagine, fourth and six and they burn us on one play. We had them on the run and had played them into the ground. How lucky can you get?" Hivner had another explanation. "I somehow felt we could do it. You feel that way around here, or you don't play for Jim Owens."

The key to success in any conference race is what a team does in November. Two conference games remained plus the final one with Washington State. No game was bigger that the Huskies battle with the Trojans. Both stood on top of the Big Five standings.

At the Sunday coaches' meeting, assistant coach Bert Clark gave his scouting report on Southern California. He said that USC is "the best team from the standpoint of physical bulk and experience that Washington will play all season. They are as strong as any team in the country." Stanford Coach Jack Curtice proclaimed, "USC will beat Washington easily."

The Huskies traveled to the Los Angeles Coliseum at almost full strength. Allen, Gegner, and Kinnune had returned as starters. Bullard would be ready for limited play, but not without some help from the trainers and pain killers. Owens vowed that the Huskies would play much better football in the last three games of the season. They would have to be ready to handle the largest linemen and backs in the conference. The USC line averaged 227 pounds, about ten pounds more than the Husky front seven; the Trojans' backs were also ten pounds heavier than the Husky backfield.

Under skies that cried a river, the Huskies took to the mud and rain and crushed the heralded Trojans 34-0. The blowout was a body blow to USC's hope for a Rose Bowl bid. Scoring twice in the first four minutes, the Huskies played tough defense against the Trojan's unimaginative attack and took a 14-0 lead into the intermission. Then, Washington's offensive pressure sent USC reeling and staggering as the Huskies added 20 second half points.

Fleming scored 16 points on a 65-yard punt return, two field goals, and four conversions. Jackson added two touchdowns and rushed for 80 yards. McKasson led the brisk blocking up front and the unrelenting pressure on defense. The Huskies outrushed the Trojans 265 to 89.

It was the greatest margin of victory for the Huskies in the history of their series with USC, which dated back to 1923. The Huskies climbed to sixth in the polls. Minnesota rose to the top spot after mauling Iowa 27-10. The Hawkeyes were number one the week before.

Over 200 boosters waited at Sea-Tac to welcome the victorious Huskies back. Clearly the team and coaches were overwhelmed by the reception. They remembered that a few years ago, they would have been mistaken for a gang of baggage handlers.

California was next. The Bears' first-year head coach was Marv Levy. He would eventually coach the Buffalo Bulls (1986-1997) to six eastern division titles and four Super Bowl appearances.

Practices during the week were crisp and sometimes light hearted. Fleming was feeling proud of himself for his outstanding performance in the USC game. Barry Bullard recalls that in a good natured way "he was strutting around and telling everybody how good he was. Well, the linemen got together and decided to lie down on the next play. We did. None of the offensive linemen blocked anybody." The defense came screaming in and Fleming started around left end and was cut off. He darted right and was cut off again. He kept going sideline to sideline and backwards until he was tackled.

Coach Walker, who was observing the whole scene, came up to Fleming and said in his melodic Texas drawl, "George, when you get the ball, you put it under your arm and run down yonder." As Fleming was panting -- he was just worn out with all the running -- Walker continued. "You don't run hither and yon, you don't run back and forth, you put the ball in your arm and go down yonder." After Walker's observations on the art of running with a football, Fleming, still huffing and puffing after running hither and yon for about 50 yards, looked at Walker and said, "Tell me, Coach, did you see my yardage?"

The Huskies were healthy again. Even Schloredt suited up for the first time since his injury in the UCLA game. The Washington fans cheered loudly as he sent booming punts far down the field in pre-game warm-ups. It would be the last home game for 20 seniors -- players who had given Husky fans some of the greatest gridiron moments they had ever seen.

The Huskies sent the Homecoming crowd home with rosy thoughts. They beat California 27-7. The game ran according to the script. Two long scoring drives and another keyed by McKasson's interception and his 38-yard run to the Bear four, helped put the Huskies up 27-0. Cal scored late in the fourth quarter. The crowd loved every minute. For once, it was a nice comfortable afternoon for the cardiacs in the crowd.

With a nostalgic sigh, almost 56,000 watched the conquerors disappear into the tunnel. The Husky thankful bid farewell to the seniors after singing the school's Alma Mater and its final ringing refrain "All Hail! Oh Washington!"

With a perfect conference record and a season sweep of the California schools -- the first time in Husky football history -- there was little doubt that Washington was going to have a repeat appearance in Pasadena. Particularly pleased was Schloredt. He flexed his mended shoulder and promised he'd be ready for the Rose Bowl. "There's no cast, no bandage -- there's nothing on it but imagination."

Kinnune, the great Husky guard, said he couldn't make up his mind "whether to be happy or sad. We have had four great years together here." McKeta, his teammate for three years, echoed

Kinnune's sentiments. "It's almost the end of the line. They've been a perfect three years, playing under the greatest bunch of coaches you ever saw." Finally, Owens talked about his seniors, "They were the kids who started with us, and there'll always be a special place for them. They had a lot of faith in the coaching staff, and they stayed with us when things were bad."

Although it was pretty clear that Washington would be in the Rose Bowl, it was not clear who would be its opponent. The Big Five conference was no longer bound to pick only the Big Ten winner but could select any team in the land. The conference representatives already had agreed not to extend an invitation to an opponent until after the Army-Navy game on November 26, a week after most teams had ended their seasons. The Husky powers wanted another shot at Navy if they beat Army.

As always, Owens and his players were focused on the next and last game of the regular season -- this one with archrival Washington State in Spokane's Memorial Stadium. The Cougars featured quarterback Mel Melin, who led the nation in total offense, and sophomore receiver Hugh Campbell. He was nearing national records for both receptions and receiving yardage. Washington State had the best passing game in the nation. Washington's weakness during the year was pass defense. They had yielded more passing yards per game -- 154.3 -- than any major college team.

Before about 29,000 fans braving a very chilly day made colder by a bitter south wind, the Huskies returned to their heart pounding ways. Shades of night were falling as Owens' invincibles reached way down once again and won by a whisker. The first three periods were scoreless. On a field strewn with sawdust to temper the muddy spots, the Cougars jammed the middle to combat Washington's traps and forced the Huskies outside. They trusted the soggy field to slow Fleming and Mitchell. The Huskies' line and secondary tried to defend the Cougars' aerial game.

The Huskies fumbled six times and lost two. Washington gave up 188 yards in the air and only 92 on the terrible turf. Campbell broke the national records and scored the Cougars' touchdown.

Washington threatened in the second period when they drove 38 yards to the Cougar ten. On fourth down, Fleming's kick was wide. In the third period after the Cougars punt rolled dead on the Husky eight, Jackson fumbled and State recovered on the five. Then, Melin carried the ball three times and lost one yard in his attempts. He then tried a field goal from the 13 but the kick went awry. The Huskies then marched almost 80 yards and were stopped just inches short of the goal. After the Cougars kicked out of danger, the Huskies put themselves in another mud-filled hole. Hivner's pass was intercepted by Cougar center, Denny Martin, who returned it to the Washington 31. Nine plays later and with four seconds gone in the fourth period, Campbell dropped to his knees to craddle a pass in the end zone. Melin's kick found the mark and now it was up to the Huskies.

Early in the second period, McKeta suffered a gaping gash in his right leg. The players were wearing mud cleats which were about an inch and a half long. At the end of the cleat was a piece of metal that capped the rubber cleat. It had a very sharp tip. That tip on the cleat of one of the Cougar tacklers ripped into McKeta's leg. He collapsed in pain as he was trying to walk off the field to the locker room. Two Husky reserves had to lift the Washington warrior and pack him off. With ten stitches in a leg wrapped with bandages, McKeta came back for the second half. All he did was to lead all ground gainers with 56 yards -- 67 for the game -- and display once again his courage and commitment to play from the heart.

None of his yards were more important than on Washington's scoring drive. It started with Mitchell receiving the kickoff and galloping for 38 yards before Bylan's touchdown saving tackle knocked the speedy sophomore down on the Cougar 47. With

Kermit Jorgensen at the helm, the Husky ship moved slowly down the watery passage. Except for a six-yard toss to McKeta for a first down on the 25, the remaining 15 plays were all just straight ahead tests of strength and conditioning and an incredible will-to-win. Jones, Jorgensen, McKeta, and Mitchell repeatedly mushed over the tackles and wings to the Cougar 11.

On one of McKeta's carries, he ran over the strong guard, a position being played by Tim Bullard. "I was lying on the ground looking up at McKeta. He was dripping his sweat all over my face, and with a great big grin on his face, he said, 'Goddam, Tim, you never could block like your brother Barry.' "

From the 11, Jorgensen went back to pass and then cut back over the middle for nine yards. On the next play, the Renton redhead dropped the ball while trying to stuff it in Jones' belly but recovered on the three. Jones clutched the ball on the next play and dove over right guard to within inches to set up Jorgensen's sneak. Washington was now within one.

No Husky fan doubted that Owens would go for two. The crowd stood tensely under the arc lights in dwindling daylight as Hivner came in to execute a short version of the Utah special. McKeta forgot about the pain and pressure and slid off the left side and was all alone as he tucked Hivner's pass safely into his chest for the 8-7 lead.

But the Cougars were not dead. They still had almost eight minutes to score. They stormed across midfield only to have McKasson pick off a Melin pitch on the 24. He returned it 20 yards. The Huskies punted the ball after three downs and the Cougars started what they hoped would be the game winning drive. The series featured the passing of Melin and the defensive resolve of the Huskies. Melin to Campbell for 14, to Kerrone for 22 down to the Husky 47, and to Campbell to the 29. After Merlin hit West for five yards, Kinnune rose up and hammered the

Cougar field general for a four-yard loss. The Cougars had time for only one play. Melin set up for a field goal attempt. Ray Jackson at 5'9", one of the smallest men on the field but one with the greatest resolve, rose up to slap the kick away.

Keith Jackson was in a hurry to interview the coaches. "I did the broadcast by myself on a local basis. I had no help and no bathroom. I was drinking coffee because it was so damn cold. I did the first interview in the men's room."

The Husky locker room was subdued. The coaches and players knew they had played in a very tough game and had high praise for their in-state rival. With another late winning drive down Cardiac Canyon, Coach Tipps couldn't take much more. "This team will be the death of me yet. We had it when we needed it. Just like we have all year." Owens felt the season had been more satisfying than the year before. "We were under more of a handicap this year. Every school was pointing for us, particularly the schools from the Northwest." The margin of victory in each of those three games was one point.

Allen felt the Huskies' will-to-win and toughness got them through the close games. Davidson reflected on the several come-from-behind victories. "Even though we were down in the fourth quarter in those games, you say to yourself, 'This isn't a big deal. Somebody, somewhere, somehow is going to do something to pull this game out.' And, sure enough, it happens." Schloredt thanked everyone for giving him a chance to play in one more game. "I'll be ready to go on January 2."

McKeta, gingerly stepping on his injured leg, was among the last to reach the shower room. His heavily taped leg was mute evidence of the rage of battle. This courageous Husky, who seemed to thrive in the toughest moments of the mayhem of football, finally emerged to get dressed. "Does it hurt?" inquired a well-wisher who had wondered into the locker room. "Nothing hurts now," McKeta said quietly, "Nothing."

CHAPTER 10

National Champions

The final Associated Press and United Press International regular season polls crowned Minnesota as the national champions. The Gophers were followed by Mississippi, Iowa, Navy, Missouri, and Washington. Arkansas, Ohio State, Alabama, and Duke rounded out the top ten in the Associated Press poll. Washington finished fifth in the UPI poll behind Minnesota, Iowa, Mississippi, and Missouri. Both polls were taken *before* the bowl games were played.

None of the top teams had an unblemished record. Minnesota (8-1-0) lost to Purdue (4-4-1) and trounced then number one Iowa 27-10 in early November. Mississippi (9-0-1) tied LSU (5-4-1) in late October. Iowa (8-1-0) lost to Minnesota. By beating Army 17-12 on November 26, Navy finished its regular season 9-1-0, losing to Duke 19-10 in early November. Missouri (9-1-0) lost to Kansas 23-7 in its next to last game of the season.

The Middies' Joe Bellino, who had become an American football folk hero, won the Heisman Trophy. His vote margin over second place Tom Brown, Minnesota's guard, was one of the biggest in Heisman history. Brown was selected as the top lineman in the nation besting Pittsburgh's Mike Ditka. Others receiving votes included Washington's Chuck Allen and Roy McKasson.

Because the Big Five conference could pick any opponent in the land, there was quite a bit of discussion about who that opponent should be. Washington players had different opinions. Some wanted to play Navy because they felt the Midshipmen had lucked out with the last second field goal to beat them. Others felt the Big Ten conference was the strongest in the country and wanted to play Minnesota.

All the discussion ended on November 22, when Minnesota was given the invitation to face Washington in the 47th Rose Bowl, to be played on January 2, 1961. It would be the Gophers' first appearance in Pasadena. The invitation was extended after the school's faculty-controlled senate, called to meet by Minnesota President Meredith Wilson, accepted a recommendation by its Intercollegiate Athletic Committee to go to the Rose Bowl if invited.

Minnesota was one of the leading opponents of the Big Ten Rose Bowl pact which expired in 1959 after a 14-year run. A year later, The Big Ten was deadlocked 5-5 on the renewal of the agreement but allowed individual schools to play in bowl games if invited and if the school so chose.

With their opponent set, the Huskies could focus their attention on preparing for the game. Meanwhile, post-season honors came in bunches for Husky players. Six were selected to the all-conference team -- Chuck Allen, Roy McKasson, and Don McKeta were unanimous choices and George Fleming, Kurt Gegner and Ray Jackson rounded out the first team. Pat Claridge, Bill Kinnune, and Charlie Mitchell were named to the second team. Allen, McKasson, and McKeta were selected to the AP's All-Coast team with Claridge, Fleming, and Gegner on the second unit. Allen, Fleming, Gegner, and McKasson were selected to the UPI's All-Coast team.

McKasson earned first team All-America honors from the Associated Press and Look Magazine. Look's team was chosen by the Football Writers' Association. Gegner was selected by ABC's TV Game of the Week sportscasters to their All-America team.

Husky Center Roy McKasson earned first team All-America honors from the Associated Press and the Football Writers Association in 1960.
Photo Credit: University of Washington Athletic Communications Department / Collegiate Images.

McKasson's choice was a popular one with everybody. Jerry Austin, McKasson's, coach at Clover Park High School, said, "Roy is a tremendous competitor. He has desire and qualities of leadership. He's clean cut and religious. I'm very happy for him."

Happier still were the coaches. Owens, speaking for all the coaches, heaped on the praise. "Pound for pound, he's a real top notch football player. He's not as big as college linemen go -- especially a center. But he makes up for it by constantly trying to improve." He would go on to say, "He's a smart player. His defensive quarterbacking has been fine. And he proved this season that he can carry an extra load, staying in there when others were hurt. Roy is a fine stabilizing influence."

Washington had the most representation of any team in the nation on the AP's's All-America teams. In addition to McKasson's first team selection, six teammates received honorable mention -- Allen, Claridge, Fleming, Gegner, McKeta, and Schloredt.

Barry Bullard received the National Football Foundation's Scholar Athlete Award and Bob Hivner was picked on the Academic All-America team.

Schloredt was honored by Navy as the most outstanding player they faced during the entire season. Fleming, Gegner, and McKasson were also chosen to the Middies' all-opponents team. Seven Huskies were selected for post-season games. Hivner and McKeta accepted bids to play for the North in the Senior Bowl in Mobile Alabama on January 7. Allen, Fleming, Gegner, McKasson, and Schloredt were chosen to play in the Hula Bowl in Honolulu on January 8.

They would be familiar with the West team's system. Its head coach would be Jim Owens. UPI selected Owens as the West Coast Coach of the Year. The American Football Coaches Association picked the Husky head man as the runner-up for National Coach of the year. Minnesota's Murray Warmath was the top selection.

Twenty Washington seniors were feted at the team's banquet. McKasson and McKeta were chosen to lead the Huskies in the Rose Bowl. For McKeta, it was the second year in a row that he had received the honor. He is the only man in Husky history to be a two-time Rose Bowl captain. Also for the second time, he received the Flaherty Award as the team's most inspirational player. He is only the second player in Husky history to receive the award two times. Coach Chesty Walker described McKeta as " a man who would charge hell with a bucket of water." The Brian Stapp award

205

was presented to quarterback Jim Everett as the most outstanding non-letter winner. Joe Bellino received the most votes on the Huskies all-opponents team.

The play of the seniors and their teammates contributed significantly to the size of the crowds during the regular season. For the first time, Washington had a higher total attendance than any of the California schools. The Huskies also led all the schools in the old Pacific Coast Conference. They attracted 429,258 total fans in their nine regular season games and averaged 49,450 for their six home games.

The other major bowl games were set. Number seven Arkansas would face tenth-ranked Duke in the Cotton Bowl. The Sugar Bowl would match number two Mississippi against unranked and twice beaten Rice. Navy would go after fifth-ranked Missouri in the Orange Bowl. Two of the major polls -- The Helms Foundation and the Football Writers' Association -- would choose a national champion after the bowl games were over.

Washington would face a much tougher opponent than Wisconsin in this Rose Bowl. Minnesota had a grinding mobile line that averaged 223 pounds, almost 20 more than the Husky front wall. The hub of the line was 243-pound Tom Brown who was acclaimed as the best interior lineman in all of the land. He received not only a fist full of national awards but also was crowned the Big Ten's Most Valuable Player. He was only the eighth lineman to receive the award in its 37-year history.

At 24, Brown was a very seasoned player. He interrupted his career at Minnesota to serve three years in the Navy. During the hitch, he played at the Great Lakes Naval Training Station near Chicago. Often, he knocked helmets with professional players, past and future, on other service teams. He was eligible for the professional draft after his sophomore year. The Baltimore Colts selected him in an early round but he elected to stay at Minnesota and complete his collegiate career.

Other heavy weights included sophomore Bobby Bell (6'4" 220), senior tackle Frank Brixius (6'4" 250) and senior center Greg Larson (6'2" 220). Junior quarterback Sandy Stephens (6'0" 215), one of the few black quarterbacks in college football, spearheaded the Gopher offense along with running backs who hit with authority. The Gophers had not failed to score when they were inside their opponents' 20-yard line all season. Their defensive play had led to more than half of their touchdowns by creating turnovers that gave them good field position. It was, in essence, a defensive team with a fullback-oriented offense.

Minnesota's defense shut out four of its nine opponents. All-American's Brown and McKasson would face off in the middle of the scrum. Brown had stormed and stomped over rival linemen all season leaving havoc in his wake. As Coach Owens viewed the films of Minnesota games, he whistled softly as he watched Brown wrecking the Iowa line. McKasson would have a very tough challenge.

The two teams matched up pretty well. Minnesota scored 221 points in nine games to Washington's 255 in ten games. Minnesota gave up 71 points, Washington 100. The Gophers big scoring quarter was the fourth -- 86 points to the Huskies' 51. One of the major differences was in the punting game. Washington allowed 3.75 yards per punt return to Minnesota's eight-yard average.

As in 1959, Owens gave the players about two weeks off to prepare for and take the quarter's final examinations. All players continued to work out on their own in order to be ready to resume team workouts in California. Owens again chose Long Beach as Husky headquarters. They would stay at the now familiar Lafayette Hotel and would practice at Long Beach City College. The city was very pleased to host Washington a second time.

The Huskies took off for Long Beach on Saturday, December 17 after a rousing rally at Sea-Tac Airport. They received a warm welcome in the California city by the sea. The coaches and players were greeted by Mayor Edward Wade, Tournament of Roses officials, and Rose Queen Carole Washburn and her court. Among the greeters were Washington's former athletic director, George Briggs, and his wife Beth. He was now a banking executive in the Los Angeles area.

The next day, the Huskies had their first workout at Veteran's Stadium, the home of the Long Beach College team, which a week earlier had won the Junior Rose Bowl championship. The workout schedule was set to prepare the Huskies for battle. Initially, the practices would put the linemen through contact drills, focus on punting drills and have the backs participate in speed and agility drills and ball handling. Except for the second day -- Monday December 19 -- which consisted of meetings with the press and a tour of Disneyland and a dinner with both teams present, the focus would be on combat. Two-a-days would resume on the 20th and continue through the day before Christmas. In the week leading up to the game, the Huskies would sharpen their defensive and offensive schemes and peak for the contest.

When the teams met in Disneyland, Jim Skaggs was asked by one of the Gophers, "I notice that most of your players have a healed-over cut on their foreheads. What's it from?" Skaggs explained that their coaches taught them to strike the first blow with their heads. "The repeated impact drives down the rim of the helmet and makes a sore spot which never heals." The Minnesota players, brows unmarred, stood in awe after the reply.

The Huskies were healthy. Schloredt was running with the second team and going through punting drills with Hivner. Owens said, "defense would come first in the Huskies' preparation. We've got to figure out a way to stop Minnesota and then see if our kids can handle it ...We have to make some changes," he explained. "Then we'll go ahead strong with our offense."

Similar preparation was taking place at East Los Angeles College. The Gophers, staying at the Huntington Hotel, were seemingly more focused than Wisconsin was in its game preparation a year earlier. It was clear in their drills that they were preparing to fight a war in Pasadena. They focused on short passes, running behind their big linemen up through the guards and tackles, and option sweeps.

After going through the regular season with a succession of injuries, the Huskies were feeling hale and hearty until two days before Christmas. That day, Joe Jones had his appendix removed. "They had Washington State apples in the hotel lobby. I just loved those apples. I had about three the day before. About 2 AM in the morning, I started complaining. I thought the apples were causing a reaction. Charlie Mitchell, my roommate, said, 'Shut up man, I got to get my sleep.' This went on for about an hour. Finally, we called Dr. Geehan (the team physician). He came in and checked me out. He said I had appendicitis. They rushed me out to the Long Beach Hospital and Dr. Neibling performed the operation." Neibling told Jones he might be on his feet in 24 hours and could watch from the sidelines during the Rose Bowl. Jones had other ideas. The fullback learned his ability was worth something. Hearing of Jones appendectomy, the odds makers increased the point spread from six-and-a-half to seven.

The loss of Jones shook the coaches and players. As a backup to Jackson, the senior fullback and outstanding linebacker saw considerable playing time during the season.

Owens voiced concern about filling the hole left by Jones' condition, especially on defense. The potential backups, Lee Bernhardi and Ron Quincy, had a total of 48 minutes of action during the 1960 season. Owens would also turn to sophomore Bob Monroe to shore up the fullback situation.

The coaches believed that one of the keys to winning the game was McKasson's ability to neutralize Brown, and the ability of other

Husky centers as well. The preparation began on picture day. The centers had board drills. Dick Dunn remembers that "they put the biggest guys on the team -- John Meyers and Ben Davidson -- at one end of the board and the centers and the quarterbacks on the other. We (McKasson, Norm Dicks, and Dunn) immediately started snapping the ball and the monsters at the other end began hitting us to see who was ready to block Tom Brown." Dunn continued. "The idea of the board was you couldn't let your feet come together. From a straddle position, you would snap the ball, make contact, and keep your feet driving without coming on the board."

During the practices that followed, the preparation for Brown would continue. Tackle Barry Bullard was fascinated by the coaching. "Tom Brown would always play toward the strong side of the offensive line. McKasson had to block him. Brown outweighed him by about 40 pounds. To block Brown, the coaches instructed Roy to crawl between his legs. After he snapped the ball, he would get down on all fours and crawl between Brown's legs. That cut down his lateral movement." Dunn would add, "In the first team meeting, the coaches showed us Minnesota game films. In one game, Brown delivered a blow to the opponent's center. The center goes backward into the quarterback who goes backward into the fullback who is supposed to get the hand-off. All three end up in a heap. They kept running that part of the film back and forth, saying, 'The guy is a monster.' If Brown could stand you up, you were in deep trouble. So the blocking scheme was to keep low and get between his legs -- not too low or he jumps over you."

Halfback Brent Wooten even paid attention to what was happening to the centers. "There never was a time in practices when the center didn't snap the ball that he didn't have guys just whacking him over the head."

The coaches also played mind games with the centers. Writers covering the Huskies reported that McKasson gave up his purple jersey in one practice because of sloppy tackling. "That was not true. Hell, they just wanted all the centers ready," Dunn said.

As Christmas Day approached, the wives of the coaches and players arrived and the holiday spirit was evident. As the players arrived at the December 24 practice, they greeted the coaches with "Merry Christmas." Ten minutes later, the coaches' greetings were not so merry. "All right, girls, suck in your guts and get in there."

As the Huskies entered the last week of practice, the coaches turned to blocking and tackling technique drills. Owens believed that when a team is outweighed more than 20 pounds to the man, "then the lighter team's major hope for victory would depend on its technical skills." Claridge remembers, "There was an exactness in our blocking and tackling. Also, we were doing it for our buddies, we were playing for each other, for the team."

Owens firmly believed that getting through, over, and around Minnesota's tough defense had to be the focus of the remaining practices. They noted in scouting reports that Minnesota liked to crash their defensive ends. So, they introduced the "Red Eye" formation. With a balanced line, they split both ends wide. The two wingbacks set up in the slots between the tackles and split ends. Only the fullback was stationed directly behind the quarterback. The wingbacks and the ends could cut off the crashes of the Gopher's defensive ends.

Another feature of the new offensive scheme was to send the slot backs in motion on wider sweeps toward the sidelines. On this variation, the weak side end would go deep, giving the Husky passers an option of throwing to the man who got loose -- either the end or the man in motion. The third variation was the quarterback option. If the defensive ends continued to crash, then the field generals would slide along the line of scrimmage, fake to the fullback, and dart forward past the end.

The overall purpose of the plan was to keep Minnesota guessing, to keep the Gophers worried about Husky runners getting outside. "We wanted to make them worry about covering the whole field," Owens stated.

The coaches also showed a new defensive alignment. Normally, Washington played a four-man front with four linebackers and three defensive backs. They started the game in a five-man front with three linebackers. The front wall was anchored by Dave Enslow in the center flanked by Kinnune and Claridge on one side and Gegner and Stan Chapple on the other. Allen lined up as the middle linebacker and Jackson and McKasson were at the corners. The 5-3 defense was designed to stop the fullbacks from running up the interior and to stuff the counter plays.

As the game neared, McKeta felt that Minnesota was going to be much tougher than Wisconsin. "We knew they were not going to lose their poise. They've been too great a fourth quarter team for that to happen." He also reaffirmed a vow that Washington would not be beaten physically on January 2. "We have a team with tremendous morale and a tough conditioned one. We'll be ready." He finished with this. "We'd like to get George Fleming loose a few times. It would help offset some of that grinding offensive power that Minnesota is going to hit us with."

Minnesota was very aware of Fleming's game breaking potential, especially on punt returns. "Go get Fleming," Warmath yelled in practice as his Gopher defenders thundered down field on punt coverage. "Run, run, run. You've got to keep running to beat Washington."

Minnesota was also interested in the condition of McKeta. He had played many of the 600 minutes of the season despite injuries. His right leg, seriously injured in the Washington State game, was still bothering him. It was reported that he was a doubtful starter. If he could not start, Minnesota might prepare differently for the game. Sid Hartman, sports editor for the Minneapolis

Tribune, wanted to determine McKeta's condition. He called John
Thompson, who had assumed the role of Assistant to the Athletic
Director, and asked him if he could interview McKeta. With
Thompson's blessing, Hartman met with the Huskies' leader. He
asked to see McKeta's injured leg. The street smart warrior pulled
up the pant leg covering his *left* leg which had about a one inch scar
from another injury. McKeta told the columnist, "It is nothing."
Hartman walked off very disgruntled. In his newspaper report the
next day, Hartman reported that McKeta's leg had healed very
nicely and that he was ready to play.

Hivner and Schloredt would share the quarterbacking duties.
Hivner deserved to start. He had done a masterful job of guiding
the Huskies to six straight victories after Schloredt went out for the
season with an injury in the UCLA game. Hivner was poised under
pressure in engineering come-from-behind wins over Oregon State
and Oregon and hitting McKeta for the two point conversion in
the 8-7 thriller over the Cougars. During the regular season, he
completed 54.4 percent of his passes and led the Huskies in total
offense and passes intercepted.

At the Football Writers Association luncheon attended by the
coaches and representatives of the various media covering the Rose
Bowl, Owens discussed Schloredt's condition. "Schloredt is in the
middle of things again. Considering that he was away for two
months, he's doing very well. He shows improvement every day.
He's still a little rusty but he'll split equal time with Hivner." A
few days later, Owens reporter that Schloredt would see plenty of
action. "He has been coming back real fast, especially the last few
days, and he is in just about the form he had before his injury."

In addition to attracting attention as a player, Schloredt was
developing a relationship with Rose Bowl Queen and Pasadena
City College student, Carole Washburn. "It started in Marineland.
I was going into the area and Carole had just been interviewed and

had been separated from her court. We walked up a ramp going into some venue. We just talked." They sat together a few days later at a dinner that she and her princesses attended as guests of the Washington team. They met a few more times during the buildup to the Rose Bowl.

The intensity rose in practices on December 29. The practice gates were closed. The Huskies concentrated on stopping the Gophers' fullbacks up the middle and the quarterbacks running wide. They discounted Minnesota's passing game and hoped to contain the halfbacks. Joe Jones returned to practice to buoy the spirits of his band of brothers. He ran in sweat clothes hoping to get Dr. Geehan's approval to put on full armor in the last intensive practice.

On the day before the game, the Huskies bussed up to Pasadena to have a look at the empty Rose Bowl. Dressed in their blue blazers and gray slacks and rep ties, they walked up and down the green turf. Some climbed up the aisles in small groups and wandered amid the empty seats. Some climbed up the west side to the very last row and sat in the shade of the press box to see the perspective the media crews and sports columnists would have the next day.

During the tour of the field, backfield coach Chesty Walker herded all the ball-carriers into the end zone. As he did the previous year, he told each of the players to pluck a blade of grass and put it in his hip pocket. Harking back to the Wisconsin game, when five backs scored, he smiled and said, "That means you will score a touchdown."

▶ *The 1960 Husky team on its visit to the Rose Bowl the day before the 1961 game against Minnesota. This team was the first Washington football team to win a national championship.*

Photo Credit: From the personal collection of Dick Dunn, a member of that team.

Schloredt stayed down on the field squinting the length of the gridiron at the northern goal posts. "That's where we made out first touchdown against Wisconsin up there. And we made another up there in the third quarter." Finishing his reflections, he added, "I'm more nervous about this game than I was for Wisconsin. Minnesota's better than Wisconsin. You can see that in the movies. There's nothing complacent about this team."

Hivner was facing an additional challenge during his preparation for the Rose Bowl. His two-week old son, Robert Philip, had been on the "critical list" at Children's Orthopedic Hospital in Seattle. Although the baby boy was getting better, he was at the top of his father's mind.

Schloredt's counterpart felt things looked bright. Stephens, the 215-pound junior said, "We've had two real good practices in a row. Not a mistake. We'll be ready. We had a lot of diversions when we first got here, but now we're ready to play football."

McKeta had little doubt about the Huskies being ready. On December 31, he stated, "We're as ready now as we've ever going to be. At least, we're ready physically. Now we have to get ourselves ready mentally. That's the hardest part. There's nothing the coach can do about that. We've got to do it ourselves."

In its long history, the Rose Bowl probably had never been shaken by such passion from the stands. Nearly 30,000 Washington fans had assembled in the stands. Two hours before kickoff, 12,000 had filled the student section. Over 300 more students with tickets stood outside the bowl throughout the whole game, unable to crowd themselves into the tiers of seats. Cards had been prepared for the student section. The cards contained an array of colors. In addition to the school colors and nicknames, the cards would be arranged to produce pictures of the State of Washington, to promote the Century 21 Exposition (the 1962 Seattle World's Fair), and, presumably in a patriotic gesture, to advertise Series E Savings Bonds.

Across the field sat the Gophers' fans whose display of maroon and gold was so vast that it gave the impression that everyone was in the bowl to cheer for Minnesota. Their pom poms soon would fall listless as Washington got off to a fast start.

Both Minnesota and Washington fans had sent enormous messages to the teams a few days before the game. An eight-pound telegram roll containing some 15,000 signatures was presented to the Gophers. Western Union officials believed that it was the largest Rose Bowl telegram ever. The Huskies received a similar package containing over 10,000 signatures. Although the players couldn't read all the names, they were clearly appreciative of the fans' support.

McKasson and McKeta met the Gophers' center, Greg Larson, in the middle of the field. The Huskies won the coin flip and elected to receive. The conditions were warm and sunny with very little wind. The field was dry.

The Huskies' speedy running back, Charlie Mitchell, took the kickoff on his eight-yard line near the right sideline and cut initially up field. As he reached the 25, Mitchell raced diagonally to his left past and around defenders to the Washington 33.

Washington immediately went into the new Red Eye formation. McKasson started to execute his blocking tactics on Brown. McKeta gained eight over left tackle and then, breaking away from four Gopher tacklers, willed his way for another six over the same side and a first down. Kinnune remembers that he pulled out left from his right guard position to hit Bell, the Gophers' right tackle. "It was like hitting a cement wall. I muttered 'Oh, Boy.' He was tough." Many of the Huskies felt he was the best Minnesota player. Their opinion was shared by the Kansas City Chiefs who drafted him two years later. He was the first Chiefs' player to be elected to the Pro Football Hall of Fame. Bell, from Shelby, North Carolina, had been advised to go to Minnesota by Jim Tatum, the Tarheels' coach. For racial reasons, Bell could not enroll at the segregated University of North Carolina.

Schloredt had another observation about the play. "It set the tone of the victory. McKeta crashed through them and they knew exactly what he was going to do. They couldn't stop him. They saw they couldn't do anything about it. You could see the funny looks on their faces."

On fourth and four, Hivner punted. The Gophers' Dave Mulholland decided not to catch the ball on the 17 and watched it bounce and roll dead on the six. The Gophers' punt receivers did not try to catch or run with a Washington punt the entire first half. Warmath couldn't understand why they did not. "I assume they thought the ball was going to roll into the end zone." Those mental lapses put the Gophers in terrible field position to start offensive play.

On its first defensive series, Washington set up in its new 5-3 scheme. It worked perfectly on the first two plays. Roger Hagberg was stuffed by Pat Claridge and lost ground. On the next play, Kinnune stood Brown up and Enslow straightened up Larson. Allen and McKeta filled the gap to hold Hagberg to three yards. The Husky interior was winning the battle in the trenches. Brown's wrist was slightly sprained.

On third down, Stephens initially set up over his center and then dropped back five yards in the end zone. He booted the ball to Fleming who took it at midfield and danced between several defenders up the middle to the Gopher 34. Four plays later Washington's kicking game would swing into action. On fourth and three, Fleming lined up on the 34. He remembers that some of the Minnesota players started laughing and saying 'No way' about his kicking a field goal from that distance. They shut up as he swung his leg perfectly into the ball, sending it sailing through the uprights for a 3-0 lead. "I got back there and just boomed it. It went about 60 yards." His 44-yard field goal was the then longest one in Rose Bowl history. It was also a personal best for Mr. Automatic.

Four plays later, the Huskies were again in Gopher ground. After Hagberg went over right guard for 13 and Minnesota's initial first down, the Gophers set up on third and eight on the 36. Stephens rolled right and threw toward Mulholland near the right sideline. Mr. Fleming, now in his role as safety, closed in front of the Gopher back on the Husky 45, and picked off the pass with his right hand and returned it to the Minnesota 47.

Schloredt, who had entered the game on the Washington defensive series, set up to take the Huskies in for another score. Minnesota's defense was ready. After two running plays, Schloredt rolled left to set up for a pass, escaped tremendous pressure from the right side, and threw toward Claridge on the 15. The pass was almost intercepted. On fourth and nine, Schloredt's punt went untouched by Mulholland and rolled dead on the eight.

Minnesota again went three and out. On third and seven, Allen fought off a blocker and drove fullback Jim Rogers to the ground a few feet short of a first down. Stephens then boomed the ball 45 yards to the Husky 38 where Fleming bobbled the ball and then dove to the ground to pull it away from the outstretched arms of a fast closing Gopher.

Several plays later, the maroon and gold section of the stands went absolutely quiet. On second down, Schloredt hid the ball on his hip as he rolled to his left behind some great interior blocking. Jackson, who had slipped out of the backfield, was open near the left sideline and tucked Schloredt's pass in on the Minnesota 48 for a 12-yard pickup. Jackson then darted over left tackle through a lane of Husky blockers down to the Gopher 29. Schloredt pitched to Mitchell, who initially cut up toward the tackle and then sped around right end for six more. Jackson for three. On third and one,

Schloredt followed the blocks of McKasson and Bullard over the left and a first down on the 18 as the quarter ended.

Four plays later, the Huskies scored. Mitchell dashed over left end for 11. Schloredt, on a rollout over the right side, slipped for no gain. He then rolled left for four behind a punishing block by Jackson. On the right side, Schloredt faked the run and overthrew Mitchell who was open in the right side of the end zone. Fourth down. Wooten initially set up on the left side and then went in motion in an arc to the right. He kept on running after the snap and was wide open when Schloredt hit him with a short toss on the one and he went untouched into the end zone.

"We were in a double-wing. I'm sure Minnesota hadn't seen it before because when I caught the pass, God, there wasn't anybody close." Fleming's kick made it 10-0 and it was beginning to look like the 1960 Rose Bowl all over again.

The fired up Huskies again held the Gophers to three and out and Stephens punted for the third time -- this time a 48-yarder. Mitchell fielded it on the Husky 23 and returned the ball a few yards before he was forced out of bounds. Washington was penalized for clipping which brought the ball back to the 13. After Mitchell was thrown for a ten-yard loss, Schloredt kicked out of his end zone. The ball was not fielded and rolled dead on the Washington 48.

Minnesota quickly picked up a first down on the Husky 35. On third and seven, Stephens' pass was dropped by Hagberg and the next pass sailed out of bounds high over the receiver's head. Washington then went 68 yards in nine plays.

Fleming, Jackson, and Schloredt got the big yardage. Jackson over left guard for 10. Fleming took it for nine yards in two carries. On third and one at the Gopher 49, Schloredt looked over an eight-man Minnesota front. He hesitated after the snap just long enough to get great blocking over the left side. He then jumped through the front wall and cut left in the secondary. At the 40-yard line, Folkins laid a terrific block outside-in on the corner back. Schloredt cut outside of Folkins to the left sideline and rumbled down to the 18 before the pursuit caught him.

Jackson bounced over right guard for three. Schloredt rolled right for eight yards and a first down at the seven. Jackson drove to the four and then again over the same spot to the goal line. Everybody in the crowd and on the sidelines thought he had scored. The referee set the ball down inches from the big white stripe. Schloredt then followed a host of linemen over the left side for the touchdown. After the successful kick, Fleming was flattened by a Gopher squarely in front of the official who presumably was only intent on making a perfect signal on the conversion. The scoreboard showed Minnesota 0, UofW 17 and 4:14 left before intermission.

On the next series, Washington survived a real scare. Minnesota again was forced to punt. From the 30, Stephens sent his fourth punt of the first half 48 yards down to the Washington 22 where Fleming let it bounce. Kermit Jorgensen, setting up on the right side to block for Fleming, got tied up with McKeta coming over from the middle to help Fleming. Jorgensen accidentally kicked the ball toward his goal line. The Renton redhead mustered all the speed he could to smother the ball on the seven. Fortunately, the play was nullified by a Gopher holding penalty. Stephens kicked again, this time to Mitchell, who returned the ball to midfield.

Hivner, along with other members of the gold unit, came in to run out the clock. He ended up fumbling and Minnesota recovered on its 43 and called time-out. With enough time for one play, Stephens let fly. The pass was wildly overthrown and Mitchell, in the deep safety spot, picked off the errant throw on the Husky 19. He brought the crowd to its feet as he raced untouched up the left side. After cutting right at the Husky 45, the speedy sophomore ran into a wall of defenders on the Minnesota 43 as time expired.

Fans had witnessed the execution of almost a perfect offensive game plan in the first half. The Huskies started by spreading the Gopher defense with the Red Eye formation. They then sent Jackson crashing inside the tackles and that set up the pass-run option, Schloredt's bread and butter play. In rapid succession, the Huskies had employed the double-slot formation, the wing-T, the double-wing, the lonesome end, backs in motion, and balanced and unbalanced lines. The coaches had staged a masterpiece.

During half-time, the spectators would see trickery of a different order. Before Christmas vacation, students from the California Institute of Technology hatched a plot with the precision and the secrecy of a wartime Office of Strategic Services operation. It involved the stealthy substitution of over 2,000 rooters' instruction cards for the half-time card stunts in the Washington student section. On one card stunt, the students were supposed to hold up cards that would show "Huskies." Instead the cards spelled "Caltech." In two other tricks "Huskies" were spelled out backwards and a beaver's head -- for Caltech -- was substituted for a Husky's head.

About a dozen Caltech students, motivated by seeing if it could be done, obtained a small sample of the small instruction cards to be tacked on the back of the students' seats and had enough cards printed to bring about the results desired by the Caltech pranksters.

While the Husky players, coaches, and others in the Washington contingent were at Disneyland, two of the Caltech contingent entered the Long Beach College dormitory where the Washington cheerleaders in charge of card stunts were staying. They merely substituted the forged cards for the originals.

Meanwhile, in the bowels of the stadium, Minnesota coaches and players were trying to figure out how to fool the Huskies in the second half. Statistics clearly showed Washington's domination in the first half. Washington had held the Gophers to 61 total yards and gained 158. Minnesota had not completed a pass -- two were intercepted -- and had only two first downs. They bested the Huskies only in punting -- averaging 44 yards to 40.3 -- but netted zero yards on returns compared to the Huskies 29.

The Washington coaches were telling the players to stay with the straight ahead running plays. Schloredt succinctly summed up the Huskies' strategy. "We were going to play it close to the vest. We wanted ball control." It was going to be conservative football. Washington did not attempt one forward pass in the second half.

Warmath wasn't too concerned. "We were such a great second half outfit all year. I thought we would tramp the Huskies in the last 30 minutes." And he was right for much of the final two periods.

At the outset, Minnesota drove to the Husky 35. On fourth and inches, Chapple, crashing in from the left tackle position, met Hagberg head on and dropped him for a one-yard loss. No chest thumping, no pointing to the sky, just the satisfaction of doing his job as the Husky senior trotted directly off the field.

The Huskies set up to put the game away early in the third quarter as they did a year ago. But not this time. On the first play, Hivner backed away from the center a wee bit early, fumbled the exchange, and Bob Deegan recovered on the Husky 32. In three plays, the Gophers reached the end zone.

On a first down on the 18, Stephens ran left on the option play and when Folkins committed to stop him, he pitched back to right halfback Bill Munsey. The left side was now wide open for most of Munsey's trip to the end zone. Fleming slowed him up at the five and then he dragged Schloredt the rest of the way for the score. Rodgers kick was good and the Gophers' fans finally had something to cheer about. With over 24 minutes left, Minnesota had plenty of time to follow their practice of beating opponents in the second half. The Husky fans were quiet and concerned.

Near the end of the third quarter, Stephens punt rolled out of the bounds on the Husky 11. The next Husky series took away the Minnesota momentum and ate up precious minutes. Through a gaping hole on the left side, Jackson ran straight ahead for nine. Next, Schloredt faked to Jackson and handed off to Mitchell circling left. He was met by the end crashing in from the right side. No gain and no minutes left in the quarter.

The Gophers set up in an eight-man front. Schloredt knew if he got past the first wave, he was going to pick up a lot of yards. He momentarily set up for a hand-off and then busted through the left side. The hole was widened by McKeta trying to get there ahead of Schloredt. The two hit the gap together. McKeta joined Folkins on his left side to take care of the corner back and make it difficult for the safety to get a good shot at Schloredt. Finally, help arrived from the other side to bring the Husky quarterback down on the Washington 42 after a gain of 22 critical yards.

Minnesota then turned the tables. They forced the Huskies into third and 19. Schloredt punted 47 yards to put the Gophers 76 yards away from making the game much tighter. In eight plays, they reached the Washington 26 where they faced fourth and two. Hagberg then fumbled and Husky sophomore Ray Mansfield recovered. But Washington had jumped offside and the Gophers had new life on the 21.

After Stephens rolled around right end for six and Judge Dickson plowed over right guard for a first down on the 11, Minnesota reached the six. On third and five, Stephens dropped straight back to pass. As he turned to throw, he found McKeta blitzing in from his corner back position. "I actually lined up as a linebacker. It was just a gut feeling to get near the line of scrimmage," McKeta recounted. "I just knew Stephens was coming my way. I had to go in and cut him off." Stephens was dropped on the 18. Coach Tipps would later say one of the keys to the victory was "...when McKeta crashed through and hit their passer for a loss -- when they were knocking at our goal line for their second touchdown."

With the crowd standing and all the coaches and players on the sidelines encouraging the men on the field, Minnesota set up for a field goal attempt on the 25. Stephens, the holder, caught the snap, rose, rolled right, right arm cocked. He continued running down to the 20 where three Huskies were converging on him. He then threw toward the goal line where a column of four Huskies had the passing lane to the lone Gopher receiver covered. McKeta was the third one in the phalanx and in front of the receiver -- Fleming was covering behind. The gutty and gritty Husky came to the rescue one last time. He stepped up to catch the underthrown pass on the one and returned it out to the nine. McKeta would later say that he didn't want to catch the ball at the goal line. "But I was afraid if I batted it into the air, a Minnesota player might grab it and we really would be in trouble. So, I caught it and ran as far as I could. My terrific speed," he laughed, "carried me all the way to the nine."

McKeta's play was sensational. And it was even more so when one considers he was still feeling the effects of the injury in the Washington State game and had taken a beating in the Rose Bowl. On one play, the veteran back from Robertsdale, Pennsylvania, was racing down to cover a Husky punt midway through the third quarter. As the receiver ran toward the right sideline, McKeta turned to race after him. At that moment, a galloping Gopher, wearing number 78 on his white jersey, crashed into McKeta on his blind side. It was Bell, the powerful 220-pound 6'4" tackle. He had come out of the twilight zone at full speed and hit McKeta with the force of an express train.

"Brother," muttered a writer high in the press box with a clear look at the unfolding collision, "they better get the shovels ready for that little guy. He just got bombed into oblivion."

McKeta got slowly to his feet and staggered to the sidelines as Owens sent in Wooten to replace him. "I thought Don was finished for the afternoon," remarked Owens. "I said 'sit down and take a rest. You've earned it.'" Owens was surprised when his tough and indestructible captain answered, "I'll be OK in a few plays, coach." Several plays later, McKeta went back into the fray. "Man I've got to hand it to that guy," sighed Bell after the game. "I had a running 20-yard start when I cracked him. He's not just tough, he's not human."

On third and 12 on the Husky seven and less than five minutes to go, Schloredt set up in his end zone to punt. With a hang time of 4.7 seconds enabling three Huskies -- Fleming, Kinnune, and McKeta -- to run down field and get set to flatten him, Stephens made a fair catch on the Husky 44. Minnesota was now getting desperate.

Stephens rolled left and lobbed a short pass to Rogers, near the left sideline on the Husky 40. As Rogers turned to head downfield, Schloredt came up from his deep corner spot at full speed. He aimed his helmet right at the opponent's right shoulder and chest and drilled it with the might of his body and extended legs. He not only straightened the Gopher fullback up but drove him back several yards and toppled him to the ground. It was the essence of the Husky defense -- hitting with the helmet to inflict pain and physical punishment on the ball carrier. The game was over.

Minnesota would turn the ball over after three incomplete passes. Washington would kick for the last time. Schloredt launched the ball skyward for 51 yards -- his longest punt of the day -- into the hands of Dickson on the Gopher 14. He returned it nine yards. Minnesota went to the air to get its last first down on the Husky 35. One more pass would fall incomplete as time expired but not before Owens tapped Joe Jones on the shoulder and directed him to get on the field. He raced into position. "It was wonderful...but a couple of seconds seemed like a whole game." He had fulfilled his goal of playing in back-to-back Rose Bowls. He was one of the happiest Huskies as the game ended.

McKasson had neutralized Brown. By the end of the devastating, destructive, and decisive first quarter, the Minnesota All-American guard was out of the game. He had more than he could handle from Washington's All-American center. Brown would return, but he was never very effective.

Jackson was the ironman. He gained 60 yards and played every minute of the game except for the few moments for which Jones had replaced him.

For Schloredt, Hollywood couldn't have scripted it any better. From a broken collar bone in October and all those gut-wrenching one point victories to get to the Rose Bowl, Schloredt had played a large part in another Rose Bowl victory. Back on the big stage, his flair, his ability, and his bruising style led the Huskies to a stirring victory over the regular season national champions. He had gained 68 yards and averaged 13.6 yards per carry. He scored one touchdown and threw for another. For the second year in a row, he was voted the game's Most Outstanding Player award -- he shared it with Fleming in 1960. He was the first player in the 47-year history of the Rose Bowl to receive the award twice.

The story continues. Carole Washburn, the Rose Festival beauty queen, greeted him with a hug and a kiss outside the locker room. Beneath her royal gown, she revealed she was wearing his warm-up pants. They would dine together at the team banquet in Long Beach. She would then say good-bye to her football hero as he departed late that evening for Honolulu and the Hula Bowl. She kept his Most Valuable Player trophy until he returned to see her once again a few days later.

It was the second straight time the Huskies, as the underdog, had risen up and smashed a Big Ten opponent with a decisiveness that left only the size of the score, never the winner, in doubt. It was the first time in the continuous series with Big Ten teams, that a West Coast team had won two Rose Bowls in a row.

The Washington seniors had faced their toughest opponent. They had played their best game. Fleming, Jackson, McKeta, Schloredt, and Wooten -- along with sophomore Mitchell -- were the monsters of the offensive assault in the first half. In the second half, Washington's defense was the obstinate fighter, exhausted but warily protecting the points piled up in the early rounds. The key to its success were seniors Allen, Barry Bullard, Chapple, Claridge, Davidson, Enslow, Fleming, Folkins, Gegner, Hivner, Hurworth, Jackson, Kinnune, McKasson, McKeta, Schloredt, and Wooten. They got lots of help from juniors Tim Bullard, Jorgensen, Meyers, Nelson, and Skaggs, and sophomores Locknane, Mansfield, Mitchell, and Scheyer. They kept their poise and provided sufficient pressure to thwart Minnesota's assaults in the third and fourth periods.

The Huskies had demonstrated their remarkable camaraderie, their close-knit team unity, and their overwhelming desire to pay the price for victory. The seniors had laid four years of work on the line to become champions.

In the final analysis, it was Owens' philosophy and system for success clearly in evidence on the battlefield. Fast lean linemen, speedy backs, two heady and confident field generals, vicious tackling, the kicking game, and finely conditioned athletes who had become a band of brothers in battle.

Washington had defeated the regular season national champions. In the pre-game venues where the players came together, the Huskies noted that the Gophers sported watches inscribed with "National Champions." The Washington coaches and players believed that the Rose Bowl game was a championship bout and that when you win a championship match, you get the title. They felt that they just didn't eke out the victory, they won decisively.

Over the two-year period -- 1959 and 1960 -- the Huskies had forged the second best record of any collegiate football team in America -- 20 wins and two losses. With 20 victories, one tie, and one defeat, Mississippi had a slightly better resume.

Clearly the evidence showed that these two teams deserved a piece of the national championship. The situation before and after the bowl games was as follows:

Regular Season Ranking	Regular Season Record	Bowl Results	Record after Bowl Games
1. Minnesota	8-1-0	Lost to Washington	8-2-0
2. Mississippi	9-0-1	Beat twice beaten and unranked Rice 14-6	10-0-1
3. Iowa	8-1-0	Did not play in a bowl	8-1-0
4. Navy	9-1-0	Lost to Missouri 21-14	9-2-0
5. Missouri	9-1-0	Beat Navy 21-14	10-1-0
6. Washington	9-1-0	Beat Minnesota	10-1-0
7. Arkansas	8-2-0	Lost to Duke 7-6	8-3-0
8. Ohio State	7-2-0	Did not play in a bowl	7-2-0
9. Alabama	8-1-1	Lost to unranked Texas 7-3	8-2-1
10. Duke	7-3-0	Beat Arkansas 7-6	8-3-0

In 1960, the system of selecting a national champion was seriously flawed. Most polls made their final selections before the bowl games were played. The Associated Press finally recognized the problem in 1965 when it selected a champion after the entire season was over.

Controversy reigned as much in 1960 as in the early 21st century. Imagine -- some were even calling for a national playoff system.

At that time, there were two polls that selected a national champion after all the evidence -- regular season records and bowl game results -- was in. They were the Helms Foundation Poll founded in 1936 and the Football Writers Association of America (FWAA) which started in 1954. The FWAA selected Mississippi. The Helms Foundation selected Washington as the national champion.

Before crowning the Huskies as national champions, the Foundation sought the opinions of a number of football coaches and sportswriters around the country. The majority favored the Huskies. In making its decision, the Foundation narrowed its analysis down to Mississippi and Washington. The Foundation staff carefully weighed the merits of the two teams as to results and strength of their opponents. As a result of the Helms Foundation decision, Washington could lay claim to the national title outright or at least to a shared title with the Rebels.

Owens and his staff and their band of football brothers had taken a program on probation and won back-to-back Rose Bowl games and a national title. Washington's football program had risen from the ashes to fields of roses and a national championship.

Epilogue

Fifty years ago, the college football environment was very different than it is today. Sports Center, the Bowl Coalition Series, 24-hour sports talk shows did not exist. College recruits didn't have press conferences to herald their commitment to the school of their choice. They were not built up by the press to the extent that they are now. There was no talk of an athlete leaving a university before he graduated thereby using the university as a farm system for his athletic objectives. There was little or no trash talking. There was no chest thumping, high five's, or end zone celebrations when an athlete made a sack, a touchdown, or some other significant play. Most coaches cared about the academic success of their players, recognizing that very few of them would be successful professional athletes.

Fans viewed the players as student athletes and expected them to cope with the demands of academic studies as well as athletic activities. Student athletes were seldom coddled, exempted from rigorous academic study, or given special academic counseling and tutoring. They were admitted to major academic institutions on the basis of their overall academic abilities, not just on their ability to play football.

Most student athletes graduated, many in four years. They chose fields of study that prepared them for a profession other than football. Many forged successful careers. They were, by and large, good representatives of the universities they attended.

The University of Washington football program in the 1950's was representative of those in other major universities in America.

There were about 50 players on the team, most playing both offense and defense. Some had to work part-time to finance their education. The single ones lived with other students in dormitories and fraternity houses. Some were married and had children.

It was an era characterized by good sportsmanship on the part of the fans, players, and coaches. Fans did not greet opposing teams with loud choruses of boos and profanity laced epitaphs. They recognized that it took two teams to play a game, and the opponent would be greeted enthusiastically when it's players came on the field. Home crowds also cheered the great plays of visiting teams.

The Huskies provided the only games in town in the fifties and early sixties. The Seattle Supersonics did not arrive until 1967, the Seahawks in 1976, and the Mariners in 1977. So the citizens of Seattle and the neighboring region followed closely the exploits of the Washington athletic program, especially its football team.

The Husky home crowd was out in great numbers when their victorious 1961 Rose Bowl team arrived home from Los Angeles on January 4. Supporters chanted, "We're Number One, We're Number One." The King County Labor Council presented its "Team Unity" trophy to the Huskies. It was accepted by the recovering appendectomy patient, Joe Jones.

The celebrations ended a special period in the lives of the players, particularly the seniors. They gathered together one more time at the 26th annual Seattle Post-Intelligencer "Man of the Year" banquet a few nights later. Jim Owens had received the honor the year before. Senior Don McKeta, was selected for the 1960 award, from among the nominees that included Ron Santo of the Chicago Cubs; the Lake Washington Rowing Club's four-without-coxswain crew that won a gold medal in the 1960 Rome Olympics; and the 1957 winner, Jo Anne Gunderson, again the top US woman golfer.

Recognizing his fellow seniors and all other members of his

team, McKeta accepted the award by saying, "I want to accept this honor in behalf of all the seniors who played with me on the Huskies. They deserve all of this. Whatever I have done is due to the help of the Washington Huskies. And I feel that I am just a small part of our football team."

There were several newspaper stories about McKeta in the days following the banquet. The scribes focused on his toughness, love of combat, emotional drive and inspirational leadership. As he reflected on his years at Washington, he looked forward.

"Last year at a banquet, I was introduced to a fellow who(was) an All-American. Here he was -- the greatest -- and he was an alcoholic. His hand was shaking. Whew! That really woke me up. I looked at him and I couldn't believe how sorry I felt. I thought to myself what a bad thing it is to keep reliving those old games -- particularly when the only guys who'll listen to you are sitting around some bar and day after day you go in and they're still your pals because you made some long run 100 years ago."

McKeta continued. " I said to myself, 'You watch it, boy. Don't let that happen to you.' It's been great playing ball here but once it's over, it's over. That's the way life is and if you learn only one thing from playing on a great team like I have here with the Huskies, the thing you should learn is just that -- once it's over, it's over."

Many young men on the 1959 and 1960 teams took what they learned in the classroom and on the football field and forged diverse and successful careers. Some started in professional football, others went into different fields of endeavor. The following is a brief summary of what some of them have done.

Chuck Allen spent his entire working career in football. He signed with the American Football League's Los Angeles Chargers who became the San Diego Chargers when they moved from Los Angeles in 1961. Allen was a middle linebacker on four AFL West championship teams and a member of the Chargers' team that won the AFL title in 1963. He was selected to two AFL Pro Bowls. He played for the Chargers for nine seasons including 1969, the last year for the AFL. After the merger of the National Football League and the AFL in 1970, the Chargers joined the NFL's American Football Conference. That year, Allen joined the Pittsburgh Steelers, where he played for two seasons. He finished his playing career in 1972 -- his 12th professional season -- with the Philadelphia Eagles. Allen was a linebacker coach on Owens' staff in 1973 and 1974. The next year, he became an Assistant General Manager for the newly formed Seattle Seahawks who entered the NFL in 1976 as an expansion team. Allen would be a mainstay of the Seahawks' football operations staff until 1995. "My whole life has been football -- two years in junior high school, four years in high school, four years at Washington, twelve years in the pros, two years coaching at Washington, and twenty years with the Seahawks."

Barry Bullard graduated from Washington with a degree in civil engineering and as the top US Air Force ROTC cadet. He served for 17 years as an officer in the Air Force. He received a masters' degree in astronautics and space facilities from the Air Force Institute of Technology. He was awarded the Bronze Star, two Meritorious Service Medals, and an Air Force Commendation Medal for his service in Phu Cat in Vietnam as well as his performance as Facilities Manager at the Air Force Academy in Colorado Springs. Bullard was promoted to Lieutenant Colonel but was unable to assume the rank because of a significant disability which forced him to retire as a Major. He then worked as a facilities manager in several hospitals before moving to Port Ludlow. For several years, he has volunteered as a tutor in mathematics for middle school children in that area.

Barry's brother, Tim, was a Marine Corps officer for several years. He then joined KOMO-TV and his 23- year career there included assignments as a producer and director, and also in public affairs and sales. He left KOMO for Edge Learning Institute where, for twelve years, he headed up its organizational training function followed by three years with Genie Industries. He shared his time and resources with Big Brothers of Seattle; as President of the Big W Club at the University of Washington; the UW Alumni Board; and as President of the 101 Club of the Washington Athletic Club.

Larry Clanton, a reserve guard in 1959 and 1960, left Washington in his senior year and returned to California where he worked as a combination fireman/policeman and received his degree at San Jose State. In 1964, he joined the US Air Force and became a pilot. He was sent to Vietnam. He became a forward air controller and flew a Birddog, a small aircraft that carried no armor or weapons on missions to spot enemy ground forces and direct aircraft with heavy weapons to destroy the enemy positions. On February 3, 1968, Captain Clanton was flying near Long Dien in support of friendly ground forces clearing that town of the enemy. He repeatedly made low passes through heavy fire and helped outnumbered friendly units to withdraw from the area. On March 23, 1968, Clanton died from wounds suffered on his mission. He was posthumously awarded the Silver Star for his heroic action.

Pat Claridge, a Canadian citizen, spent several years with the B.C. Lions and Calgary Stampeders in the Canadian Football League. He then had a successful career as an investment broker with Merrill Lynch and as a venture capitalist.

Mike Crawford received his degree in civil engineering and served three years as a platoon leader in the US Marines. He then began a 38-year career in construction. For much of that period, he was the co-owner of, and an executive with, Concrete Nor'West who provided ready-mixed concrete and sand and gravel to customers primarily in Skagit and Whatcom Counties. He has served on numerous civic, community and economic development organizations in Skagit County. Crawford received several leadership awards including Skagit Valley College's Distinguished Service Award and the Skagit Business Leader of the Year citation.

Ben Davidson, a geography major, traveled the country with several professional football teams. In 1961, he joined the New York Giants. After three games, he was traded to the Green Bay Packers for a fifth-round draft choice. As a backup defensive end, he helped the Packers defeat the New York Giants 31-0 in the NFL championship game in his rookie season. After a pre-season game against Dallas in 1962, Davidson was traded to the Washington Redskins, again for a fifth-round draft choice. He spent the 1962 and 1963 seasons with Washington and was released in pre-season camp in 1964.

Davidson quipped that "In my first seven years of football (he did not play in high school), I was only a starter one year and that was in my second year at East Los Angeles Junior College. I had an inauspicious beginning."

Things would get much better after the AFL's Oakland Raiders signed a contract with him in 1964. He played eight seasons for the Raiders and was selected to play in the AFL's Pro Bowl in 1966, 1967, and 1968, and the NFL's Pro Bowl in 1972. In 1967, Oakland won the AFL championship and lost to the NFL's champion Green Bay Packers in Super Bowl II. In 1973 and 1974, he was placed on the taxi squad. In 1974, Raider's Coach John Madden gave Big Ben the choice of staying in Oakland on the taxi squad or being released. Davidson took a release and played with the Portland Storm of the World Football League.

Davidson also worked in television and in some movies. "I had a teammate with the Raiders -- Fred Williamson. In 1969, he called and said 'you want to be in the movies?' The movie was MASH." His biggest role was in Miller Lite commercials that ran from

1975 until 1991. "I did 27 of those commercials. There were more Raiders in those than any other team. Having grown up in East Los Angeles and having spent a lot of time traveling in Mexico, Spain, and other Spanish speaking countries, I speak the language and so I did three commercials in Spanish for them and that was a lot of fun."

Norm Dicks, a sophomore on the 1960 team, received his law degree from Washington in 1968. Later that year, he joined the staff of Washington's US Senator Warren Magnuson. He served on "Maggie's" staff until 1976 when he began his successful campaign for the United States Congress. He has been re-elected ever since. He now serves as the senior member of the House Appropriations Committee. He has been an influential member of Congress on defense, national security issues, and environment initiatives. Dicks has been very effective in getting economic development funds for local communities in the State of Washington.

Dick Dunn spent three years as an officer in the US Army Transportation Corps. He recently retired from a 31-year career in investment and trust management sales, primarily as an officer with US Bank in Seattle.

Dave Enslow, known as the "Bear" to his teammates, became a math teacher and football coach after graduating from Washington in 1961 with a degree in education. He added a masters degree in education with a focus on real estate math. He played for six years with three semi-professional teams -- the Edmonds Warriors, the Seattle Ramblers, and the Seattle Rangers. Enslow was the head football coach at East High in Bremerton, Mercer Island High School, and Chimacum High School on the Olympic Peninsula as well as an assistant coach at O'Dea High School in Seattle. He also coached wrestling. Teams that he coached won championships in both football and wrestling in the Kingco, Metro and Olympic leagues.

Carver Gayton, a history major, had a brief stint as a graduate assistant coach at Washington and then became a special agent for the FBI. He returned to Seattle in 1968 to become the first black assistant coach at Washington. He resigned during the turmoil surrounding the dismissal of four black players in October 1969 and was named the University's Director of Affirmative Action in 1970. During his seven-year tenure in that office, he also completed his Masters in Public Administration and Ph.D in Political Science. He joined Boeing in 1979 where, for 18 years, he was the company's Director of Training and Educational Relations and its Corporate Director of College and University Relations. During his career at Boeing, he and the company received several awards for its innovative and effective human resources program and for leadership in, and contributions to the field of workforce development.

In 1997, he became the Commissioner of the Washington State Employment Security Department, a position he held for four years. He is currently the Director of the Northwest African American Museum in Seattle and is also a workforce development consultant and teaches at the Evans School of Public Affairs at the University of Washington. He has served on a wide variety of national, state, and local boards including the University of Washington Alumni Association, where he served as President, and Chairman of the Board of the National Center for Occupational Research and Development. Two hallmarks of his career have been his ability to bring about change without being confrontational and getting things done "without holding a press conference."

Kurt Gegner graduated with a degree in mechanical engineering in 1961 and was a student assistant coach that year. He entered the Marine Corps as an officer in December 1961 and was a platoon leader until his honorable discharge in 1964. He joined the engineering department of Pacific Northwest Bell in 1964 and left in 1966, to become an engineering manager with Kaiser Aluminum in Tacoma. Three years later, he and his family moved to Jamaica where Gegner was a member of Kaiser's management team in a joint venture with Reynolds Aluminum. In 1974, he came back to Tacoma as the Maintenance Manager for Kaiser and joined other key people in managing the Tacoma operations. In 1978, he was diagnosed with Non-Hodgkin lymphoma, a form of cancer arising from lymphocytes, a type of white blood cells. His widow, Susan Gegner Kreigel, tells of his courage and will to beat the disease and the tremendous support of his teammates and coaches. "He never thought he wouldn't beat the disease. He was real tough -- that carried over from his experience as a Husky." He passed away in 1981.

George Fleming was drafted by the Oakland Raiders as an all-purpose player -- receiver, running back, kicker, punt and kickoff returner. In the 1961 season, he saw limited action except for running back punts and kickoffs and kicking extra points and field goals. He set an AFL field goal record with a 54-yard gem. He had a no-cut contract for $15,000 but the financially strapped Raiders claimed he was a specialist and not an all-purpose player and decided to cut his contract to $8,500. "They told me to take it or leave it. I told them to stick it. I sat out the 1962 season and worked at Boeing."

In 1963, he contacted the Toronto Argonauts who had drafted him second in 1961. The Argonauts signed him for more than the Raiders had offered. After the last exhibition game, Toronto cut him. "Fortunately, Bud Grant (who would become the head coach for the Minnesota Vikings in 1967) called and asked me to come to Winnipeg. I led the league in scoring with 135 points, only ten short of the record. The next year, I got banged up and missed the last seven or eight games and that was the end of my football career."

239

After his professional football career, Fleming, went to work in the office of Washington's Secretary of State and then US West. In 1968, he was elected to the Washington State Legislature. He served for two years in the House and for 20 years in the State Senate, 18 of which were in leadership positions. Fleming was the first African American member of the Washington State Senate. He received the US Justice Department's highest award for community service. During his distinguished career, Fleming focused on education, economic development, civil rights, senior citizens, and affordable housing.

In 1997, the Pritchard Fleming Building in Bellevue was named for Joel Pritchard, the former Washington State Lieutenant Governor and State Senator Fleming. The building houses historically valuable records from several counties in the Puget Sound region for public access and research.

Lee Folkins spent five years in professional football -- with Green Bay in 1961 when they won the NFL championship, three with the Dallas Cowboys (1962-1964) and in 1965 with the Pittsburgh Steelers. He and Don Meredith, a former quarterback for the Cowboys, started a business making plastic pipe which they eventually sold. With his mechanical engineering academic background, he then entered the construction business and became a partner in a construction company in Norman, Oklahoma. On a mid-July afternoon in 1972, he was with his superintendent, Herman Wood, testing a new backhoe that they wanted to use to dig ditches for sewer pipe. Above the long boom of the backhoe were 66,000-volt electrical transmission wires supported by metal towers. Folkins ambled over to the machine to check an oil leak and touched it. At that moment, the current in the wires overhead jumped to the raised boom and shot through Folkins.

Folkins suffered severe electric shock that changed his world. Over the next three years, he had memory loss, lacked the ability to concentrate, and had many periods of discomfort laced with desperate and bizarre acts. Finally, tests confirmed that Folkins had acute brain syndrome, a reversible condition. Ever so slowly, he improved, and after about three years, he was able to handle the demands of business again. After taking a job in Saudi Arabia for six years, he returned to the United States and started another construction company and shuttled back and forth to assignments in Saudi Arabia, Indonesia, and the West Indies. Still actively working, he quipped, "I probably should have retired, but I have too much of the Owens/Tipps/Walker discipline and work ethic in me."

Joe Jones received his degree in marketing and advertising. After working with IBM for three years, he became the Sales and Promotion Manager for KYAC, a newly formed black radio station, and soon became its Station Manager. Jones used the station as a forum to address some of the racial issues going on at the University of Washington in the late 1960's. In 1973, he started Impact Communications and has been involved in the firm to the present time. For awhile, he put the firm on the back burner when he joined Paccar's Kenworth Division as its National Advertising and Sales Promotion Manager. In 1982, he reactivated Impact Communications, which is now mainly involved in the publishing and marketing of his wife's books. Dr. Mona Jones is a writer, orator, educator, and model of the African American woman on the move. She is the Poet Laureate for King County.

Kermit Jorgensen received his degree in forestry and joined Scott Paper as a logging engineer. After two years with Scott, he embarked on a 35-year career with H.B. Fuller where he became a sales executive. Fuller is a global company with over $1.5 billion in revenue and worldwide markets in specialty chemicals.

Bob Hivner returned to California after graduate work in education at Washington and started a long-time career in coaching and teaching. In 1963, he became the youngest head football coach in the Los Angeles County School District. For eight years, he coached at his alma mater, Southgate High School. In 1971, he became the head coach at Mission Viejo High School. Five years later, he took a leave of absence to help his wife and three children provide love, care and support for his fourth and youngest child, Sue. She had been diagnosed with cancer and died a few years later at the age of 8. After she passed on, Hivner returned to Mission Viejo as an assistant football coach and world history teacher where he retired in 1990.

Ray Jackson worked as a patrolman in the King County Sheriff's Office until 1969 during which period he was also a student assistant coach at Washington. He joined Puget Sound Power and Light in 1969 as a personnel manager. In 1971, the utility company granted him a leave of absence to become an assistant coach for the Huskies during Owens' last four years and Don James' first year in 1975. He rejoined Puget Sound for the remainder of his professional career. "I still have pictures of the Rose Bowl teams in my house (in Waco, Texas). I look at them almost every day."

Bill Kinnune got his start in business by selling real estate while completing his degree in business administration. In November 1961, he joined Western Kraft headquartered in Portland, Oregon. He soon moved to Portland to assume sales management responsibility for the states of Oregon and Washington. He rose to become the Executive Vice President for corrugated containers and bags in what had become Willamette Industries. Just before it was sold to Weyerhaeuser in 2002, its sales were $5 billion. He has served on several corporate boards as well as the UW's Business School Advisory Board. He spends some time on his two ranches in Eastern Oregon.

Ray Mansfield was a second round choice of the Philadelphia Eagles in 1963. He played his rookie season for the Eagles and then was traded to the Pittsburgh Steelers where he played from 1964-1976. He was a member of the 1974 and 1975 teams that won the Super Bowl. He still holds the Steelers' record for consecutive games played -- 182. He became a legend in the Steel City for his ability to inspire his teammates. After his playing career ended, he served as vice-president of the NFL Alumni Association. Mansfield was called *The Ranger* for his love of hiking. He often backpacked in the Grand Canyon. He and his 24-year old son, Jimmy, and one of his son's pals set out on the south rim of the canyon in early November 1996. After the first day of hiking, he told the young men to go on ahead and set up camp. He didn't show up, and, since it was dark, Jimmy and his friend couldn't find him. The next morning, they found him dead, sitting with his back against a rock facing a beautiful vista, a serene expression on his face. He was 55.

Roy McKasson, a history major, played one year with the Edmonton Eskimos in the CFL and then joined the staff of Young Life. He ministered to high school students in Dallas and Chicago and was widely know for his Christian witness, his friendliness, kindness, and generosity. He died in late January 1998 at age 59. His teammates honored him at a memorial service. "He was like a brother to me," Bob Schloredt said. "He was as common as an old shoe and every time he spoke to you he made you feel you were the only person in the world he was talking to...He was everybody's friend." Don McKeta added, "Roy had all the things that make someone great: dedication, high values, and his conviction to Christ. He was someone everybody looked up to."

McKeta had served in the Navy for four years before he came to Washington. Most of his service was in the Far East, some during the Korean War. After graduation, he played one season in the CFL with the Saskatchewan Roughriders. He was a Husky assistant coach for two years and then started a career in corporate sales and public relations. He started his own company in the apple orchard business in Wenatchee and became the head football coach for Wenatchee Junior College during some of the years he lived there. One of McKeta's biggest thrills in athletics was when he was coaching a Special Olympics slow-pitch softball team in Wenatchee in the regional championship game. "One gentleman on our team had one arm and his leg and ankle were turned in completely deformed. He never had a hit all year. The bases were loaded in the bottom of the last inning. Everybody wanted me to pinch hit for him and I said 'No, we are going to let him hit.' And he hit a single. The emotions of his teammates swarming all over that guy was just unreal. Everybody was in tears of joy. It was a very special moment."

McKeta provided significant support to Chuck Carroll, the former King County Prosecuting Attorney and the second Husky consensus All-America selection in 1928. Carroll died in 2003 at the age of 96 and McKeta visited him several times a week during his last few years and was with Carroll when he died. McKeta was inducted in the "Unsung Heroes" category of the All-American Football Foundation in 1998. He was enshrined in the Pennsylvania Sports Hall of Fame in 2001.

John Meyers spent six years in professional football -- with the Dallas Cowboys in 1962 and 1963 and the Philadelphia Eagles from 1964-67. He then started a career in Seattle which eventually led to the ownership of a beverage distributorship in Kirkland. He was President of the UW Tyee Board and was very active in the UW's Husky Fever financial support program. Meyers passed on in May 1998 at age 58. "He was a special person who helped me a great deal when I arrived at the University of Washington," said then Washington's Athletic Director Barbara Hedges. McKeta added, "He was a big, mean, and agile player. He was a good football player and a good guy. He extended his hand to a lot of people."

Don Millich spent 21 years as a production manager with

Portland Stevedoring and General Brewing and ended his career with the Internal Revenue Service. For 13 years, he was a group manager and lead instructor in tax law for the IRS staff in the Portland, Oregon, district.

Charles Mitchell played six years in the NFL -- five with the Denver Broncos and one with the Buffalo Bills. He then began a career in education. He received his Masters and Doctorate degrees in Education from Brigham Young University. In 1981, Mitchell started a long relationship with the Seattle Community Colleges as Dean of Students at Seattle Central. He became president of Seattle Central Community College in 1987 and served in that capacity until 2003 when he became Chancellor of the Seattle Community College District which educates over 55,000 students in several locations. It is the largest two-year system in the state.

Under his leadership, Seattle Central established a reputation for developing innovative curricula and student services, which were acknowledged by Time Magazine's "College of the Year" award in 2001. Mitchell has served on the boards of Seattle University, the Seattle Foundation, Virginia Mason Medical Center's Board of Governors, and the Seattle Art Museum.

Bob Schloredt was the first Husky to sign a professional football contract. On January 9, 1961, he cast his lot with the British Columbia Lions where he played two seasons. Schloredt also spent considerable time in coaching. He was an assistant coach at Washington from 1963-1974, ending his Husky coaching career when Jim Owens resigned following the 1974 season. Then, he became the offensive coordinator for the World Football League team in Honolulu for several seasons, after which he spent a number of years as Corporate Sales Manager for the Western International Hotel facilities in Hawaii and Washington. He now works part-time for the Department of Urban Development inspecting homes and apartment houses. Schloredt was admitted to the National

Football Foundation's College Football Hall of Fame (1989) and the Rose Bowl Hall of Fame (1991).

Jim Skaggs signed with the Philadelphia Eagles after graduating in 1962. He played 11 seasons with the Eagles. He then started a 29-year career with State Farm Insurance Company rising from an agent to a field executive.

Dan Wheatley began his 42-year coaching and teaching career at Kelso High School and finished it at Rainier High School in Oregon. Along the way, he was selected the State of Oregon's Coach of the Year (1974) and coached six football teams to the state playoffs and 14 basketball teams to playoff action, including a state championship in 1974. He helped coach track teams that won six state championships. He never had a sick day in his entire educational career. Apparently his good health contributed to the proliferation of his progeny -- six children and 23 grandchildren!

After coaching at Columbia Basin College for two years following graduation, Brent Wooten coached and taught for 37 years at Eastern Washington University. Wooten said, "I got to go out to my classroom every day which was the golf course."

More players from the 1959 and 1960 teams have been individually inducted in the Husky Hall of Fame than from any other two teams in Husky history -- Allen, Fleming, Mansfield, McKasson, McKeta, Mitchell, and Schloredt. The entire 1959 team was selected in 1994 -- the first football team in Husky history to be selected. The Appendix that follows includes the names of the players inducted and the players on the 1960 national championship team.

Jim Owens coached for another 14 seasons after the 1960 season. His 1963 team would go to the 1964 Rose Bowl. Led by Junior Coffey, Bill Douglas, and Rick Redman, it was his last team to go to a bowl game. The Huskies faced third-ranked Illinois in Pasadena. The Illini, with Jim Grabowski at fullback and consensus All-American Dick Butkus at linebacker, defeated Washington 17-

7. This loss was the only blemish on Owens' record in bowl games. He played in three winning bowl games as a player at Oklahoma, was an assistant to Bear Bryant when Kentucky won the Cotton Bowl in 1952, and coached the Huskies to victory in the 1960 and 1961 Rose Bowls. He finished his 18-year Husky coaching career with 99 wins, 82 losses and six ties for a .545 winning percentage.

Owens' teams thrived in the one platoon era. When free substitution was allowed in 1965 and two platoon football was implemented, it had a very significant impact on Husky football. Owens did not like the new rule. He believed that one platoon football was how the game should be played. The change undermined the basis for Washington's success in the eight seasons he had been the head coach. The stress on defense and physical conditioning that enabled the Huskies to punish its opponents, particularly in the fourth quarter, was not so important with players going only one way and having significant sideline "breathers." Two platoon football required a change in the recruiting process. Owens said he and his coaches were slow to select high school and junior college players that focused on just offense or defense. "Looking back on it, we made some mistakes. We should have picked some people who were more specialized. But we hadn't been experienced in that type of football."

Another major change came in the mid-to-late sixties. It was a time of much campus unrest brought about by the war in Vietnam, racial turmoil, and other social issues in the country. The attributes of discipline, commitment to pay the price, and team unity that characterized the 1959 and 1960 teams were no longer being completely embraced by college athletes. Many students and some athletes also began to challenge the "authority" of leaders in business, government, universities, and coaching staffs. In addition, the Huskies were not winning.

In early 1968, 14 black student athletes demanded the hiring of a black coach or administrator because of alleged discriminatory practices in the athletic department. In August of that year, Carver Gayton joined the staff as an assistant football coach. Individual and group counseling sessions were initiated. A wide variety of community events took place to connect the student athletes with the local black community. Although the 1968 season ended with a 3-5-2 record, Gayton felt that the overall situation was beginning to move in a positive direction.

Washington lost the first six games of the 1969 season. The coaches and players became frustrated. At the end of October, several days before the UCLA game in Los Angeles, Coach Owens met with university officials to discuss the situation. After the meeting, he decided to present a loyalty oath to each one of the 80 players. Owens talked with each player and asked each of them to pledge 100 percent unconditional loyalty to him, the team, and the university. Four players refused and were suspended. All were black. Gayton resigned in protest because he felt that the process, and the result, undermined his relationship with the athletes.

Tension, fear, and rage became pervasive in the black *and* white communities of Seattle. A University of Washington Human Rights Commission was appointed in 1970 and issued its report in late January 1971. The report contained many recommendations including the firing of coach Owens and athletic director Joe Kearney -- who had replaced Owens as AD in 1969 -- and the hiring of a black assistant coach and a black assistant athletic director. The Board of Regents rejected the recommendation to fire Owens and Kearney.

Reflecting on the situation, Gayton said, "The irony of the situation was that the same qualities that had led to the success in the late 1950's were part of what led to the difficulties ten years later. The players began to question authority and a strong disciplined approach. Some could not accept pledging loyalty to the coach and the university. And, Owens, who personified the qualities of discipline, hard work, team unity, and paying the price, was not the type of person who would sit down and say 'let's talk' or apologize for his treatment of the players -- for example, the Death March."

Mitchell could see the explosion coming. "Did racism exist when I played (in 1960-62)? Yes. Was it different than in other programs? No. Does that necessarily make it right? No. We didn't have that many black ball players on the 1960 team. And all of us were playing. And, it was before the time of the civil rights movement. We didn't have a lot of episodes. All the episodes started after that. I don't believe Washington coaches were prepared to handle what came later."

Dr. Odegaard, the President of the University, remarked in a staff meeting that he didn't think Owens was racist. He thought Owens and some of the coaches were color blind. They treated everybody equally. Odegaard felt that the situation in the late sixties required a different approach. University officials had to understand what was happening to blacks around the country. They had to discuss and evaluate the demands of organizations like the Black Student Union, meet with their leaders, and determine what changes were required to ease the tension.

When the 1970 season started, the turmoil had subsided somewhat. Husky football fortunes also got better. Led by Sonny Sixkiller, a sophomore quarterback from Ashland, Oregon, Washington recorded a 6-4 record, its best since the 1966 season. Washington was acclaimed the most improved team in the country in the wake of the 1-9 record in 1969. The Huskies finished tied for second in what then had become the Pacific-8 conference with the addition of Washington State in 1962 and Oregon and Oregon State in 1964. Stanford, featuring Heisman Trophy winner Jim Plunkett at quarterback, won the conference title and stunned the football world by beating previously unbeaten Ohio State 27-17 in the 1971 Rose Bowl.

Off the field, changes were being made to improve the relationships between the coaches and student athletes. In January 1971, Ray Jackson become an assistant coach. Later that month, Don Smith was named assistant athletic director. Smith, a black, had worked for the Seattle Times and Pacific Northwest Bell before taking a public relations position in New York for AT&T. Through the ensuing months, Smith worked tirelessly to heal wounds, to develop better relationships between the various factions, and to gain the confidence of all parties that the situation would be improved.

Smith also selected Gertrude Peoples, a member of the newly created Office of Minority Affairs' Black Student Division, to establish an outreach program for student athletes, especially the blacks. "I provided a friendly voice for the athletes. I was kind of like a mom, a good friend." She and her small staff started an academic counseling program which provided a host of services to those who needed help in what, for some, was a very different environment. Peoples recalls, "The Athletic Department became a lot more sensitive." As a result of the changes, the Black Athletes Alumni Group led by Joe Jones, reversed its stand to discourage black athletes from attending Washington.

Owens continued to coach for four more seasons. In both 1971 and 1972, the Huskies won eight and lost three and finished third in the conference. The 1971 season included one of the wildest games ever played in Husky Stadium. In an old fashioned shoot-out, the Huskies came from behind four times to beat Purdue 38-35. With under four minutes to play, Purdue scored on an 80-yard pass play to go ahead 35-31. Heeding Owens' advice to "stay cool and score," Sixkiller needed just five plays to get in the end zone. He hit Tom Scott from 33 yards out for the victory.

On November 27, 1974, at the end of the football team's annual post-season banquet, Owens announced his retirement from coaching. Athletic Director Joe Kearney remarked. "Today marks the end of an era -- the Jim Owens' era. All who have shared this span of football history can take pride in the past 18 years. The Owens' years included more drama, change, and excitement than any comparable span of time in Washington athletics. Many shared in the halcyon years when the purple gang terrorized the nation's best in Pasadena. During some of those years, controversial issues swirled around the football program but in the final analysis, what was evident was the stature of the man. Jim Owens has been a credit to the University, the State of Washington, and to the coaching profession. He has conducted the Husky football program in an ethical manner and has exemplified the highest ideal of the coaching profession. Today, we mark the end of an era. But it most certainly marks the beginning of a legend that will grow from this day on. The legend of Jim Owens, the coach, and Jim Owens, the man."

Owens was inducted as a charter member into the Husky Hall of Fame in 1979, the year it was established. He was inducted as a player in the National Football Foundation's College Football Hall of Fame in 1982 and as a coach in the Rose Bowl Hall of Fame in 1992. More than ten years later, on October 25, 2003, a statue of Owens was placed in front of the northwest entrance to Husky Stadium. Some in the black community, because of the events in 1969 and 1970, were angry over the erection of the statue. Owens helped heal the wounds when, in his acceptance speech before 72,000 Husky fans, he gave a heart-felt apology to his players for the pain he may have caused them. For Gayton and others, Owens' apology ended one of the most excruciating sagas in the history of Husky sports.

When Owens retired from coaching at age 47, he had many productive working years left. He became an executive with Universal Services, a company that supplied food, housing and logistics services to oil exploration companies in areas such as Alaska, the Gulf of Mexico, and the North Sea. After ten years with Universal, he joined Houston- based Rowan Drilling and continued as an executive with that company until 1994. He then retired to Big Fork, Montana, where he and his wife had, some years before, purchased waterfront property and built a permanent home as they neared retirement.

Tom Tipps continued to coach at Washington through the 1969 season. He left to become a talent scout in the National Football League. He retired in 1987 after a heart attack When he was in the hospital recovering, Tipps' wife, Frances, called Bill Kinnune and said Tom wanted to talk. Kinnune had remembered that in a grueling practice, Tipps exhorted the linemen by yelling, "It's 90 percent mental and 10 percent physical." Kinnune asked Tipps how he was doing. "Not so good." Kinnune then said to his coach, "A wise man once told me it's 90 percent mental and 10 percent physical." At the other end, there was a long pause and then the question. "A wise man told you that?"

Kinnune told Tipps he was correct. "Tom you get your butt out of that hospital and I'll take you up to Alaska fishing." About a week later Kinnune got a another call. This time, Tipps' wife asked, "What did you tell Tom? He's out walking around the lake about six times a day to get in shape to go fishing with you." Kinnune exclaimed, "Oh boy." So Kinnune and his beloved coach went fishing in Alaska and had the best time they had ever had together. Tipps passed away in February 2007 at age 90.

Chesty Walker coached at Washington through the 1965 season and then joined the Dallas Cowboys' organization as a talent scout. For nine seasons at Washington, he had been the father-confessor to scores of young football players and the chief architect of a Husky offense that helped earn three trips to the Rose Bowl. When he left, Owens wrote a letter to the Husky football players.

"There is no way to express or evaluate what Chesty has meant to Husky football, the players who were privileged to know him, the coaching staff, and myself. He has been like a second father to me, and we will all miss him greatly." He died in 1968 at age 64.

Many football seasons have come and gone since the 1959 and 1960 teams rose to the top of collegiate football. When you talk today about the Husky tradition -- endurance, passion, pride, tenacity, and toughness -- it all started with them. Jim Murray, the noted sports columnist for the Los Angeles Times, once said of those teams, "I won't say Owens gets the hungriest football players in the West each year, but if they were in the Roman Coliseum, the lions wouldn't come out."

Don James, who followed Owens as the Husky football coach in 1975, remarked, "Those teams laid the foundation for Husky football."

The collegiate football years of a band of brothers who came together almost 50 years ago laid the foundation for their lives. From the conditioning, the physical toughness drills, and playing through pain, they learned to never quit or give up. Davidson once asked Gegner about the Marine Corps. "Kurt, what was tougher, the Marine Corps or Husky football?" "He looked at me like I was stupid and said, 'Are you serious?' "

Davidson would also observe that the Husky practices were much harder than in his professional football career. "My first season after graduation was with Vince Lombardi. Practices were supposed to be tough, hard, and brutal. At the time, I said, 'Man, he can't hurt me. After what I have been through at Washington, this is a breeze.' " He continued on about what he carried forward from his Husky experience to the rest of his life. "If you have been through brutal practices and you think you can't make it and it's suddenly over, you think 'Man, I've survived another one.' The mind really does control the body and that can hold you in good stead."

Allen reflected that the coaches felt that there were opposing players with more talent but that with our better conditioning, mental toughness, and greater will to succeed, we could accomplish great things. "Basically, they taught us to believe in ourselves and that is the key which opens doors to any field of endeavor."

They learned the importance of team work, a quality that is expounded so frequently by current management writers and teachers. They believed that it took a whole team to get the job done. They appreciated what they accomplished as a team. "Nobody got bent out of shape thinking he was better than a teammate. We all paid the price," McKeta observed. "All sorts of people stepped up and did what was needed at the time. It might have been a lineman making a big hole and who never got credit or a back making 10 or 15 yards. It might have been a quarterback on a roll-out, a safety intercepting a pass. Someone always seemed to step up and make something happen to get a victory. And, it wasn't the first 11, it was all 45 guys. We all contributed. It was a nice fraternity."

They learned that everybody was in the battle together. "As a team we were very close. With one platoon football, you couldn't point to the defense for something that got screwed up or the offense or special teams. We all were the offense, we were the defense, and we were the special teams," Schloredt observed. "And we had much smaller teams than today. We could come together much more easily. We had no gravy trains. The coaches recruited people who had character and didn't expect extra or different treatment. The coaches had integrity. There were no outside influences. Nobody expected anything except hard work."

Tipps felt that football players have to get together and do something for somebody else to win a football game. "It's the same thing you have to do to lead a good life."

Gayton would credit the team concept instilled by the coaches for the fundamental underpinning of his management style. "The ingredients for a good team in any organization include talent, commitment, discipline, leadership, and a willingness to leave egos at the door. But just like the cook who has what is assumed to be the best recipe and ingredients to bake the perfect cake, you can have the cake fall flat. There are intangibles that are not in the recipe that make the cake a winner. Our 1959 team had those intangibles and the result was an euphoric experience."

The 1959 and 1960 Huskies also had a great impact on future Washington teams and players. Rick Redman, only one of two Huskies in history to be twice (1963 and 1964) named a consensus All-American, chose Washington over several other big-time programs because of what he saw at Washington in 1959 and 1960 when he was a high school player at Blanchet High School in Seattle. When Redman heard the 1959 team was having its 40th reunion in October 1999, he went to its dinner for a few minutes. He felt very strongly that somebody who followed in their footsteps as a Husky needed to tell them the very significant impact they had made on future Husky players. "I had to come here. I hate to break in on your festivities. But I just wanted to say a few words about why I decided to come to Washington. I remember the way you guys played football, the way you hit, the discipline you had, the way you believed in yourselves when few did in 1958, the way you carried yourselves, and what you accomplished. When I saw you in practice and in games, I made up my mind to become a Husky. Thanks for giving me so much encouragement and drive."

Redman, after playing nine seasons with the San Diego Chargers, joined Sellen Construction Co., where he is its Chairman. Sellen is one of the most successful construction companies in the Northwest. He attributes much of his success from playing under Owens, Tipps, and Walker and with his teammates on the 1962, 1963, and 1964 teams. "I was fortunate to be around people early in my career that helped me understand and appreciate the life skills that you get from being involved in a challenging team sport. And it's those kind of basic life skills that have given me a level of confidence to do whatever I wanted to do. I also learned how to be able to take directions, to communicate with and trust your teammates, to overcome obstacles, to operate in a team environment, and to prepare through visualization, situation analysis, setting objectives and letting your creative subconscious figure out how to reach your objectives."

Before the 1999 reunion dinner, the 1959 team was honored at the end of the third quarter of the Stanford game on October 30 in Husky Stadium. The 1999 Huskies were behind. Quarterback Marques Tuiasosopo looked out at the gray-haired men spreading across the field at the west end of the stadium.

"I thought to myself, 'Those are the real dawgs. They are the ones who turned it around in the first place.' " Tuiasosopo continued. "Man I can't express how I feel about these guys and all they've done for Washington. I thought to myself, 'We can't lose in front of these guys.' "

After the older generation was given a thunderous applause from the fans, the Huskies huddled up at midfield, turned to wave to the legends leaving the field, and then came from behind to beat the Cardinal 35-30 -- in the fourth quarter, just like the old guys had done. It was a game in which Tuiasosopo ran for 207 and passed for 302, the first time a collegiate player had ever put together a 200/300 game. And just like his 1959 heroes, he played hurt. On the opening offensive series, he had been dumped on his backside while completing a rollout pass. He played the rest of the game with a severely bruised hip and buttocks.

The legacy of the teams in the late 1950's lives on in the minds of coaches, players, fans, and historians. Those Husky teams picked up an entire state and region and revitalized it. People were drawn to the teams because of their commitment, sacrifices, courage, and focus. The coaches and players provided an example of what people with those attributes can achieve. They were heroes and they provided hope to thousands. Not just then but for many decades to come.

Dave Enslow penned a poem in 1992 that included these lines:

As athletes we once were the best
Models for all of the rest

Appendix

Players on the 1959 Team Inducted in the
Husky Football Hall of Fame

Ricardo Aguirre

Chuck Allen

Lee Bernhardi

Barry Bullard

Tim Bullard

Don Carnahan

Jim Carphin

Stan Chapple

Larry Clanton

Pat Claridge

Keith Cordes

Mike Crawford

Gary Dasso

Ben Davidson

Dick Dunn

Bob Echols

Dave Enslow

Jim Everett

George Fleming

Lee Folkins

Carver Gayton

Kurt Gegner

Serge Grant

Bob Hivner

Sam Hurworth

Ray Jackson

Joe Jones

Kermit Jorgensen

Bill Kinnune

Gary Kissell

Roy McKasson

Don McKeta

John Meyers

Don Millich

John Nelson

Ed Peasley

George Pitt

Jim Quessenberry

Bob Schloredt

Jerry Schwarz

Jim Skaggs

Barney Therrien

Jack Walters

Dan Wheatley

Bob White

John Wilson

Brent Wooten

Players on the 1960 National Championship Team

Ricardo Aguirre
Andy Alkire
Chuck Allen
Lee Bernhardi
Chuck Bond
Barry Bullard
Tim Bullard
Don Carnahan
Stan Chapple
Larry Clanton
Pat Claridge
Gary Clark
Ben Davidson
Norm Dicks
Dick Dunn
Dave Enslow
Jim Everett
George Fleming

Lee Folkins
Kurt Gegner
Pete Greenlee
Vance Hansen
Pete Hanson
Lynn Hewitt
Bob Hivner
Jim Hornell
Sam Hurworth
Ray Jackson
Joe Jones
Kermit Jorgensen
Glen Kezer
Bill Kinnune
Gary Kissell
Tony Kopay
Jake Kupp

Duane Locknane
Ray Mansfield
Roy McKasson
Don McKeta
John Meyers
Charlie Mitchell
Bob Monroe
John Nelson
Dave Phillips
Ron Quincy
Bob Ridgway
Rod Scheyer
Bob Schloredt
Bill Siler
Jim Skaggs
Barney Therrien
Brent Wooten

Acknowledgments

First, I want to acknowledge the coaches and players of the 1959 and 1960 teams who forged an extraordinary record in Husky football history. Many of them helped in developing this book.

Former Washington athletic director George Briggs, head coach Jim Owens, and sports publicity director John Thompson spent many hours with me and provided perspective and a wealth of information about the 1956-1960 period in Husky football history. Assistant coaches Tom Tipps and Norm Pollom provided extensive input on the philosophy and techniques used to develop team unity and implement offensive and defensive schemes. Former head coach Darrell Royal provided perspective on the season of 1956 and the factors which set the stage for the great success in the years that followed.

Several prominent sports columnists of the period -- Georg Meyers, John Owen, and Dick Rockne -- provided insights about the major factors related to the success of the 1959 and 1960 teams. The renowned football announcer, Keith Jackson, was the KOMO sports director during the mid-to-late fifties. He shared his reflections on not only what the teams accomplished but how they picked up the entire state and region and revitalized it.

I interviewed many players from the 1955-1960 period. They willingly shared many personal stories and perspectives about the teams on which they played and how the 1959 and 1960 teams became a football band of brothers with the mental and physical toughness to overcome adversity and to rise to the highest level in collegiate football.

They are: Chuck Allen, Barry Bullard, Tim Bullard, Luther Carr, Pat Claridge, Whitey Core, Mike Crawford, Ben Davidson, Dick Dunn, Dave Enslow, George Fleming, Lee Folkins, Carver Gayton, Bob Hivner, Ray Jackson, Joe Jones, Kermit Jorgensen, Bill Kinnune, Corky Lewis, Reese Lindquist, Don McCumby, Don McKeta, Don Millich, Charles Mitchell, George Pitt, Bob Schloredt, Jim Skaggs, Dan Wheatley, and Brent Wooten.

Thanks also to Don James who provided comments about football in the fifties and the impact the 1959-60 teams made on Husky football. And to Rick Redman, who played on the 1962-64 Husky teams, for his comments on Owens' coaching philosophy and the impact of the 1959-60 teams on Husky players that followed.

I appreciate very much the information and perspective Carver Gayton and Gertrude Peoples provided on issues of minority students and the program initiated by the University of Washington athletic department in the late 1960's.

Two former ASUW presidents -- Frank Gustin (1955) and Don Nielsen (1960) -- were helpful in explaining the role of the ASUW in the administration of the athletic department and the student support of the athletic programs in the period. Artie Buerk, student football manager in 1954-57, provided broad perspective of the football program in those years.

I received significant perspective and reflections on the State of Washington, Seattle and the region, and the University of Washington during the mid-to-late fifties from former Governors Albert Rosellini and Dan Evans, former Seattle Mayor Gordon Clinton, and Jim Ellis, an extraordinary community leader.

Many many thanks to those who reviewed all or parts of the

manuscript. They are Tim Bullard, George Briggs, Dick Dunn, Carver Gayton, Jim Owens, John Thompson, my good friend Tim Rich, and another good friend, my wife Dixie Jo. Tim and Dixie transformed my drafts from opaque into translucent and flawed into the complete.

I thank the staff of the University's Manuscript, Special Collections, and University Archives Division of the University of Washington Libraries. The Athletic Communications staff provided much information on the coaches and players about whom the book is written. A special thanks to Brian Tom.

Finally, thanks to Jim Daves, my co-author on two previous books -- The Glory of Washington: The People and Events that Shaped the Husky Athletic Tradition and Husky Stadium: Great Games and Golden Moments. He provided great counsel in the planning stages for this book. He would have been my co-author of this book had he not left the University of Washington to become the Media Relations Director at the University of Virginia in 2005.

Research Methodology

I used many sources of information in the research for this book. There were three primary sources. One was the University of Washington Athletics Communications Department located in the Graves Building. Another was the University Manuscripts, Special Collections, and University Archives Division (UWMssSCUA) located in Allen Library. The third was the Microfilm and Newspaper Collections Department in Suzzallo Library.

The Athletics Communications Department publishes annual media guides on each sport and has files on individual athletes. It also has extensive references including NCAA and PAC-10 publications.

The MssSCUA Department has data related to early university and athletic history including a complete set of the Tyee (the university yearbook), original copies of the campus newspaper (the Pacific Wave, the Wave, and the Daily) and many photographs of early athletes and teams.

The Microfilm Department contains microfilm on local newspapers, including the Seattle Post-Intelligencer, the Seattle Times, and the University Daily. Many of the quotes in the book came from newspaper articles related to the events described.

I used the following articles, books, and unpublished theses in my research.

Articles

_____. Boosters Mess It Up In Washington. Sports Illustrated, February 20, 1956

_____. One Eye on the Rose Bowl. Sports Illustrated, October 3, 1960

_____. The Wildest Rose. Sports Illustrated, January 9, 1961

Blank, Joseph. Shock! The Extraordinary Story of What a 66,000 Volt Charge Did to a Man's Life. Reader's Digest, July 1974

Gayton, Carver. Carver Gayton Reflects on the Jim Owens Statue at Husky Stadium, University of Washington. (see www.historylink.org)

Riffenburgh, Beau. The Helmet: An Excerpt from The Official NFL Encyclopedia. (see www.riddell.com/history.htm)

Books

Ambrose, Stephen. Band of Brothers: E Company, 506th Regiment, 101st Airborne from Normandy to Hitler's Eagle Nest. New York: Simon & Schuster, 1992

Boyles, Bob and Guide, Paul. Fifty Years of College Football. Wilmington, Delaware: Sideline Communications, Inc., 2005

Burke, Roger. Once a Husky, Always a Husky. Kennewick, Washington: Columbia River Book Co., 2005

Daves, Jim and Porter, W. Thomas. The Glory of Washington:

The People and Events That Shaped the Husky Athletic Tradition. Champaign, Illinois: Sports Publishing, Inc., 2001.

Dent, Jim. The Junction Boys. New York: St. Martins Press, 1999

Dent, Jim. The Undefeated: The Oklahoma Sooners and the Greatest Winning Streak in College Football. New York: St. Martins Press, 2001

Durgard, Martin. Chasing Lance: The 2005 Tour de France and Lance Armstrong's Ride of a Lifetime. New York: Little, Brown and Company, 2005

Egan, Timothy. The Worst Hard Time: The Untold Story of Those Who Survived the Great American Dust Bowl. New York: Houghton Mifflin Company, 2006

Gates, Charles M. The First Century at the University of Washington, 1861-1961. Seattle: University of Washington Press, 1961

Halberstam, David. The Fifties. New York: Villard Books, 1993

Hamlin, Rick. A 100 Year Celebration - Tournament of Roses. New York: McGraw Hill Publishing, 1988

Hammerbeck, Bernard A., editor, Pacific Coast Conference Record Book. Los Angeles, 1959

Hendrickson, Joe. Tournament of Roses - The First 100 Years, A History in Words and Pictures. Los Angeles: The Knapp Press, 1988

Johnston, Norman J. The Fountain & the Mountain. Seattle: Documentary Book Publishers and the University of Washington, 1995; second edition 2003

Owen, John. Press Pass. Seattle: The Seattle Post-Intelligencer, 1994

Quirk, James. The Ultimate Guide to College Football: Rankings, Records, and Scores of the Major Teams and Conferences. Champaign, Illinois: University of Illinois Press, 2004

Porter, W. Thomas and Daves, Jim. Husky Stadium: Great Games and Golden Moments. Chattanooga, Tennessee: Parker Hood Press, Inc., Seattle: University of Washington Intercollegiate Athletic Department, 2004

Rockne, Dick. Bow Down to Washington. Huntsville, Alabama: The Strode Publishers, 1975

Rudman, Steve. Celebrating 100 Years of Husky Football. New York: Professional Sports Publications, 1990

Seaborg, Glenn T., with Colvig, Ray. Roses from the Ashes: Breakup and Rebirth in Pacific Coast Intercollegiate Athletics. Berkeley, CA.: Institute of Government Studies, 2000 .

Torrance, Roscoe C. Torchy!. Mission Hill, S.D.: Dakota Homestead Publishers, 1973

Unpublished Theses

Hewitt, Lynn R. The History of Intercollegiate Football at the University of Washington from its Origin through 1965. An Unpublished Thesis, University of Washington, 1967

Maurer, Bruce L. A Compendium of Head Coaches of Intercollegiate Sports at the University of Washington, 1892 to 1970. An Unpublished Thesis, University of Washington, 1970

I interviewed and received correspondence from those acknowledged in the previous section of this book. Many stories in the book came from the interviews.

Dick Rockne gave me his tapes of interviews used as research material for his book cited above. The interviews were very helpful in the discussion of the events leading up to Washington's being placed on probation in Chapter 1.

Glen Seaborg's book provided much information for Chapter 1 about why several Pacific Coast Conference schools were put on probation in the mid-1950's. It also helped in the discussion of the demise of the conference in Chapter 4.

Timothy Egan's book provided valuable insights on the Dust Bowl devastation discussed at the beginning of Chapter 2.

James Quirk's book contained information used in the discussion of the history of collegiate football in Chapter 5.

Tom Porter and Jim Daves' book on Husky Stadium was the source for the history of Washington football presented in Chapter 5.

Charles Gates' book provided extensive information about the history of the University of Washington discussed in Chapter 7. Norm Johnston's book provided additional material related to the discussion of the University in Chapter 7.

I watched the video of the 1960 and 1961 Rose Bowl games countless times in order to accurately describe the action on the field in Chapters 8 and 10.

Roger Burke's book provided information about Larry Clanton's heroism discussed in the Epilogue.

Joseph Blank's article in the July 1974 issue of Reader's Digest was the source about Lee Folkins' electric shock and recovery discussed in the Epilogue.

Carver Gayton's article presented valuable and balanced insights into the racial turmoil in the late 1960's discussed in the Epilogue.

Much of the Epilogue material about the players on the 1959 and 1960 teams came from a questionnaire I sent to many of them.

SPECIAL ORDER FORM

for

A FOOTBALL BAND OF BROTHERS

FORGING THE UNIVERSITY OF WASHINGTON'S FIRST NATIONAL CHAMPIONSHIP

To get this book for a friend or family member with a personal inscription from the author, please complete and mail this order form (or a copy thereof) to the address shown below.

			Number of Books	Total Order
(1)	Book price	$24.95		
(2)	Sales tax (if a resident of the State of Washington)	2.20		
(3)	Shipping and handling	4.00		
(4)	Total per book	$31.15 X	_____ =	_____

If you want a note to the recipient(s) of the book(s), please enter the name(s) of the people to whom you want the book(s) inscribed and any personal information you want included in the inscription (e.g., love of the Huskies, graduate of UW).

_____

_____

_____

_____

Please make a check payable for your total order to BAND of BROTHERS and send it to National Championship, 5183 NE Laurelcrest Lane, Seattle WA 98105

Please provide the following shipping information to fulfill your order. Thanks

Name: _____

Company (if appropriate): _____

Address: _____

City: _____ State: _____ Zip: _____

Phone number: _____ Fax number: _____

Email: _____

CPSIA information can be obtained at www.ICGtesting.com
Printed in the USA
LVOW08s2156141214

418841LV00001B/101/P